☆☆☆ Forbes

TRAVEL GUIDE

Formerly Mobil Travel Guide

NORTHERN CALIFORNIA

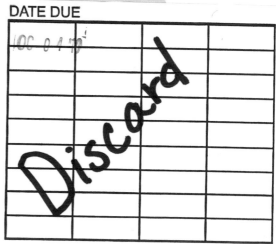

ACKNOWLEDGMENTS

We gratefully acknowledge the help of our representatives for their efficient and perceptive inspections of the lodgings listed. Forbes Travel Guide is also grateful to the talented writers who contributed to this book.

Some of the information contained herein is derived from a variety of third-party sources. Although every effort has been made to verify the information obtained from such sources, the publisher assumes no responsibility for inconsistencies or inaccuracies in the data or liability for any damages of any type arising from errors or omissions.

Neither the editors nor the publisher assume responsibility for the services provided by any business listed in this guide or for any loss, damage or disruption in your travel for any reason.

ISBN: 9-780841-61421-5   Manufactured in the USA

10 9 8 7 6 5 4 3 2 1

TABLE OF CONTENTS

STAR ATTRACTIONS

If you've been a reader of Mobil Travel Guide, you will have heard that this historic brand partnered with another storied media name, Forbes, in 2009 to create a new entity, Forbes Travel Guide. For more than 50 years, Mobil Travel Guide assisted travelers in making smart decisions about where to stay and dine when traveling. With this new partnership, our mission has not changed: We're committed to the same rigorous inspections of hotels, restaurants and spas—the most comprehensive in the industry with more than 500 standards tested at each property we visit—to help you cut through the clutter and make easy and informed decisions on where to spend your time and travel budget. Our team of anonymous inspectors are constantly on the road, sleeping in hotels, eating in restaurants and making spa appointments, evaluating those exacting standards to determine a property's rating.

What kind of standards are we looking for when we visit a proprety? We're looking for more than just high-thread count sheets, pristine spa treatment rooms and white linen-topped tables. We look for service that's attentive, in-dividualized and unforgettable. We note how long it takes to be greeted when you sit down at your table, or to be served when you order room service, or whether the hotel staff can confidently help you when you've forgotten that one essential item that will make or break your trip. Unlike other travel ratings entities, we visit the places we rate, testing hundreds of attributes to compile our ratings, and our ratings cannot be bought or influenced. The Forbes Five Star rating is the most prestigious achievement in hospitality—while we rate more than 8,000 properties in the U.S., Canada, Hong Kong, Macau and Bei-jing, for 2010, we have awarded Five Star designations to only 53 hotels, 21 restaurants and 18 spas. When you travel with Forbes, you can travel with confidence, knowing that you'll get the very best experience, no matter who you are.

We understand the importance of making the most of your time. That's why the most trusted name in travel is now Forbes Travel Guide.

STAR RATED HOTELS

Whether you're looking for the ultimate in luxury or the best value for your travel budget, we have a hotel recommendation for you. To help you pinpoint properties that meet your needs, Forbes Travel Guide classifies each lodging by type according to the following characteristics:

★★★★★These exceptional properties provide a memorable experience through virtually flawless service and the finest of amenities. Staff are intuitive, engaging and passionate, and eagerly deliver service above and beyond the guests' expectations. The hotel was designed with the guest's comfort in mind, with particular attention paid to craftsmanship and quality of product. A Five Star property is a destination unto itself.

★★★★These properties provide a distinctive setting, and a guest will find many interesting and inviting elements to enjoy throughout the property. Attention to detail is prominent throughout the property, from design concept to quality of products provided. Staff are accommodating and take pride in catering to the guest's specific needs throughout their stay.

★★★These well-appointed establishments have enhanced amenities that provide travelers with a strong sense of location, whether for style or function. They may have a distinguishing style and ambience in both the public spaces and guest rooms; or they may be more focused on functionality, providing guests with easy access to local events, meetings or tourism highlights.

★★The Two Star hotel is considered a clean, comfortable and reliable establishment that has expanded amenities, such as a full-service restaurant.

★The One Star lodging is a limited-service hotel or inn that is considered a clean, comfortable and reliable establishment.

For every property, we also provide pricing information. All prices quoted are accurate at the time of publication; however, prices cannot be guaranteed.

STAR RATED RESTAURANTS

Every restaurant in this book comes highly recommended as an outstanding dining experience.

★★★★★Forbes Five Star restaurants deliver a truly unique and distinctive dining experience. A Five Star restaurant consistently provides exceptional food, superlative service and elegant décor. An emphasis is placed on originality and personalized, attentive and discreet service. Every detail that surrounds the experience is attended to by a warm and gracious dining room team.

★★★★These are exciting restaurants with often well-known chefs that feature creative and complex foods and emphasize various culinary techniques and a focus on seasonality. A highly-trained dining room staff provides refined personal service and attention.

★★★Three Star restaurants offer skillfully-prepared food with a focus on a specific style or cuisine. The dining room staff provides warm and professional service in a comfortable atmosphere. The décor is well-coordinated with quality fixtures and decorative items, and promotes a comfortable ambience.

★★The Two Star restaurant serves fresh food in a clean setting with efficient service. Value is considered in this category, as is family friendliness.

★The One Star restaurant provides a distinctive experience through culinary specialty, local flair or individual atmosphere.

Because menu prices can fluctuate, we list a pricing range rather than specific prices. The pricing ranges are per diner, and assume that you order an appetizer or dessert, an entrée and one drink.

STAR RATED SPAS

Forbes Travel Guide's spa ratings are based on objective evaluations of more than 450 attributes. About half of these criteria assess basic expectations, such as staff courtesy, the technical proficiency and skill of the employees and whether the facility is clean and maintained properly. Several standards address issues that impact a guest's physical comfort and convenience, as well as the staff's ability to impart a sense of personalized service. Additional criteria measure the spa's ability to create a completely calming ambience.

★★★★★Stepping foot in a Five Star spa will result in an exceptional experience with no detail overlooked. These properties wow their guests with extraordinary design and facilities, and uncompromising service. Expert staff cater to your every whim and pamper you with the most advanced treatments and skin care lines available. These spas often offer exclusive treatments and may emphasize local elements.

★★★★Four Star spas provide a wonderful experience in an inviting and serene environment. A sense of personalized service is evident from the moment you check in and receive your robe and slippers. The guest's comfort is always of utmost concern to the well-trained staff.

★★★These spas offer well-appointed facilities with a full complement of staff to ensure that guests' needs are met. The spa facilities include clean and appealing treatment rooms, changing areas and a welcoming reception desk.

NORTHERN CALIFORNIA

A DREAM OF GOLD EVEN BEFORE IT BECAME A STATE, CALIFORNIA HAS ENTICED WORLD travelers for more than 150 years. Over land and across the Pacific Ocean, in sunshine and in fog, travelers keep coming to cruise along 1,200 miles of coastline and picnic among vineyards, lounge on beaches and play in the surf, climb mountains and ski snowy peaks, look down on the Golden Gate Bridge from the heights of San Francisco and gaze up at gargantuan redwoods.

With the oldest-known trees on Earth—a stand of bristlecone pines said to be more than 4,700 years old—and with the lowest and highest points in the continental United States—Death Valley and Mount Whitney—only 80 miles from one another, the Golden State does things in a big way.

Even if you haven't made it to this strip of coast yet, you've surely tasted its treasures. California leads the nation in producing grapes, peaches, apricots, nectarines, figs, dates, olives, lemons, avocados, walnuts, rice, eggs, turkeys, honey and dozens of additional crops and goods.

Home state to the aircraft and missile industries, California generally likes to entertain. The electronics industry is booming again in Silicon Valley, starting in South San Francisco, and the large and small silver screens debuted here. Take about an hour's flight from San Francisco International Airport and stroll among the stars on Hollywood Boulevard.

Spaniards, Mexicans, English, Russians, Chinese and others helped write the state's rich history. Many streets and buildings in California bear the name of Juan Rodríguez Cabrillo, a Portuguese explorer and the first European to venture into California waters in 1542. English explorer Sir Francis Drake is believed to have landed just northwest of what is now San Francisco in 1579.

It took almost 200 years more, however, for the first towns to develop around Spanish missions, beginning in 1769. For five years, the Mexican flag flew over California after Mexico won independence from Spain. In 1826, American settlers revolted against Mexican authorities and formed the short-lived Bear Flag Republic (commemorated by the state flag). The 1848 Treaty of Guadalupe Hidalgo ended the Mexican-American War—during which the U.S. cut Mexico in half—and led to California's becoming part of the developing coastal boundary of the United States.

The same year, a glimmer of gold in the American River set off a mass migration of a half-million California dreamers from around the world whose arrival enlivened the drowsy countryside and split the Far West wide open. The 49ers who came for gold stayed to enjoy the geographic and agricultural splendors of what would become the most populous state in the union. Now it's your turn. www.gocalif.ca.gov

BERKELEY

See also Oakland, San Francisco

One of the most progressive cities in the nation, Berkeley is home to the flagship campus of the University of California and a population of well-heeled, aging hippies who want to enjoy the good life organic-style, even as they yearn for their politically radical pasts.

During the 1960s, it seemed like students protested at Berkeley almost as often as they went to class, clashing repeatedly with the administration and memorably with the National Guard and President Reagan over "People's Park," a strip of land that has never been developed. The university has mellowed since then, and the once hair-raising Telegraph Avenue, including its tattoo parlors, has gentrified.

The city takes its name from George Berkeley, Bishop of Cloyne, an 18th-century Irish philosopher, famous for a theory summed up in the phrase, "To be is to be perceived," words that the city's inveterate protesters (not to mention California's abundance of celebrities) seem to have taken to heart.

WHAT TO SEE
AMOEBA RECORDS
2455 Telegraph Ave., Berkeley, 510-549-1125; www.amoeba.com

Since it opened in 1990, this independent record shop has offered music lovers an array of tunes from top 40 to indie rock, underground rock and hip-hop, world music and much more. Since then, Amoeba has opened stores in San Francisco and Hollywood. With new and used music filling the racks, you can find pretty much anything you want to listen to. Unlike larger music chains, independent Amoeba focuses on creating a community for independent musicians and music lovers. Located on Telegraph Avenue, Amoeba is at the center of free-spirited Berkeley.

ASHKENAZ MUSIC & DANCE COMMUNITY CENTER
1317 San Pablo Ave., Berkeley, 510-525-5054; www.ashkenaz.com

Since 1973, Ashkenaz community center has brought together people of all walks of life to experience live world and roots music. This nationally recognized, nonprofit venue offers nightly live music, dance classes and programs for children featuring African, Balkan, Brazilian, Cajun, Reggae, Bluegrass and more. Ashkenaz welcomes people of all ages and has plenty of options for young children. Founded by David Nadel, a human rights activist and folk dancer, Ashkenaz was first a dance hall for international and contemporary roots music and dance. Nadel was murdered in 1996, in his own club, a place that stood for nonviolence. Since then, Ashkenaz evolved into what it is today through the help of many community members to keep this unique place that Nadel created alive.

BERKELEY ART MUSEUM & PACIFIC FILM ARCHIVE
2626 Bancroft Way, Berkeley, 510-642-0808; www.bampfa.berkeley.edu

Founded in 1963, this UC Berkeley campus museum contains Abstract Expressionist Hans Hofmann paintings and many important historical and contemporary art including artists Jackson Pollock, Paul Gauguin and Joan Brown. There is also an outdoor sculpture garden, museum store, cafe and the Pacific Film Archive Library and Film Study Center. The museum showcases temporary exhibitions, which explore international art.

Gallery admission: adults $8, non-UC Berkeley students, senior citizens, disabled persons, young adults 13-17 $5, UC Berkeley students, faculty and staff, children 12 and under free. Admission: adults $9.50, non-UC Berkeley students, UC Berkeley faculty and staff, seniors, disabled persons, children 17 and under $6.50, UC Berkeley students, BAM/PFA members $5.50. Additional feature $4. Show times may vary. First Thursday of every month free. Wednesday-Sunday 11 a.m.-5 p.m.

BERKELEY FARMERS' MARKETS
Center Street and Martin Luther King Jr. Way, Berkeley, 510-548-3333;
www.ecologycenter.org
At this pair of outstanding farmers' markets, held year-round on Tuesdays, Thursdays (all organic) and Saturdays, local farmers and chefs set up booths vending a far-flung range of delicacies, including olives, avocados, coffee beans and vegan Mexican food, along with baked goods, jams, plants and flowers. More than half the markets' produce is organically grown. Musicians often provide entertainment; food activists and social justice activists have been in attendance since the markets began in 1987.
Saturday 10 a.m-3 p.m., Tuesday 2-7 p.m. and Thursday 3-7 p.m.

BERKELEY MARINA
201 University Ave., Berkeley, 510-981-6740; www.ci.berkeley.ca.us/marina
The Berkeley marina's public fishing pier, at 3,000 feet long, juts out into 52 acres of water for those who want to fish (no license required) or enjoy the view. There are 1,100 berths along with a launching ramp, an area for car and boat trailer storage, and a marine fueling facility along with restaurant options. Also located in the marina are the Adventure Playground, for children, and the Shorebird Park Nature Center, which offers wildlife exhibits and a 100-gallon saltwater aquarium.
Daily sunrise-sunset.

BERKELEY REPERTORY THEATRE
2025 Addison St, Berkeley, 510-647-2949; www.berkeleyrep.org
This Tony-award winning theatre earned respect since its opening in 1968 for its outstanding theatrical productions and talented, reputable actors, directors and playwrights. It is also home to the Berkeley Repertory School of Theatre, which provides theater education for children and adults. Each season consists of various plays and schedules; and in the past three years, it sent five of its hit plays to Broadway, including Eurydice, Bridge & Tunnel and Taking Over.

BERKELEY ROSE GARDEN
1200 Euclid Ave., Berkeley, 510-981-5150; www.ci.berkeley.ca.us
Opened in 1937 after four years of construction, this historic rose garden consists of 3,000 rose bushes with 250 varieties. The best time to visit the garden is in mid-May, when most of the roses are in full bloom. Also in May is the Rose Day Celebration on Mother's Day. Many people believe that this

beautiful and fragrant rose garden is the best in northern California. Daily sunrise-sunset.

BOTANICAL GARDEN

200 Centennial Drive, Berkeley, 510-643-2755; www.botanicalgarden.berkeley.edu

The University of California at Berkeley's Botanical Garden has many unusual plants from all over the world, covering most continents, including Asia, Australia and South America collections along with many native California plants. With over 34 acres of 12,000 varieties of plants, there is a lot to see.

Admission: adults $7, seniors and children 13-17 $5, children 5-12 $2, children under 5 free. First Thursday of every month free. Daily 9 a.m.-5 p.m.; closed first Tuesday of every month. Tours: Thursday, Saturday-Sunday 1:30 p.m.

FREIGHT & SALVAGE COFFEEHOUSE

1111 Addison St. Berkeley, 510-548-1761; www.thefreight.org

Since 1968, Freight & Salvage Coffeehouse has operated as a non-smoking, alcohol-free all-ages coffee house and performance venue. Over time, with changes in its location and owner, it still acts as a nonprofit community resource for traditional music from many different cultures. On a given night, you might find musicians performing traditional blues, bluegrass, worldbeat, gospel, jazz or folk. You can pick up some coffee, tea and a snack at the Freight food counter and kick back and enjoy the diverse music.

INTERNATIONAL HOUSE

2299 Piedmont Ave., Berkeley, 510-642-9490; www.ihouse.berkeley.edu

This Mission Revival structure serves as a home and program center for 600 students from the United States and abroad. Built in 1930, this was the second such institution in the world part of the "International House movement." The first house opened in New York City in 1924 and was founded by Harry Edmonds and funded by John D. Rockefeller, Jr. It is a place for students to understand other cultures. Its impressive dome is visible for miles. It also acts as a conference and event facility. Daily.

TILDEN PARK GOLF COURSE

10 Golf Course Drive, Berkeley, 510-848-7373; www.tildenparkgc.americangolf.com

Tilden Park isn't very long (a few yards under 6,300), but the many challenging tees require careful club selection. Several holes dogleg, and most are lined with large trees likely to swallow errant drives. Three of the four par-threes measure longer than 200 yards and provide perhaps the biggest overall challenge to the layout. The course is usually very crowded (about 75,000 rounds are played there each year), so arrive early and hope that you play behind someone who is fast.

Daily 6 a.m.-9 p.m.

TILDEN REGIONAL PARK

2501 Grizzly Peak Blvd., Berkeley, 510-843-2137, 888-327-2757;
www.ebparks.org/parks/tilden

The park's 2,079-acre recreational area offers a swimming beach with a bath-house, fishing at Lake Anza, picnicking, nature hiking, bicycle and bridle trails, an 18-hole golf course, carousel, steam train rides and a botanical garden of native California plants. The park connects with East Bay Skyline National Trail at Inspiration Point. Daily 5 a.m.-10 p.m. Carousel: Saturday-Sunday.

UNIVERSITY OF CALIFORNIA, BERKELEY

2200 University Ave., Berkeley, 510-642-5215; www.berkeley.edu

More than 35,000 students attend this vast campus in the foothills of the east shore of San Francisco Bay. Founded in 1873, it is the oldest of the 10 University of California campuses and later became the system's flagship institution. The university's white granite buildings are surrounded by groves of oak trees and its 307-foot tower, known simply as the "Campanile," can be seen from a distance. The campus is known for its high-ranked public research library, discoveries in research, and the history that surrounds the city of Berkeley and the free thinkers who have lived there over the years. UC Berkeley boasts many famous alumni including William Randolph Hearst, newspaper publisher; Steve Wozniak, co-founder of Apple; Gregory Peck, actor; Jack London, author; Alice Waters, chef and author; and Tom Anderson, co-founder of MySpace, to name a few. Visit room 101 of University Hall where Visitor Services is located for more information.

WILLIAM RANDOLPH HEARST GREEK THEATRE

Gayley Road and Hearst Road, Berkeley, 510-809-0100; www.apeconcerts.com

Located on the University of California Berkeley campus, this theater was a gift from newspaper tycoon William Randolph Hearst to the university in 1903. This intimate outdoor amphitheater features regular performances from leading pop and jazz artists and has hosted performances by the likes of Bob Dylan, Grateful Dead, Phish, Dave Matthews Band as well as speakers including Theodore Roosevelt and the 14th Dalai Lama. Nestled in the foothills, this legendary theater overlooks the San Francisco Bay with views of the Golden Gate and Bay Bridges. May-October.

SPECIAL EVENTS
BERKELEY WORLD MUSIC FESTIVAL

Telegraph Ave., Berkeley; www.berkeleyworldmusic.org

This early summer celebration brings together an array of world music (from Jamaican Reggae to Celtic fiddlers to Argentinean tango) to stages on the streets of Berkeley. Musicians also fill the cafes and book and music stores; there is also a craft fair in People's Park and an after party at Ashkenaz Music & Dance Community Center. Early June

WHERE TO STAY
★★★THE CLAREMONT RESORT & SPA
41 Tunnel Road, Berkeley, 510-843-3000, 800-551-7266; www.claremontresort.com

Set on 22 acres of lush gardens in Berkeley's Oakland Hills, this country retreat is only 12 miles from San Francisco and just a glance from a bay view. The hotel recently underwent a renovation that left the cheerful rooms stocked with down-duvet topped beds and flat-screen TVs. With two pools, 10 tennis courts, a comprehensive fitness center and a full-service spa, there's plenty to do. The resort's three restaurants turn out Pacific Rim and American dishes. While at press time the signature restaurant was closed for a renovation that will transform it into Meritage at the Claremont, a contemporary-casual dining room with a menu that focuses on food and wine pairings, the Paragon Bar & Cafe still offers a café-style menu with amazing views of the San Francisco bay and live music four nights a week.

279 rooms. Restaurant, bar. Business center. Fitness center. Spa. Pets accepted. $251-350

★★HOTEL DURANT
2600 Durant Ave., Berkeley, 510-845-8981; www.jdvhotels.com/durant

This green-certified boutique hotel underwent a major renovation in 2008. With its Spanish Mediterranean architecture and decor, it offers not only comfortable guest rooms, but also luxurious amenities and a prime location. Each room is complete with organic bathrobes, 300-thread count linens, 37- or 42-inch flat-screen televisions, an honor bar and complimentary Internet access.

144 rooms. Restaurant, bar. Business center. Pets accepted. $151-250

WHERE TO EAT
★★AJANTA
1888 Solano Ave., Berkeley, 510-526-4373; www.ajantarestaurant.com

With a menu that constantly changes, there is always something new to try at this green-certified restaurant. The kitchen offers a prix fixe menu for both lunch and dinner. A meal arrives with plenty of accompaniments, including naan, mango chutney and basmati rice among others. Dishes are creative and come from a variety of regions in India; the artwork that adorns the walls was inspired by caves in Ajanta.

Indian. Lunch, dinner. Reservations recommended. $16-35

★★CAFÉ ROUGE
1782 Fourth St., Berkeley, 510-525-1440; www.caferouge.net

Cafe Rouge features a meat market and oyster bar, so it's no surprise that the menu here focuses on fresh organic meats and house-made charcuterie. The menu changes every two weeks, with dishes such as grilled flat-iron steak with marble potatoes, and the half-pound Rouge burger with fries making regular appearances.

Mediterranean, American. Lunch, dinner (Tuesday-Sunday), Sunday. brunch. Outdoor seating. Bar. $35-85

★★CÉSAR
1515 Shattuck Ave., Berkeley, 510-883-02222; www.barcesar.com

Located in the "gourmet ghetto" of Berkeley, César serves fresh Spanish tapas, and offers an extensive list of wines, beers and spirits. Chef Maggie Pond continues to travel through Spain every year to find new ingredients and recipes to bring back to incorporate into her menu. A few of the most popular dishes are salt cod and potato; toasted palacios ham and cheese sandwich; and to complete the meal, bread pudding with orange-caramel sauce. Spanish. Lunch, dinner, late night. Outdoor seating. Bar. $16-35

★★★CHEZ PANISSE AND CAFÉ
1517 Shattuck Ave., Berkeley, 510-548-5525; www.chezpanisse.com

Chez Panisse is celebrity chef Alice Waters' finest creation, and one of the best arguments anywhere for relying on organic, locally grown meat and produce. The charming, long-standing restaurant pioneered the farm-to-table movement, with an ever-changing menu of Mediterranean dishes that make the most of whatever's in season. A casual upstairs café serves an à la carte menu. Make reservations several weeks in advance for the prix fixe menu offered in the formal downstairs dining area (a $25 credit card deposit is required per person).
Californian, Mediterranean. Lunch, dinner. Closed Sunday. Reservations recommended. $36-85

★HENRY'S PUB
Hotel Durant, 2600 Durant Ave., Berkeley, 510-809-4132; www.henrysberkeley.com

Although this is a gastropub, you won't find typical bar food here. The menu is inspired by chef Eddie Blyden's childhood in West Africa and his formal training from New York to Switzerland and the British West Indies. He also follows the slow-food movement, using locally grown produce and organic, free-range meats.
International. Breakfast, lunch, dinner, late-night, Saturday-Sunday brunch. Bar. $15 and under

★★LALIME'S
1329 Gilman St., Berkeley, 510-527-9838; www.lalimes.com

This two-level restaurant housed in a cottage serves organically produced fruits and vegetables from local farmers. The menu features tasty options such as wild mushroom and ricotta crepes, and roasted Australian rack of lamb. Special event meals include menus crafted with wines or beers; after a recent jaunt in Belgium, chef Steve Jaramillo offered a Belgian food and beer prix fixe dinner.
California, Mediterranean. Dinner. Bar. $36-85

★★O CHAMÉ
1830 Fourth St., Berkeley, 510-841-8783

For those who enjoy Japanese fare, O Chamé combines a subtle Californian influence that's just right. A popular dish is the udon noodles with a choice of topping, from Monterey squid to pork tenderloin to grilled grouper. The menu is paired with an extensive wine list and plenty of sake options.
Japanese. Lunch, dinner. Outdoor seating. $16-35

★★★SKATES ON THE BAY
100 Seawall Drive, Berkeley, 510-549-1900; www.skatesonthebay.com
From two levels of tables, you can sample creative California cuisine paired with stellar views through large picture windows that frame the bay, Golden Gate Bridge, Bay Bridge and San Francisco skyline. The menu features steaks, seafood and fresh oysters, and the extensive wine list includes wine flights. Take a seat at the bar for happy hour and try the Smoky Martini, made with vodka and garnished with a slice of pepperoni and a blue cheese-stuffed olive.
Steak, seafood. Lunch (Monday-Friday), dinner, Saturday-Sunday brunch. Reservations recommended. Children's menu. Bar. $36-85

BIG SUR
See also Carmel, Carmel Valley, Monterey
Dominated by the Santa Lucia Mountains, the sparsely developed Big Sur region gives nature room to breathe. Drivers need travel only 30 miles south of Monterey on Highway 1, considered an American National Scenic Byway, to see the beautiful rocky Big Sur bluffs, redwood forests, canyons, waterfalls, secluded beaches and sheer mountains—and gain access to several state parks south of Carmel. A great time to visit Big Sur is in the fall when humpback and blue whales migrate from Alaska to Mexico and California condors fly above. On the southern part of Big Sur, elephant seals, protected by the Marine Mammal Protection Act, congregate to mate in the winter months. Monarch butterflies are also found in Big Sur in October and migrate north in January. It is not unlikely to see many butterflies in the morning in Eucalyptus trees in Andrew Molera State Park.

WHAT TO SEE
BIXBY BRIDGE
www.beachcalifornia.com
A registered historic landmark, the Bixby Bridge, completed in 1932, is one of the highest single-arch bridges in the world and straddles a large canyon along the Big Sur coastline. This two lane bridge reflects the time period in which it was built, with an Art Deco style. All-weather photographers come to capture this engineering marvel, whether clouds partially obscure the bridge's vast body or sunlight makes its white structural supports gleam.

JULIA PFEIFFER BURNS STATE PARK
Big Sur Station 1, Big Sur, 831-667-2315; www.parks.ca.gov
Stretching from the Big Sur coastline into nearby 3,000-foot ridges, the park holds a variety of trees—redwood, tan oak, madrone and chaparral—and an 80-foot waterfall that drops from granite cliffs into the ocean from the Overlook Trail. While at Overlook Trail, be sure to keep watch for whales that come close to the shore. Hike the backcountry via several trails, or check out the 1,680-acre underwater reserve (between Partington Point and McWay Creek), which protects a spectacular assortment of marine life, to look for seals, sea lions and sea otters in the cove. Experienced scuba divers can explore with special-use permits at Partington Cove. Daily sunrise-sunset.

POINT SUR STATE HISTORIC PARK

Big Sur Station 1, 831-625-4419; www.parks.ca.gov

Poised 361 feet above the surf on a large volcanic rock, the park is home to the Point Sur Lightstation, which is visible from the highway, and an active U.S. Coast Guard light station. The lightstation is only open to the public during docent-led tours (which are three-hour long walking tours). From 1889 to 1974, lighthouse keepers and their families lived at the site when the lightstation was automated. There is even a moonlight tour, which tells tales of the "ghosts" of the lightkeepers from the past. Guided tours available. Admission: adults $10, children 6-17 $5, children 5 and under free.

WHERE TO STAY
★★★★POST RANCH INN

Highway 1, Big Sur, 831-667-2200, 800-527-2200; www.postranchinn.com

Perched on a cliff overlooking Big Sur's rugged coastline, the inn is an ideal romantic getaway. Designed to blend with the Santa Lucia Mountains, the buildings resemble sophisticated modern treehouses. Each of the 40 guest rooms has an ocean or mountain view, king-size bed, wood-burning fireplace, indoor spa tub, private deck and digital music system. The wet bar and minibar are filled with complimentary snacks, juices and half-bottles of red and white wine. What you won't find: TVs or alarm clocks. Wake up when you want to and head to the Post Ranch Spa for a massage or body treatment. Take a private yoga class or a guided hike through the Santa Lucia and Ventana Mountains. End your evening at the Sierra Mar restaurant, which serves a superb prix fixe menu and has an extensive wine list.

40 rooms. Restaurant, bar. Complimentary breakfast. Fitness center. Pool. Spa. No children allowed. $351 and up

★★★VENTANA INN & SPA

48123 Highway 1, Big Sur, 831-667-2331, 800-628-6500; www.ventanainn.com

This stylish resort speaks to nature lovers with a soft spot for luxury. From its perch 1,200 feet above the coastline on the Santa Lucia Mountains, the property sprawls across 243 acres of towering redwoods, wildflower-filled meadows and rolling hills. Each guest room is complete with a private balcony or patio with mountain or ocean views. After swimming, hiking or a guided Big Sur tour, indulge in a treatment at the Allegria Spa or dine at the Restaurant at Ventana, where the inventive cuisine competes with the panoramic view.

60 rooms. Restaurant, bar. Complimentary breakfast. Business center. Fitness center. Pool. Spa. No children allowed. $351 and up

WHERE TO EAT
★★★THE RESTAURANT AT VENTANA

Ventana Inn, 48123 Highway 1, Big Sur, 831-667-4242; www.ventanainn.com

This restaurant at the Ventana Inn shows off nature's bounty from its wide, rustic, outdoor patio with sturdy redwood tables shaded by market umbrellas. If you can't sit outside, the dining room is warm and cozy, with tall windows, a large stone fireplace, wood-beamed ceilings and a bird's-eye view of the exhibition kitchen, where you'll watch as plates of Mediterranean fare are prepared from California's finest ingredients.

Mediterranean. Lunch, dinner. Bar. Reservations recommended. Outdoor seating. $36-85

★★NEPENTHE
48510 Highway 1, Big Sur, 831-667-2345; www.nepenthebigsur.com
Located in the Santa Lucia Mountains, this restaurant has been a welcoming spot for artists, poets and travelers for 60 years. Comfort food favorites fill the menu, including naturally raised rib-eye steak, vegetarian lasagna and roast chicken with sage stuffing.
American. Lunch, dinner. Outdoor seating. Children's menu. Bar. $16-35

★★★★SIERRA MAR
Highway 1, Big Sur, 831-667-2800; www.postranchinn.com
This acclaimed restaurant, located in the Post Ranch Inn, blends comfort with elegance in natural surroundings— –cliffs, mountains and the ocean below. Executive chef Craig von Foerster's menu focuses on California cuisine with French and Mediterranean influences. His four-course, prix fixe menu changes daily and utilizes seasonal organic products. You might find butter poached Maine lobster as a course, saffron seafood soup with gulf prawns and wild salmon, artichoke ravioli or roast rabbit. Desserts are equally appealing with options such as baked Valrhona milk chocolate crepes with hazelnut brown butter sauce, a hazelnut lace cookie and bittersweet Valrhona chocolate sorbet. The restaurant has one of the most extensive wine cellars in North America with well-known wine producers and hard-to-find bottles from boutique vineyards. They also offer all guests a complimentary breakfast buffet.
American. Lunch, dinner. Reservations recommended. Outdoor seating. Bar. $86 and up.

SPAS
★★★★POST RANCH SPA
Highway 1, Big Sur, 831-667-2200, 800-527-2200; www.postranchinn.com
This spa focuses on nature-based therapies, such as the wildflower facial with organic plants and Big Sur flowers, or the skin-renewing Hungarian herbal body wrap, which blends organic herbs (including sage, ivy, cinnamon and paprika) with a Hungarian thermal mud body masque. Several treatments also draw from Native American rituals, including the Big Sur jade stone therapy, which uses jade collected from nearby beaches and basalt river rocks with massage to relieve sore muscles, and cooled marble to release inflammation. Massages are offered on your private deck or in your room, and the spa also offers private guided hikes, meditation sessions, yoga and couples massage instruction. You can work out in the fitness room, and then relax by one of the two pools or plunge in; the basking pool overlooks the ocean.

BODEGA BAY
See also Santa Rosa
This gorgeous stretch of shoreline on California's north coast is a favorite of day-tripping San Franciscans. Covering eight miles of coast, there are sandy

beaches to swim, surf, windsurf, and just enjoy the scenery. There are also plenty of restaurants, the marina and shopping to keep busy. Bodega Bay is a great spot to go whale watching or horseback riding through the mountains, and it's close enough to Sonoma county wineries for some wine tasting.

WHAT TO SEE
DORAN REGIONAL PARK
201 Doran Beach Road, Bodega Bay, 707-875-3540; www.sonoma-county.org/parks
Build a sandcastle on two miles of sandy beach or wander out onto a rock jetty at the harbor mouth for crabbing or fishing. You can also go surfing or hiking. Campgrounds are open year round and offer a beautiful place to relax and picnic. Dogs are permitted on a leash only, and facilities include a fish-cleaning station, boat-rinsing station, picnic areas, restrooms with electrical outlets and showers. Just past the Bodega Harbor Golf Course, you can fit in a day of golfing and fun at the beach.

WHERE TO STAY
★★★BODEGA BAY LODGE AND SPA
103 Coast Highway 1, Bodega Bay, 707-875-3525, 888-875-2250;
www.bodegabaylodge.com
Just an hour north of San Francisco, this lodge overlooks the ocean, a nature preserve, Doran Beach State Park and the bluffs of Bodega Head. The comfortable guest rooms feature ocean views and most have fireplaces, private balconies, bathrobes, minibars, CD players and European-style bedding. After a day of pampering at the onsite spa, snag a table at the Duck Club, which overlooks the ocean and serves up seasonal local seafood, meats and regional ingredients.
84 rooms. Restaurant. Pool. Spa. 251-350

★★★THE INN AT THE TIDES
800 Coast Highway 1, Bodega Bay, 707-875-2751, 800-541-7788;
www.innatthetides.com
From the bay and harbor views in the guest rooms to the staff's attentiveness, this resort is all about relaxation. Book a King Fireplace, King Vault Fireplace or Sonoma Fireplace room, which all include wood-burning fireplaces along with views of the harbor or bay. Take a dip in the indoor/outdoor heated pool, and renew in the Finnish sauna. Dine at one of two restaurants, the Tides Wharf or the Bay View, both of which feature views of either the bay or the harbor.
86 rooms. Restaurant, bar. Complimentary breakfast. Fitness center. Pool. $151-250

WHERE TO EAT
★★THE BAY VIEW RESTAURANT AND LOUNGE
The Inn at Tides, 800 Coast Highway 1, Bodega Bay, 707-875-2751,800-541-7788;
www.innatthetides.com
Located at the Inn at the Tides, this upscale restaurant offers views of Bodega Bay and the harbor. The menu includes fresh, local seafood, meats and produce including dishes such as Sonoma duck breast with duck confit, beluga lentils and cherry-sage sauce; and pistachio-crusted rack of lamb with garlic-

Yukon Gold mashed potatoes and a rosemary zinfandel glaze.
American. Dinner. Closed Monday-Tuesday. Bar. $16-35

★★★THE DUCK CLUB
103 Coast Highway 1, Bodega Bay, 707-875-3525, 888-875-2250;
www.bodegabaylodge.com
Head out to the southern fringes of Bodega Bay for fine dining at the Bodega
Bay Lodge and Spa. The lodge's restaurant overlooks a bird sanctuary and
Doran Beach, with Bodega Head and the Pacific Ocean as a backdrop. Ask
for a seat on the dining room's western side for a sea view through large picture windows. Chef Patrick Tafoya's menu offers local, sustainable seafood,
meats, cheeses and produce. You'll find options such as crab cakes, seafood
chowder, crab cioppino, maple-roasted acorn squash and crispy sole with
golden raisin-caper chutney.
American. Breakfast, dinner. $36-85

CALISTOGA
See also Napa, Rutherford, St. Helena, Santa Rosa, Sonoma
Calistoga lures travelers to the north end of Napa Valley with its famed geo-
thermal hot springs and mineral water, as well as its wineries. California's
first millionaire, Samuel Brannan, arrived here in the 1840s and opened the
area's first hot springs resort, setting the tone for a city that blends nostalgia
with shrewd business sense. The downtown has an Old World look, thanks
to 19th-century architecture, and a modern feel that comes with plenty of
luxurious spas, top-notch restaurants and appealing shops.

WHAT TO SEE
CALISTOGA INN AND BREWING COMPANY
1250 Lincoln Ave., Calistoga, 707-942-4101; www.calistogainn.com
Visit the first company to begin brewing beer commercially in Napa since
Prohibition. With a full-time brewmaster, the facility creates award-winning
beers and ales but limits production to just 450 barrels a year. The brewery
serves four types of beer, which include Calistoga Wheat Ale, Pilsner, Red
Ale and Porter. Most of it is served on draft at the adjacent Calistoga Inn,
where you'll find a restaurant, English-style pub and beer garden. On weekends, hit the pub for live music or come Wednesday for open mike night. You
can even schedule a tour of the brewery with the brewmaster. Daily.

MOUNT ST. HELENA
Highway 29, Calistoga 707-942-4575; www.parks.ca.gov
Broke, ill and newly married, Scottish author Robert Louis Stevenson hon-
eymooned on the slopes of this extinct volcano in 1880. Bring a copy of *The
Silverado Squatters*, Stevenson's travel memoir describing those two memo-
rable months, and hike to the nearby Silverado Mine. The five-mile hike up
Mount St. Helena is not easy, but is certainly worth the view from the top; on
clear days, you might be able to see Mount Shasta, which is 192 miles away.
The trail begins in Robert Louis Stevenson State Park and takes you through
the forest at first, and then a steep uphill climb over rock, trees and bushes.
Free. Daily sunrise-sunset.

OLD FAITHFUL GEYSER OF CALIFORNIA

1299 Tubbs Lane, Calistoga, 707-942-6463; www.oldfaithfulgeyser.com

It's safe to expect a show from Old Faithful, one of only three regularly erupting geysers in the world. Nearly every half-hour—for about three minutes each time—a towering plume ascends from the source, unless an earthquake disrupts the geyser's timing. An underground river boils up to 350 degrees fahrenheit, causing vapor and steam to escape to heights of 60 to 100 feet. Also on site is a petting zoo containing goats, sheep and llamas and a gift shop.

Admission: adults $8, seniors $7, children 6-12 $3, children 5 and under free. Daily 9 a.m.-5 p.m.

THE PETRIFIED FOREST

4100 Petrified Forest Road, Calistoga, 707-942-6667; www.petrifiedforest.org

Some three million years ago, a volcanic eruption turned a forest of giant redwoods into solid quartz and stone. Discovered in 1857, these preserved trees offer insight into geological formations and give visitors a glimpse of a prehistoric world. At the museum and rock shop, children can take a closer look at some geological wonders. You can also take a guided meadow walk to learn more about the volcanic activity, among oak, douglas fir, madrone and manzanita trees, wildflowers and views of Mount St. Helena. In 1880, Robert Louis Stevenson wrote about his visit here in his book *The Silverado Squatters*.

Admission: adults $7, seniors and children 12-17 $6, children 6-11 $3, children 5 and under free. Daily 9 a.m.-7 p.m. Meadow walk tours: Sunday 11 a.m., weather permitting.

ROBERT LOUIS STEVENSON STATE PARK

Highway 29, Calistoga, 707-942-4575; www.parks.ca.gov

Commemorating the famous author who spent his 1880 honeymoon here, the park provides a rugged respite from the wine crowds. Little of the 3,000 acres are developed, but there is a good, five-mile trail up to the summit of Mount St. Helena, an extinct volcano and the highest peak in the Napa Valley at 4,343 feet. On the way up to the top, look for the marker identifying the site of the bunkhouse of the abandoned Silverado Mine, where Stevenson and his bride, Fanny Osbourne, slept. Daily sunrise-sunset.

SCHRAMSBERG VINEYARDS

1400 Schramsberg Road, Calistoga, 707-942-4558; www.schramsberg.com

Schramsberg is one of Napa's oldest vineyards and a mandatory stop for anyone who enjoys sparkling wine. Elaborate gardens surround the 19th-century home of the winery's founder, Jacob Schram. But the real treat comes on the tour, as guides take you through caves hand-dug by Chinese laborers in the late 19th century, revealing a collection of nearly two million bottles. The tour fee includes a sampling of three sparkling wines and one still variety (opt for the cabernet sauvignon if available).

Tours: 10 a.m., 11:30 a.m., 12:30 p.m., 1:30 p.m. and 2:30 p.m. Reservations required. No children allowed.

STERLING VINEYARDS

1111 Dunaweal Lane, Calistoga, 800-726-6136; www.sterlingvineyards.com

Take the aerial tramway up to Sterling Vineyards for the view, but stay for the wine. The view from the top of the 300 foot hill, which rises over Calistoga, offers a panoramic view of Napa Valley. From a whitewashed building modeled after villages on the Greek island of Mykonos (the founder of Sterling once lived there), this winemaker helped establish chardonnay and merlot grapes in California. Take your time on a self-guided tour of the premises and watch the winemaking operations from elevated walkways, sample current releases in the main tasting room or check out the Reserve Tasting and Cellar Club Rooms. General admission includes the aerial tram, self-guided tour, and a complimentary tasting of five wines.

Admission: adults $20, children 2-21 $10, children 3 and under free. Daily 10 a.m.-4:30 p.m.

SPECIAL EVENTS
NAPA COUNTY FAIR

Napa County Fairgrounds, 1435 N. Oak St., Calistoga, 707-942-5111;
www.napacountyfairgrounds.com

Celebrate Independence Day with a four-day festival including fireworks, a country music concert, rides, a parade, a barbecue contest, exhibits and a wide range of food concessions in a festive country atmosphere.

Admission: adults $7, children 6-12 $3, children 5 and under free. July 4 weekend.

WHERE TO STAY
★CALISTOGA INN

1250 Lincoln Ave., Calistoga, 707-942-4101; www.calistogainn.com

Known for its restaurant and brewery, the Calistoga Inn offers a basic place to stay, refreshing brews and live entertainment. This European-style hotel features guest rooms that have shared baths and low rates. The Calistoga Inn Restaurant features outdoor dining along the Napa River. After a meal at the restaurant, stop in the one of the inn's rustic pubs to try one of Napa Valley Brewing Company's ales.

18 rooms. Complimentary breakfast. Restaurant, bar. $61-150

★★★★CALISTOGA RANCH

580 Lommel Road, Calistoga, 707-254-2800, 800-942-4220; www.calistogaranch.com

Located in a private canyon right outside of Calistoga in upper Napa Valley, this 46-room resort offers a quiet retreat after a day spent exploring local vineyards. Each room is housed in a free-standing lodge surrounded by oak trees, a private lake and hilly terrain. Rooms are decorated using natural materials with fireplaces and duvet-topped beds. The deluxe lodges feature outdoor patios with fireplaces and private outdoor rain shower gardens. There is enough on the property to keep you busy, including bocce ball courts, a heated outdoor swimming pool, a full-service fitness facility, acres of hiking trails, wine seminars and special club events and programs. The onsite restaurant, the Lakehouse, has an American menu created by chef Eric Webster that is paired with local wines, which are stored in a custom-designed private wine cave. The Bathhouse spa offers a luxurious retreat with a yoga deck, lakeside outdoor treatment tents, watsu warm water therapy and programs and classes. Try one of the signature private baths in an outdoor tub to take in the natural surroundings.

46 rooms. Restaurant, bar. Fitness center. Pool. Spa. $351 and up

★★★MOUNT VIEW HOTEL AND SPA

1457 Lincoln Ave., Calistoga, 707-942-6877, 800-816-6877; www.mountviewhotel.com

This hotel is located in downtown Calistoga at the north end of Napa Valley and features a full range of guest rooms, suites and cottages, each with a mix of Art Deco décor and amenities such as featherbeds and duvets, complimentary room service breakfast, cotton terry-cloth bathrobes and Aveda bath products. The hotel also has an outdoor heated pool and jacuzzi, private cabanas and a weekly poolside wine tasting. The Spa offers a full menu of treatments, which include facials, massages body wraps and baths. Jole, the hotel's restaurant, features all-natural organic ingredients.

31 rooms. Restaurant, bar. Complimentary breakfast. Pool. Spa. $151-250

★★★SOLAGE CALISTOGA

755 Silverado Trail, Calistoga, 866-942-7442; www.solagecalistoga.com

Sister to the luxurious Calistoga Ranch and Auberge du Soleil, Solage offers a more casual but equally upscale place to come back to after a day of wine-country indulgence. The contemporary rooms feature a long list of amenities such as vaulted ceilings, polished concrete floors, signature artwork, private patios, luxurious Italian linens, down bedding, plush robes, all-natural bath products, HDTV, DVD players and iPod hookups. Some also offer steam showers, deluxe bathtubs and fireplaces. Even pets are pampered, with their own bed, bowls and treats.

89 rooms. Restaurant, bar. Business Center. Fitness center. Pool. Spa. Pets accepted. $351 and up

ALSO RECOMMENDED

THE CHANRIC INN

1805 Foothill Blvd., Calistoga, 707-942-4535, 877-281-3671; www.thechanric.com

The Chanric Inn is a culinary haven that provides stylish wine country rooms with pillow-top mattresses with down comforters and private baths stocked with Aveda products. In the morning, enjoy a complimentary three-course brunch inside, outside or on the patio. Most ingredients come from the inn's own organic garden.

7 rooms. Complimentary breakfast. Pool. $151-250

COTTAGE GROVE INN

1711 Lincoln Ave., Calistoga, 707-942-8400, 800-799-2284; www.cottagegrove.com

This cluster of private cottages, shaded by a grove of elm trees on the north end of downtown Calistoga, is a short walk from restaurants, shops and the town's hot mineral spas. The individually decorated cottages have soaking tubs, fireplaces, flat-screen TVs, DVD players and down comforters and pillows. Other amenities include complimentary bicycles, packed picnic bas-

kets for day trips, and a private porch with rocking chairs.
17 rooms. Complimentary breakfast. No children under 12. $251-350

SILVER ROSE INN AND SPA
351 Rosedale Road, Calistoga, 707-942-9581, 800-995-9381; www.silverrose.com
This bed and breakfast has 20 rooms in two Tudor-style buildings. Each room
is one-of-a-kind, with themes ranging from western to oriental or safari and
has a private bath and views of the mountains and vineyards. The spa is open
only to hotel guests, and many of the treatments reflect the location, including the champagne facial and body treatment. The Silver Rose Inn even has
its own winery, offers tastings daily.
20 rooms. Complimentary breakfast. Pool. Spa. Tennis. Closed December-
mid-April. $151-250

WHERE TO EAT
★★ALL SEASONS BISTRO
1400 Lincoln Ave., Calistoga, 707-942-9111; www.allseasonsnapavalley.net
The menu at this cozy bistro changes depending on what's fresh and in season. All of the meat served here is organic, and the produce is chemical-free
and produced locally. Sample dishes such as pan-seared crab cakes or spice
dusted-halibut with tropical fruit salsa and black rice.
American. Lunch, dinner. Closed Monday. Bar. Bar. $16-35

★★BRANNAN'S GRILL
1374 Lincoln Ave., Calistoga, 707-942-2233; www.brannansgrill.com
Brannan's Grill serves organically farmed fish, free-range poultry and locally
raised beef that is hormone and antibiotic-free. The menu offers creative options such as pan-roasted grouper, steamed mussels and stuffed olives. With
a large wine, port, scotch and sherry list, there is a complementary match for
each course. Choose to dine alfresco or at a booth by the fireplace.
American. Lunch, dinner. Bar. $36-85

★FLATIRON GRILL
1440 Lincoln Ave., Calistoga, 707-942-1220; www.flatirongrill.com
In the heart of downtown Calistoga, you'll find this cozy steakhouse. Start
with a drink in the wine bar and then dig into satisfying comfort food such as
burgers, pasta, steaks, ribs and fresh seafood.
American. Dinner. Reservations recommended. Bar. $16-35

★HYDRO BAR AND GRILL
1403 Lincoln Ave., Calistoga, 707-942-9777
Located in a historic brick building at the intersection of Lincoln and Washington streets, this casual spot has high ceilings, exposed brick walls, a cement floor and upscale bar food. At the rear of the dining room sits the U-
shaped bar, where more than 20 microbrews from the western United States
are available on draft. Live music is performed on weekends.
American. Breakfast, lunch, dinner. Bar. $16-35

★★★SOLBAR

Solage Resort and Spa, 755 Silverado Trail, Calistoga, 707-226-0850, 866-942 7442;
www.solagecalistoga.com/dining

Located within Solage Calistoga, Solbar is a casual yet sophisticated restaurant and lounge with an eco-chic interior. Dine inside or alfresco on the terrace, and try fresh, locally sourced ingredients in dishes such as gazpacho with griddled sourdough and seasonal vegetables, or steak with twice-fried potatoes. The signature cocktails incorporate fresh juices, local herbs and spices, as in the Ginger Strawberry Mojito made with local strawberries and fresh ginger.

New American. Breakfast, lunch, dinner. Outdoor seating. Children's menu. Bar. $36-85

★★WAPPO BAR AND BISTRO

1226 Washington St., Calistoga, 707-942-4712; www.wappobar.com

The menu at this casual bistro has a Mediterranean bent, but global influences can be seen in eclectic dishes such as chiles rellenos with walnut pomegranate sauce, and Tandoori chicken with basmati lemon ginger pilaf, sauteed spinach with cheese, watercress raita and warm curry naan. The outdoor courtyard, shaded by a grapevine trellis, is a comfortable spot for sipping local wines.

International. Lunch, dinner. Closed Tuesday. Reservations recommended. Outdoor seating. Bar. $16-35

SPAS

★★★★THE BATHHOUSE

Calistoga Ranch, 580 Lommel Road, Calistoga, 707-254-2820, 800-942-4220;
www.calistogaranch.com

The Northern California town of Calistoga is famous for its natural hot springs and mineral clay baths, and as such is a haven for spagoers. The Bathhouse at Calistoga Ranch caters to them with five treatment rooms inspired by the native landscape and designed with organic elements such as copper, stone, wood and water. Four of the treatment rooms feature large terraces with soaking tubs and showers, and all are tailor-made for treatments involving a bath: buttermilk baths, mud baths or thermal mineral pool soaks. The spa draws water from the local hot springs and uses Napa Valley ingredients, including honey, grapeseed and bay laurel in many of the treatments. Other body treatments include a mud wrap said to boot immunity, and an oat and brown sugar scrub to sooth dry skin. The Bathhouse also offers private and group yoga classes and pilates; guests of the lodge can schedule private spa treatments in their rooms.

CARMEL

See also Big Sur, Carmel Valley, Monterey, Pebble Beach

Colonized by the Spanish in 1769, this city became the headquarters for the state's 21 Christian missions. Its striking architecture reflects the inspired whims of the artists and writers who have claimed it as their own since the early 20th century. Other artistic types have lived here including Clint Eastwood, who was the town's mayor from 1986 to 1988. With an abundance of art galleries and beaches, Carmel-by-the-Sea is an enduring tourist's delight.

WHAT TO SEE
ANTIQUE AND ART GALLERIES
San Carlos Street and Fifth Avenue, Carmel, 831-624-2522; www.carmelcalifornia.org
With more than 90 galleries displaying a wide variety of art and antiques, you can get a glimpse into what life is like as an artist in this beach community. Galleries showcase many different types of art from original oil paintings, figurative sculpture, contemporary artwork, emerging artists, expressionist art, etchings and much more.

THE BARNYARD SHOPPING VILLAGE
3618 The Barnyard, Carmel, 831-624-8886; www.thebarnyard.com
Nearly an acre of terraced flower gardens surround rustic, old-style California barns that house shops, galleries and restaurants. Boutique shops include apparel for men, women and children; jewelry, gifts and a florist. There are also salons, galleries and different restaurants including a pub, a pizzeria, a bistro, a sushi bar, and more.
Monday-Saturday 10 a.m.-6 p.m., Sunday 11 a.m.-5 p.m.

CARMEL CITY BEACH AND OCEAN STREET BEACH
Ocean Avenue, 831-624-4909; www.carmel.com
Carmel City Beach and Ocean Street Beach, located at the foot of Ocean Avenue, are easily accessible, have white sands and surfer-friendly waters. Carmel City beach holds a sand castle competition annually. Dogs can run freely on the beach and bon fires are permitted south of 10th Avenue. This is a great beach to gather friends for an afternoon picnic or a late-night bonfire. Carmel beaches are the most photographed beaches in the region and often an inspiration for many of the artists who live here.
Daily 6 a.m.-10 p.m.

CARMEL RIVER STATE BEACH
Carmelo Street and Scenic Road, 831-649-2836; www.parks.ca.gov
At Carmel River State Beach, south of Carmel on Scenic Road, find calm waters, tide pools and an adjacent bird sanctuary in a lagoon. The Wetlands Natural Reserve is also here and there are many waterfowl, ducks, mallards and coots around the lagoon. You can also see egrets, herons and hawks. This state beach is a great place for hiking, kayaking, bird-watching and sunbathing. Monastery Beach, which is also part of the park is usually frequented by scuba divers.

EARTHBOUND FARMS
7250 Carmel Valley Road, Carmel, 831-625-6219; www.ebfarm.com
A major player in the produce field—their products are in 75 percent of all supermarkets—Earthbound Farms started in 1984, producing herbs and a variety of organic greens for restaurants in the area. Their pre-washed salads put them on the map and the rest is history. The 30 acres in Carmel are devoted to research and development these days, the fruits of which are sold

at the farm stand right up front. You'll find pink lemons, golden raspberries, multi-colored beets (prepared in a delicious salad) and, of course, more than 60 varieties of lettuce. Also sold are foamy lattes, warm panini sandwiches, freshly baked breads, sweet treats and more.
Monday-Saturday 8 a.m.-6:30 p.m., Sunday 9 a.m.-6 p.m.

POINT LOBOS STATE RESERVE
Highway 1, Carmel, 831-624-4909; www.ptlobos.org
With its natural grove of Monterey cypresses, hundreds of plant, bird and animal species, you'll understand why this state reserve has often been called "the crown jewel of the State Park System." From Point Lobos, you can see many marine mammals in their natural habitat, such as sea lions, different types of seals, sea otters, whales and dolphins. On land, you will probably see gray foxes, coyotes, raccoons, skunks, opossums, bobcats and deer. Occasionally, but not often, mountain lions and badgers will come through the reserve looking for food. There is a picnic area, naturalist programs and scuba diving is permitted with proof of certification. Dogs are not allowed in the reserve.
Admission: $10 per car. Daily 8 a.m.-sunset.

RANCHO CAÑADA GOLF CLUB
4860 Carmel Valley Road, Carmel, 831-624-0111, 800-536-9459; www.ranchocanada.com
If golf is your game, and you're up for a challenge, then put your skills to the test at the acclaimed Rancho Cañada Golf Club in the heart of Monterey Peninsula at the entrance of Carmel Valley. There are two 18-hole championship courses: the East Course, with the Carmel River crossing the course five times, and the West Course, which has both broad and narrow fairways with the Carmel River intersecting three times. The Santa Lucia Mountains serve as a backdrop. There is a driving range, a golf shop, dining in the Golfers' Grill and a full bar. Daily.

SAN CARLOS BORROMÉO DE CARMELO MISSION
3080 Rio Road, Carmel, 831-624-1271; www.carmelmission.org
This is the oldest church in Carmel and headquarters for the California missions, which were founded in 1771 by Father Junipero Serra, the Spanish Franciscan priest and explorer. The Convento Museum is dedicated to Father Serra, who lived and worked there. The Mora Chapel Gallery holds a life-size memorial cenotaph, which is also dedicated to Father Serra. You can tour the Basilica, which is surrounded by gardens and fountains.
Admission: adults $5, seniors $4, children 5-17 $1. Monday-Saturday 9:30a.m.-5p.m., Sunday 10:30 a.m.-5 p.m.

SPECIAL EVENTS
CARMEL ART FESTIVAL
Devendorf Park, Carmel, 831-642-2503; www.carmelartfestival.org
Come to this juried art show for the full range of Carmel's creative denizens: artworks, sculptures and even a painting performance with live music accompaniment. This non-profit festival uses donations to support local youth

art programs. There are gallery events, lectures and demonstrations. Live music accompanies festival-goers as they browse through the art. Mid-May.

CARMEL BACH FESTIVAL

San Carlos Street and Ninth Avenue, Carmel, 831-624-2046; www.bachfestival.org

Set amidst the stunning architectural and natural landscapes of Carmel, the Carmel Bach Festival is a world-class 16-day celebration of the music of Johann Sebastian Bach, his contemporaries and musical heirs. For 72 years, the festival has brought Baroque music to music lovers from both the United States and abroad. Concerts, recitals, lectures and special events fill the days of this festival. You can attend a pre-concert talk to learn background information and tips on what to listen for during the concert; ask questions to the festival musicians; or attend a courtyard serenade outside. Mid-July-early August.

WHERE TO STAY

★★★CYPRESS INN

Lincoln Lane and Seventh Street, Carmel, 831-624-3871, 800-443-7443; www.cypress-inn.com

Built in 1929, this landmark Mediterranean-style hotel is steps away from the town center's boutiques, art galleries and great restaurants. A courtyard off the main lobby welcomes dogs and cats, and the inn also offers pet-sitting services. (Hollywood actress and animal advocate Doris Day is a co-owner.) The sophisticated rooms include bathrobes, pet blankets, fresh flowers, fruit bowls and sherry decanters. Some deluxe rooms come with a jet tub, a fireplace and a private entrance. The two-story tower suite offers an ocean view with a living area and sleeper sofa on the first floor. Terry's Lounge serves afternoon tea, lunch, tapas and dinner along with a long list of specialty cocktails and wines.

44 rooms. Restaurant, bar. Complimentary breakfast. Fitness center. Pets accepted. $151-250

★★★HIGHLANDS INN, A HYATT HOTEL

120 Highlands Drive, Carmel, 831-620-1234; www.highlandsinn.hyatt.com

Open since 1917, this sophisticated rendering of a mountain lodge is well suited to its rustic setting. The hotel's décor incorporates an abundance of wood and stone, and the rooms and suites are outfitted in contemporary, earth-tone furnishings. This inn features two restaurants and one lounge. California Market has a casual setting, with optional alfresco dining, and is open for breakfast, lunch and dinner. A more upscale option, Pacific's Edge features glass walls that allow views of the ocean and a wine list featuring over 1,400 labels. The Sunset Lounge delivers views of Point Lobos State Reserve, cocktails and live jazz music on Friday and Saturday nights. Take a complimentary mountain bike out for a ride through Carmel.

48 rooms. Restaurant, bar. Fitness center. Pool. $351 and up

★★★LA PLAYA HOTEL
Camino Real and Eighth Avenue, Carmel, 831-624-6476, 800-582-8900;
www.laplayahotel.com

This renovated Mediterranean-style villa has rooms with tropical décor and ocean, garden or village views. There are five cottages with private gardens, and the hotel's location is only one block from the beach. Dine alfresco on the Terrace Grill's charming heated terrace, which overlooks the garden. Get a massage, facial, or reflexology treatment in the garden or in your room.
80 rooms. Restaurant, bar. Business center. Pool. Spa. $151-250

★★★MISSION RANCH
26270 Dolores St., Carmel, 831-624-6436, 800-538-8221;
www.missionranchcarmel.com

Former Carmel mayor Clint Eastwood bought this 1850s farmhouse and saved it from demolition in the 1980s. Since then, it has been restored, expanded and filled with antiques and custom-designed rustic pieces. Surrounded by cypress and eucalyptus trees along with new gardens, the Bunkhouse is the oldest building on the ranch. The cozy guest rooms have quilted beds and patios from which to enjoy tranquil sunsets. There are six championship tennis courts on property along with a fitness center. Mission Ranch's restaurant serves dinner nightly and a Sunday jazz and champagne brunch. The Piano Bar is a fun place to frequent any night of the week.
31 rooms. Complimentary breakfast. Restaurant, bar. Fitness center. Tennis. $151-250

★★PINE INN
Ocean Avenue and Monte Verde Street, Carmel, 831-624-3851, 800-228-3851;
www.pine-inn.com

The Pine Inn was built in 1889 and was the first inn to open in Carmel-by-the-Sea. The European- and Asian-themed guest rooms have canopy beds, antique furnishings, and marble baths. The inn's restaurant, Il Fornaio, features authentic Italian cuisine with fresh-baked breads from the onsite bakery, which also serves pastries, breads, cookies and sandwiches.
49 rooms. Restaurant, bar. Complimentary breakfast. $151-250

WHERE TO EAT
★★★ANTON AND MICHEL
Mission Street between Ocean and Seventh avenues, Carmel, 831-624-2406;
www.antonandmichel.com

Though this long-standing restaurant's interior is ready for an update, the reliable French-inspired dishes are still as flavorful and satisfying as ever. Entrées include filet mignon, fresh-farmed abalone, rack of lamb and Châteaubriand carved tableside in the classic European tradition. Finales include flambé desserts, also prepared tableside. Choose a wine from a list that features more than 800 selections.
French. Lunch, dinner. Reservations recommended. Outdoor seating. Bar. $16-35

★★★CASANOVA

Fifth Street and Mission Street, Carmel, 831-625-0501; www.casanovarestaurant.com

One of the first restaurants in Carmel to offer a European bistro experience, Casanova has been open since 1977. All four dining rooms (one of which includes Vincent Van Gogh's table from Auberge Ravoux) feature a unique charm. The cuisine is influenced by the flavors of France and Italy and includes dishes such as pan-roasted wild salmon with Dijon mustard-citrus olive oil sauce, and pasta with roasted tomato coulis and goat cheese pesto sauce. The hand-dug wine cellar lies 14 feet beneath the restaurant and holds the more than 30,000 bottles.

French, Italian. Lunch, dinner. Reservations recommended. Outdoor seating. Children's menu. $36-85

★THE COTTAGE RESTAURANT

Lincoln Lane between Ocean and Seventh avenues, Carmel, 831-625-6260; www.cottagerestaurant.com

American. Breakfast, lunch, dinner (Thursday-Saturday). Reservations recommended. $16-35

★★FLYING FISH GRILL

Mission Street and Seventh Avenue, Carmel, 831-625-1962

Asian, American. Dinner. Reservations recommended. $36-85

★★THE FORGE IN THE FOREST

Fifth and Junipero avenues, Carmel, 831-624-2233; www.forgeintheforest.com

American. Lunch, dinner. Reservations recommended. Outdoor seating. Children's menu. Bar. $36-85

★★★THE FRENCH POODLE

Junipero and Fifth avenues, Carmel, 831-624-8643

This restaurant is an intimate hideaway known for artfully presented fare prepared in the French style. Sample truffles, foie gras with truffle dressing, filet mignon and fresh local abalone. For dessert, try the French flan or the flourless chocolate cake.

French. Dinner. Closed Sunday. Reservations recommended. $36-85

★★THE GRILL ON OCEAN AVENUE

Ocean Avenue between Dolores Street and Lincoln Lane, Carmel, 831-624-2569; www.carmelsbest.com

American. Lunch, dinner. Reservations recommended. Children's menu. Bar. $16-35

★★LE COQ D'OR

Mission Street and Fifth Avenue, Carmel, 831-626-9319

French, German. Dinner. Reservations recommended. Outdoor seating. $36-85

★★LITTLE NAPOLI

Dolores Street and Seventh Avenue, Carmel, 831-626-6335; www.littlenapoli.com

Italian. Lunch, dinner. $16-35

★★★PACIFIC'S EDGE RESTAURANT

Highlands Inn, 120 Highlands Drive, Carmel, 831-622-5445; www.pacificsedge.com

Enjoy the Pacific view, an extensive selection of mostly American wines and the local catch—Monterey spot prawns, for instance—which is usually richly accented with fresh herbs and plated with seasonal ingredients. The restaurant is located in the Highlands Inn.

American. Dinner. Reservations recommended. Bar. $36-85

★★THE RESTAURANT AT MISSION RANCH

Mission Ranch, 26270 Dolores St., Carmel, 831-624-6436, 800-538-8221; www.missionranchcarmel.com

American. Dinner, Sunday brunch. Outdoor seating. Children's menu. Bar. $36-85

★★RIO GRILL

101 Crossroads Blvd., Carmel, 831-625-5436; www.riogrill.com

Southwestern. Lunch, dinner. Reservations recommended. Outdoor seating. Children's menu. Bar. $16-35

★★ROCKY POINT RESTAURANT

36700 Highway 1, Carmel, 831-624-2933; www.rocky-point.com

American. Breakfast, lunch, dinner. Bar. $16-35

CARMEL VALLEY

See also Carmel, Big Sur and Monterey

Inland from the famed seaside village of Carmel, Carmel Valley is equally picturesque, with rolling hills, wildflower meadows and plenty of resorts, restaurants and golf courses. The village of Carmel Valley is home to many wineries with vineyards located along the winding Carmel Valley Road.

WHERE TO STAY

★★★★BERNARDUS LODGE

415 Carmel Valley Road, Carmel Valley, 831-658-3400, 888-648-9463; www.bernardus.com

Long considered one of the finest winemaking estates in California, the Lodge has a scenic Central Valley location and impressive views of the surrounding mountains and countryside. The spacious guest rooms include feather beds, fireplaces and oversized bathtubs for two. A spa also offers a wide variety of treatments. The Lodge's restaurant, Marinus, is an epicurean's delight.

57 rooms. Restaurant, bar. Business center. Fitness center. Pool. Spa. Tennis. $351 and up

★★CARMEL VALLEY LODGE

Carmel Valley and Ford roads, Carmel Valley, 831-659-2261, 800-641-4646; www.valleylodge.com

31 rooms. Complimentary breakfast. Pool. $151-250

★★★CARMEL VALLEY RANCH

1 Old Ranch Road, Carmel Valley, 831-625-9500, 866-282-4745;
www.carmelvalleyranch.com

This resort is set on 400 rolling acres in the secluded Carmel Valley countryside. The lodge-style architecture houses modern and spacious guest rooms with vaulted ceilings, floor-to-ceiling windows, wood-burning fireplaces and large decks. The resort includes an 18-hole, Pete Dye-designed golf course, tennis facilities, fitness center, pool and three dining venues, including the exquisite Citronelle, by chef Michel Richard, which serves modern French cuisine set in a sophisticated dining room. Opt for an in-suite spa treatment selected from a menu which includes massage therapies, skin care services and nail care.

144 rooms. Restaurant, bar. Fitness center. Pool. Golf. Tennis. $151-250

WHERE TO EAT

★★CAFÉ RUSTICA

10 Del Fino Place, Carmel Valley, 831-659-4444; www.caferusticacarmelvalley.com
American. Lunch, dinner. Closed Monday. Reservations recommended. Outdoor seating. $16-35

★★★★MARINUS

Bernardus Lodge, 415 Carmel Valley Road, Carmel Valley, 831-658-3595;
www.bernardus.com

This warm, country inn-style restaurant located inside Bernardus Lodge features exposed-beam ceilings, vintage tapestries and a 12-foot-wide limestone fireplace. Dishes are prepared using organic and fresh ingredients—in fact, neighbors often stop by with extra tomatoes or fishermen come in with their catch of the day. Chef Cal Stamenov then turns the goods into fresh salads and main courses such as salmon with English peas, braised leek and buerre blanc. The huge wine cellar, which stocks more than 1,800 selections, is impressive, even in wine country. Try the tasting menu, which gives you the option of choosing between a four-, five-, six- or eight-course menu.
American. Dinner. Closed Monday-Tuesday. Reservations recommended. $86 and up

★★WILL'S FARGO DINING HOUSE & SALOON

16 East Carmel Valley Road, Carmel Valley, 831-659-2774; www.willsfargo.com
American. Dinner. Bar. Reservations recommended. Outdoor seating. $16-35

SPAS

★★★★THE SPA AT BERNARDUS LODGE

Bernardus Lodge, 415 Carmel Valley Road, Carmel Valley, 831-658-3400, 888-648-9463; www.bernardus.com

This wine country spa has seven treatment rooms, an open-air "warming pool," steam and sauna rooms, and a fountain-filled meditation garden. Indigenous herbs, flowers, essential oils and healing waters are incorporated into the spa's treatments. Book the Vineyard Romance treatment, which includes a body exfoliation, lavender-grape seed bath, warm grape seed oil massage and a tea service of grape seed herbal tea. Or try the Chardonnay Facial, an 80-minute, hydrating treatment that incorporates chardonnay grape seeds, which are loaded with antioxidants. The spa's signature treatment, the Carmel Valley Escape, includes a massage, facial, spa lunch and manicure and pedicure.

FORT BRAGG
See also Mendocino, Ukiah, Willits
This lumber, agricultural, recreational and fishing center lies on the edge of the rocky coastline where the military post of Fort Bragg first stood in 1857. When the fort was abandoned in 1867, a lumber town sprang up in its place, only to be rebuilt after the 1906 earthquake. Driftwood and shell hunting are popular on nearby beaches, and the local botanical gardens that lie just beyond the surf and are the only ones in the U.S. that are directly in front of the ocean.

WHAT TO SEE
JUG HANDLE STATE RESERVE ECOLOGICAL STAIRCASE
Highway 1, Mendocino, 707-937-5804; www.parks.ca.gov
Within this state reserve is the Ecological Staircase, a 2 1/2-mile self-guided nature trail that has a series of five terraces that were formed by either waves, glaciers or tectonic activity. From the ocean, each terrace is raised at a higher level than the last, similar to a staircase. There is about a 100,000 year time span between when each terrace was uplifted from the sea, and there is about 100 feet between each terrace. You can understand the succession of the terraces by the plant life that abounds on each: the first and lowest terrace is prairie, followed by a pine forest, then a redwood forest, and the last terrace has pygmy trees which are only knee-high, showing that they've been around for decades.

MACKERRICHER STATE PARK
Highway 1, Mendocino, 707-964-9112; www.parks.ca.gov
Located three miles north of Fort Bragg, this state park covers about 10 miles of beach and ocean access. Lake Cleone's shores are stocked with picnic tables, fire pits with grills, and running water. There are four campgrounds with restrooms, showers, food storage lockers and fire rings. Guided activities here include hikes, a junior ranger program, organized whale watches and campfire programs. Near the park's entrance by the visitor center, there is a mounted skeleton of a 30-foot gray whale; whale migration occurs from mid-December to early April, when visitors come to watch the animals from the overlooks. There is also a stretch of sand dune that contains wetlands and freshwater ecosystems.

MENDOCINO COAST BOTANICAL GARDENS
18220 N. Highway 1, Fort Bragg, 707-964-4352; www.gardenbythesea.org
These gardens have about 47 acres of flowers and depending on what is in bloom, you might see rhododendrons, heathers, perennials, fuchsias, magnolias, heritage roses, hydrangeas, lilies, wild mushrooms, cactus, and others. Bird-watchers flock to the garden to view over 150 bird species, from hawks and osprey to the red-throated loon or the rare savannah sparrow.

Admission: adults $10, seniors $7.50, residents $5, children 13-17 $4, children 6-12 $2, children 5 and under free. March-October, daily 9 a.m.-5 p.m.; November-February, daily 9 a.m.-4 p.m.

NOYO HARBOR
19101 S. Harbor Drive, Fort Bragg, 707-964-4719; www.fortbragg.com
This scenic harbor is hidden in the forested hills of the south end of Fort Bragg. There are fishing centers that offer excursions and crabbing cruises, or you can a charter cruise and spend the day whale watching.

SPECIAL EVENTS
RHODODENDRON SHOW
1197 Chestnut St., Fort Bragg, 707-964-4435; www.mendocinocoast.com
More varieties of rhododendrons grow in Northern California than anywhere else in the world. The best way to get a glimpse of these varieties is to visit this show and plant sale over the first weekend in May. This juried show features over 700 entries, which include flowers, photos, bonsai and arrangements. A new hybrid will also be introduced. Refreshments and admission are free. Early May.

WHALE FESTIVAL
707-961 6300; www.mendowhale.com
In spring, the area's largest tourists—gray and humpback whales—pass through. The town stops to celebrate with not one, but two festivals. The first is the Mendocino Whale Festival, which is held the first weekend in March and features wine tasting and whale-watching. There are guided walks, exhibits, activities at state parks and at the Point Cabrillo Lighthouse. The second festival takes place the third weekend in March in Fort Bragg and includes almost everything the first one does, as well as a 10K/5K Run, a 5K competitive walk, a 5K fun walk, and microbrew beer and barbecue tastings. March.

WINESONG
Mendocino Coast Botanical Gardens, 18220 N. Highway 1, Fort Bragg, 707-961-4909; www.winesong.org
More than 100 vintners gather each September for a music festival and charity art and wine auction. Artists, local and world-famous, submit artwork to be auctioned. Over 50 of Mendocino County's best restaurants pass out samples of food to accompany the wine. Musicians perform in the gardens, making this event a great way to close out the summer. Saturday after Labor Day.

WHERE TO STAY
★★PINE BEACH INN
16801 N. Highway 1, Fort Bragg, 707-964-5603, 888-987-8388; www.pinebeachinn.com
50 rooms. Restaurant, bar. Tennis. Pets accepted $61-150

ALSO RECOMMENDED
THE LODGE AT NOYO RIVER
500 Casa Del Noyo Drive, Fort Bragg, 707-964-8045, 800-628-1126;
www.thelodgeatnoyoriver.com
Built in 1868, this bed and breakfast along the Noyo River offers rooms with cherry wood floors, and cherry and oak paneling and beams throughout. 17 rooms. Complimentary breakfast. $251-350

WHERE TO EAT
★★★THE RENDEZVOUS RESTAURANT
647 N. Main St., Fort Bragg, 707-964-8142; www.rendezvousinn.com
On the Mendocino Coast, 10 miles from the village of Mendocino, this historic redwood house holds a charming bed and breakfast with French influences and a French-trained chef. Sample dishes such as sautéed petrale sole stuffed or grilled quail with ginger-blood orange glaze. For dessert, there's roasted banana ice cream with a peanut butter swirl, and a superb pistachio soufflé.
French. Dinner. Closed Monday-Tuesday; January-February, Wednesday. Reservations recommended. $36-85

★★★THE RESTAURANT
418 N. Main St., Fort Bragg, 707-964-9800; www.therestaurantfortbragg.com
Situated in a historic building filled with original art, this restaurant has been a favorite of locals and visitors since 1973. The chef and owner, Jim Larsen, personally cooks most dishes and his wife, Susan manages the restaurant. This duo have created a charming restaurant where almost everything is made from scratch in-house using fresh ingredients. The meat, produce and seafood all come from local vendors, as does the coffee and wine.
American. Dinner. Closed Tuesday-Wednesday. Reservations recommended. Children's menu. $16-35

FORT ROSS STATE HISTORIC PARK
See also Bodega Bay, Guerneville, Healdsburg
One of the oldest parks in the California state park system, a Russian settlement was established at this site in 1812. It served as a thriving fur-trading outpost for years. The Rotchev House, which is the only building remaining, is now a National Historic Landmark. There's a beach, steep bluffs, a cove and plenty of forest to explore.

WHAT TO SEE
FORT ROSS STATE HISTORIC PARK
19005 Coast Highway 1, Jenner, 707-847-3286; www.parks.ca.gov
The fort was once a distant outpost of the Russian empire and, for nearly three decades in the early 1800s, an important center for the sea otter trade set up by the Russian-American Company of Alaska. A Californian bought the entire "Colony Ross of California" in 1841. Look for a reconstructed Russian Orthodox chapel, the original seven-sided and eight-sided blockhouses, the Commandant's house, officers' barracks and stockade walls. While on the

beach or surrounding bluffs, you might see migrating grey whales and sea lions or harbor seals lounging in the sun.
Daily sunrise-sunset.

KRUSE RHODODENDRON STATE RESERVE
Jenner, 707-847-3221; www.parks.ca.gov
Adjacent to Salt Point State Park, this 317-acre reserve is overflowing with rhododendrons. Five miles of hiking trails lead past Douglas firs, grand firs, tanoaks and rhododendrons, which bloom in April and May.
Daily.

SALT POINT STATE PARK
25050 Coast Highway 1, Jenner, 707-847-3221; www.parks.ca.gov
Sandstone from Salt Point was used to build the streets and structures of San Francisco in the 1800s. Geology buffs can look for drill holes along the rocks, as well as eyebolts left from ships anchored to load up the sandstone. Fisk Mill Cove supplies an area for picnicking with tables, barbecues, restrooms and drinking water. One of the first underwater parks, the Gerstle Cove Marine Reserve, is located here and offers a good spot for scuba diving. There are more than 20 miles of hiking and riding trails, fishing, pygmy forests and campgrounds.
Visitor center. April-October, Saturday-Sunday 10 a.m.-3 p.m. Daily sunrise-sunset.

SONOMA COAST STATE BEACH
Jenner, 707-875-3483; www.parks.ca.gov
On 4,200 acres along the coastline, running from Bodega Bay to Jenner, these sandy beaches, rocky headlands and sand dunes provide a scenic place to play. The rocky headland forming the entrance to the Bodega Harbor is a popular crabbing area. Goat Rock has a sandy beach where seals congregate to sunbathe, while Shell Beach offers plenty of tide pools to explore. Dogs are prohibited on most beaches. Daily.

WHERE TO STAY
★★★TIMBER COVE INN
21780 N. Coast Highway 1, Jenner, 707-847-3231, 800-987-8319;
www.timbercoveinn.com
A soaring cathedral ceiling, large stone fireplace and picture windows welcome guests to this lodge-like inn, located on the Sonoma Coast. The lobby is filled with leather couches, fresh flowers and a grand piano. Guest rooms are just as comfortable with spacious patios, which offer views of the ocean or the inn's quaint Japanese pond. There are 26-acres of trails and a a half-mile of ocean frontage on the grounds.
50 rooms. Restaurant, bar. $151-250

FRESNO
See also San Jose
In the state's geographic center and the heart of the San Joaquin Valley— the great central California "Garden of the Sun"—Fresno (Spanish for "ash

tree") and Fresno County are undergoing tremendous growth and extensive renovation to preserve their historic architecture. The town of Fresno grew around the railroad station when floods drove the population of nearby Millerton to seek higher ground. Fresno County claims the greatest agricultural production of any in the United States, handling more than $3 billion worth annually. The world's largest dried fruit packing plant, Sun-Maid, is here. With the diverse landscape of mountains, foothills, lakes, rivers, forests and countryside, Fresno ofers recreational activities year-round including white-water rafting, kayaking and sailing to skiing, horseback riding and rock climbing.

WHAT TO SEE
CALIFORNIA STATE UNIVERSITY, FRESNO
5241 N. Maple Ave., Fresno, 559-278-4240; www.csufresno.edu
"Fresno State" was founded in 1911 as Fresno State Normal School, and then became a teacher's college in 1921. Today, it is part of the 23 campuses that make up California State University and enrolls more than 22,000 students. The 388 acre campus, including a 1,011 acre farm, is set at the foot of the Sierra Nevada Mountains. While on campus, visit the Downing Planetarium, which has a theater and museum; the Conley Art Gallery; the campus farm and arboretum. Tours available.

FORESTIERE UNDERGROUND GARDENS
5021 W. Shaw Ave., Fresno, 559-271-0734; www.undergroundgardens.info
This subterranean, sky-lit, natural world was created single-handedly over 40 years by Baldassare Forestiere, one of three Italian immigrants who each hand-crafted residences in California. These 10 acres of underground tunnels, courtyards and rooms are filled with citrus plants, grape vines, rose bushes and other flora.
Tour admission: adults $12, seniors $10, children 13-17 $8, children 5-12 $7, children 4 and under free.

FRESNO ART MUSEUM
2233 N. First St., Fresno, 559-441-4221; www.fresnoartmuseum.org
The only modern art museum between Los Angeles and San Francisco, the Fresno Art Museum has been the centerpiece of Radio Park since it opened in the 1950s. The museum exhibits works by an international group of contemporary artists, as well as an impressive collection of Mexican art, dating from the pre-Columbia era to the present day. It also plays host to a series of performances, lectures and films.
Admission: adults $5, seniors and students $5, children 5 and under free. Free on Sunday. Tuesday-Sunday 11 a.m.-5 p.m., Thursday 11 a.m.-8 p.m.

FRESNO CHAFFEE ZOO
894 W. Belmont Ave., Fresno, 559-498-2671; www.fresnochaffeezoo.com
This 18-acre zoo has more than 650 animals representing 125 species, and has a reptile house, elephant exhibit, Sunda forest (with orangutans, siamangs and tigers) and a tropical rainforest exhibit containing plants and animals found primarily in South American regions. The zoo has 18 species

that are part of the Species Survival Plan, which helps to develop breeding management strategies to protect rare animals, such as the red wolf, Malayan tiger, keel-billed toucan, fennec fox and radiated tortoise.
Admission: adults $7, seniors $3.50, children 2-11 $3.50. Daily 9 a.m.-4 p.m.

FRESNO METROPOLITAN MUSEUM OF ART & SCIENCE
1555 Van Ness Ave., Fresno, 559-441-1444; www.fresnomet.org
This recently renovated museum has collections that include the photographs of Ansel Adams, landscape paintings of California from the 19th and 20th century, European and American paintings form the 16th-20th century and a Native American collection of baskets and cradleboards from the Central Valley of California. Other displays have included hands-on science exhibits, artwork and hands-on art exhibits where children can learn about famous artists while learning how to create their own art.
Admission: adults $9, seniors and students $7, children 3-12 $5, children under 3 free. Tuesday-Sunday 10 a.m.-6 p.m. First Thursday of the month 10 a.m.-8 p.m.

KEARNEY MANSION MUSEUM
7160 W. Kearney Blvd., Fresno, 559-441-0862; www.valleyhistory.org
This restored historic mansion was the home of M. Theo Kearney, known as the "Raisin King of Fresno". He cultivated a raisin vineyard business in Fresno County which eventually became Sun-Maid brand raisins. The mansion contains original furnishings including European wallpapers and Art Nouveau light fixtures. There is also an adjacent servants' quarters house, ranch kitchen and museum gift shop to explore. To see the mansion, take a narrated 45-minute tour.
Admission: adults $5, seniors and students $4, children 3-12 $3, children under the age of 3 free. Tours: Friday-Sunday 1 p.m., 2 p.m. and 3 p.m.

KINGSBURG
Chamber of Commerce, 1475 Draper St., Kingsburg, 559-897-1111; www.kingsburgchamberofcommerce.com
Settled by Swedes in the early 1870s, this town's architecture reflects their fondness for color and light. Flags and Dalecarlian horses (simple wooden horses painted red with colorful bridles) decorate the streets. By 1921, ninety-four percent of the population within a three-mile radius of Kingsburg were of Swedish descent. Festivals are held throughout the year to celebrate traditional Swedish food, clothing and traditions.

ROEDING PARK
890 W. Belmont Ave., Fresno, 559-621-2900; www.fresno.gov
Located in the city of Fresno, this party has a lake, several ponds and a variety of trees and shrubs, ranging from high-mountain to tropical species, all spread across 159 acres. There is also a tennis course, two dance pavilions, horseshoe pits, a children's playground and many picnic areas with tables, picnic shelters and barbecue pits.
Admission: adults $7, seniors and children 2-11 $3.50, children under 2

free. April-October, daily 6 a.m.-10 p.m.; November-March, daily 6 a.m.-7 p.m.

SIERRA NATIONAL FOREST

1600 Tollhouse Road, Clovis, 559-297-0706, 877-444-6777; www.fs.fed.us

The Sierra National Forest is made up of nearly 1.3 million acres ranging from rolling foothills to rugged, snow-capped mountains. The forest includes two groves of giant sequoias, hundreds of natural lakes, 11 major reservoirs and unique geological formations. The topography can be rough and precipitous in higher elevations, with deep canyons and many beautiful meadows along streams and lakes. The John Muir Wilderness area is the largest and most-visited in California and covers 584,000 rugged acres. Permits are required for overnight trips to the area. You can go rafting, boating, sailing, canoeing, white-water rafting, fishing, hunting, downhill and cross-country skiing, picnicking, and camping here. Due to the presence of Sierra black bears, it's important to follow rules and regulations for storing food and enjoying the forest.

SIERRA SUMMIT MOUNTAIN RESORT

59265 Highway 168, Lakeshore, 559-233-2500; www.sierrasummit.com

Located 65 miles northeast of Fresno, this mountain resort has over 45 trails and 25 ski runs, with the longest run at 2 miles and the biggest vertical drop is 1,600 feet. There are three freestyle parks, a halfpipe and areas designed for families. Onsite is a kid's camp, a ski school and a rental shop. Mid-November-mid-April, daily.

WILD WATER ADVENTURE PARK

11413 E. Shaw Ave., Clovis, 559-299-9453, 800-564-9453; www.wildwater.net

This 52-acre water park has more than 20 attractions and 38 slides, and contains one of the West's largest wave pools, the Blue Wave. The park features a special section young children.

Admission: adults $25, children 48" tall and under $18.99, seniors $10.99, children under 2 free. Late May-early September, daily.

SPECIAL EVENTS
THE BIG FRESNO FAIR

1121 S. Chance Ave., Fresno, 559-650-3247; www.fresnofair.com

This fair is the largest annual event in the Central Valley and has been held since 1884. The festival features a carnival, horseracing, arts and crafts, and concessions. October.

FRESNO COUNTY BLOSSOM TRAIL

2220 Tulare St., Fresno, 559-262-4271; www.goblossomtrail.com

Plan to take this 62-mile self-guided driving or biking tour of California agriculture during peak season from late February to mid-March. You'll see fruit orchards, citrus groves, vineyards and provincial towns. Late February-mid-March.

HIGHLAND GATHERING AND GAMES

Roeding Park, 890 W. Belmont, Fresno, 559-439-5553; www.scottishsociety.org

This annual festival features traditional Scottish competitions including dancing, piping, drumming and athletics.

Admission: adults $15, seniors and military $10, children 6-12 $5, children 5 and under free. Mid-September.

WHERE TO STAY
★★FOUR POINTS BY SHERATON FRESNO

3737 N. Blackstone Ave., Fresno, 559-226-2200; www.starwoodhotels.com

204 rooms. Restaurant, bar. Business center. Fitness center. Pool. $151-250

★★RADISSON HOTEL & CONFERENCE CENTER FRESNO

2233 Ventura St., Fresno, 559-268-1000, 800-395-7046; www.radisson.com

321 rooms. Restaurant, bar. Fitness center. Pool. $61-150

WHERE TO EAT
★★RIPE TOMATO

5064 N. Palm Ave., Fresno, 559-225-1850

French. Lunch, dinner. Closed Sunday-Monday. Reservations recommended. Outdoor seating. $36-85

GILROY

See also Salinas, San Jose, San Juan Bautista

Located in Santa Clara County, Gilroy is known for its garlic crops. The annual Gilroy Garlic Festival, held each July, is one of the area's most popular and unique events. With its Mediterranean climate and quality of life, it has been rated as the fastest growing city in Silicon Valley.

WHAT TO SEE
FORTINO WINERY

4525 Hecker Pass Highway, Gilroy, 408-842-3305; www.fortinowinery.com

This small family-run winery is located in the Santa Clara Valley and offers tours, free wine tasting and a picnic area. The winery produces chardonnay, burgundy reserve, carignan, maribella, cabernet sauvignon, sangiovese, two sparkling wines and fruit wines.

Tuesday-Saturday 10 a.m.-5 p.m., Sunday 11 a.m.-5 p.m.

GILROY PREMIUM OUTLETS

681 Leavesley Road, Gilroy, 408-842-3729; www.premiumoutlets.com/gilroy

These outlets draw shopoholics to their nearly 150 outlet stores which include J. Crew, BCBG Max Azria, American Apparel, Gap, Hugo Boss, Kenneth Cole, Jones New York, DKNY Jeans, Calvin Klein and Puma among many others.

Monday-Saturday 10 a.m.-9 p.m., Sunday 10 a.m.-6 p.m.

SPECIAL EVENTS
GILROY GARLIC FESTIVAL
Christmas Hill Park, 7050 Miller Ave., Gilroy, 408-842-1625;
www.gilroygarlicfestival.com
Since 1979, garlic lovers have come out to take part in this festival of the local crop. The Great Garlic Cook-off is a popular competition featuring amateur chefs whipping up their best garlic recipes to be tasted by celebrity judges. Booths feature foods made with garlic. Last full weekend in July.

WHERE TO STAY
★★★★CORDEVALLE, A ROSEWOOD RESORT
1 Cordevalle Club Drive, San Martin, 408-695-4500, 888-767-3966;
www.cordevalle.com
CordeValle sprawls over 1,700 acres in the foothills between San Jose and Monterey, attracting small business groups as well as golfers and those looking for a romantic weekend. The spacious, high-ceilinged modern bungalows overlook a rolling 18-hole Robert Trent Jones, Jr. golf course. Rooms feature goose-down comforters, original artwork, flat-screen TVs and a fireplace. The Villa Suites are 1,100 square feet and offer the same amenities as the bungalows but also have a bathroom with steam shower and jetted tub and an enclosed patio with another outdoor shower and private whirlpool. Each treatment room in the resort's spa, Sense, has a private garden. Treatments include massages, body wraps, body scrubs and facials. Guests also get access to the spa's whirlpool, and steam room, outdoor heated pool, fitness center, tennis courts, outdoor yoga deck and hiking trails. The onsite vineyard produces the wine and cheese placed in guest rooms as a welcome gift.
45 rooms. Restaurant, bar. Fitness center. Pool. Spa. Golf. $351 and up

★QUALITY INN, MORGAN HILL
16525 Condit Road, Morgan Hill, 408-779-0447, 877-424-6423; www.qualityinn.com
83 Rooms. Complimentary breakfast. Pool. Pets accepted. $61-150

SPAS
★★★★SENSE, A ROSEWOOD SPA
CordeValle, 1 Cordevalle Club Drive, San Martin, 408-695-4500, 888-767-3966;
www.cordevalle.com
This top-notch facility treats its guests to luxurious amenities, elegant interiors and a full-service spa menu. Classic contemporary is the reigning style at this spa, where earth tones and sandstone fireplaces create a serene atmosphere. The services blend European traditions with modern philosophies, and most of the treatments use locally grown herbs, flowers and even grapes from the hillsides just outside the window. Several treatments have been created specifically with golfers' needs in mind. The restful pace found here is perhaps best enjoyed from the private gardens accompanying each treatment room.

GLEN ELLEN
See also Calistoga, Napa, St. Helena, Santa Rosa, Sonoma
Famous for its wineries, this Sonoma Valley community was home to writers

Jack London and Hunter S. Thompson. Only 45 minutes from San Francisco, Glen Ellen is a popular spot for weekend getaways.

WHAT TO SEE
JACK LONDON STATE HISTORICAL PARK
2400 London Ranch Road, Glen Ellen, 707-938-5216; www.parks.sonoma.net.com
A memorial to the writer Jack London, this park is located on the site of his mansion, where he lived from 1905 until his death in1916. The grounds include the gravesite of London and his wife, Charmian.
Daily 9:30 a.m.-5 p.m.

SPECIAL EVENTS
WINE COUNTRY FILM FESTIVAL
12000 Henno Road, Glen Ellen, 707-935-3456; www.winecountryfilmfest.com
This festival features outdoor screenings at Glen Ellen's wineries and parks. Although the schedule is not announced until two weeks before the festival's opening, the screenings and other events often sell out well in advance. For out-of-towners, the festival has special travel packages as well as all-inclusive passes. July-August.

WHERE TO STAY
★★★ST. ORRES
36601 Coast. Highway 1, Gualala, 707-884-3303; www.saintorres.com
This inn is located three hours north of San Francisco on more than 50 acres of coastal sanctuary. Local craftsmen built the Russian dacha-like house, working with materials found in the area to form its distinct onion-domed towers, stained glass features and woodwork. Rooms have a rustic atmosphere and amenities such as wood-burning stoves, fireplaces, soaking tubs, French doors or decks. Most rooms provide an ocean view, and the restaurant offers a myriad of fine cuisine.
21 rooms. Complimentary breakfast. Restaurant, bar. $151-250

ALSO RECOMMENDED
GAIGE HOUSE INN
13540 Arnold Drive, Glen Ellen, 707-935-0237, 800-935-0237; www.gaige.com
At this woodsy yet luxurious resting spot, the guest rooms give the impression of outdoor living, with the large windows looking out onto the countryside. Rooms are individually designed—some with fireplaces or private Japanese gardens. Four off-site cottages are even more secluded and ideal for longer visits.
23 rooms. No children under 12. Complimentary breakfast. Pool. Spa. $251-350

WHERE TO EAT
★★THE FIG CAFÉ AND WINE BAR
13690 Arnold Drive, Glen Ellen, 707-938-2130; www.thefigcafe.com
Located in the center of Glen Ellen, this restaurant, which is housed in a craftsman cottage accented with flower-filled window boxes, serves fresh, seasonal French-influenced dishes in a casual setting. The menu features

dishes such as stuffed brioche French toast, baby artichoke pizza, and steamed mussels and fries.

French. Dinner, Saturday-Sunday brunch.. Reservations recommended. Bar. $16-35

★★GLEN ELLEN INN
13670 Arnold Drive, Glen Ellen, 707-996-6409; www.glenelleninn.com

This chef-owned and -operated restaurant is located in the village of Glen Ellen. The California menu features dishes such as ginger tempura calamari, braised lamb shank, and a pulled Kahlua pork sandwich. The oyster grill and martini bar make this quaint restaurant a local favorite. The extensive wine list features more than 550 local wines.

American. Lunch (Friday-Tuesday), dinner. Outdoor seating. $16-35

★★SAFFRON RESTAURANT
13648 Arnold Drive, Glen Ellen, 707-938-4844

Owned by chef Christopher Dever, this intimate café features a daily changing menu of eclectic California cuisine. The restaurant's 11 tables are dressed with burgundy and white cloths and topped with sunflowers. A small, enclosed patio with heaters and a fountain provides additional space for alfresco dining.

American. Dinner. Closed Sunday-Monday. Reservations recommended. Outdoor seating. $16-35

HALF MOON BAY
See also Mountain View, Palo Alto

Perched on a gorgeous stretch of California coastline, this resort community has a charming, well-preserved historic downtown. The close proximity to San Francisco (only 28 miles away) and many upscale restaurants, galleries and resorts make this town a popular choice for weekend visits. With mild temperatures, visitors can take in local beaches, parks and golf courses. As you make your way into Half Moon Bay, you'll notice many roadside stands selling fresh local vegetables and herbs.

WHAT TO SEE
HALF MOON BAY BREWING COMPANY
390 Capistrano Road, Half Moon Bay, 650-728-2739; www.hmbbrewingco.com

This oceanfront restaurant and brewing company is located about four miles north of Half Moon Bay on Pillar Point Harbor in Princeton-by-the-Sea. The restaurant and brewpub features ocean views, live music and dancing, and serves sustainable seafood. The eight brews are tasty and refreshing with a light ale, amber ale, hefeweizen, and more.

Monday-Thursday 11:30 a.m.-9 p.m., Friday 11:30 a.m.-10 p.m., Saturday 11 a.m.-10 p.m., Sunday 11 a.m.-9 p.m.

HALF MOON BAY GOLF CLUB
2 Miramontes Point Road, Half Moon Bay, 650-726-1800; www.halfmoonbaygolf.com

Just off historic Highway 1 on the Pacific Ocean, this golf club has two courses, the Old Course and the Ocean Course, which vary slightly in their makeup. The Old Course resembles Pebble Beach with its traditional American design, while the Ocean course lets wild grasses overtake the rough and looks more like a links layout. A cart is included in the $182 price, and walking is not permitted.

SPECIAL EVENTS
COASTSIDE FARMER'S MARKET
Shoreline Station at Kelly Avenue & Highway 1, Half Moon Bay, 650-726-4895; www.coastsidefarmersmarket.org

This farmer's market features farm-fresh produce, seafood and local art and live music. Pick up some wild king salmon, regional honey or artisan goat cheese from local farms and enjoy the scenic surroundings while listening to music.
May-late December, Saturday 9 a.m.-1 p.m.

WHERE TO STAY
★★CYPRESS INN ON MIRAMAR BEACH
407 Mirada Road, Half Moon Bay, 650-726-6002, 800-832-3224; www.cypressinn.com
18 rooms. Complimentary breakfast. $251-350

★★★MILL ROSE INN
615 Mill St., Half Moon Bay, 650-726-8750, 800-900-7673; www.millroseinn.com
Just two blocks from the center of Half Moon Bay and many shops, restaurants and art galleries, this handsome inn's stylish interiors are matched by its well-manicured grounds and blooming gardens. Each room or suite has a private entrance, European antiques, a hand-painted fireplace, claw-foot tub, complimentary stocked refrigerator, wireless Internet access and Japanese dressing robe. A complimentary gourmet breakfast is served daily, either in room, in the dining room, or outdoors in the garden courtyard. The breakfast features housemade breads, crepes, omelets and quiche.
6 rooms. Complimentary breakfast. $251-350

★★★★THE RITZ-CARLTON, HALF MOON BAY
1 Miramontes Point Road, Half Moon Bay, 650-712-7000; www.ritzcarlton.com
From its cliff-top setting to its shingled architecture, this hotel looks like a slice of Scotland on the Northern California coast. But while the windswept dunes and emerald links hint of a foreign land, this exquisite resort—only 30 miles from San Francisco—has a decidedly West Coast flavor. The guest rooms and suites are the essence of relaxed sophistication, with soft colors, floral or striped fabrics and nautical artwork. Golfers will develop a soft spot for the resort's 36 oceanfront holes, while others can go horseback riding on the secluded beach or play volleyball, basketball or croquet. Navio restaurant serves coastal Californian cuisine with fresh local seafood in a romantic setting. For a more casual atmosphere, try the Conservatory Lounge which has floor-to-ceiling windows with ocean views. Or stop in ENO, a wine, chocolate and cheese cellar where you can get a flight of wine or cheese and try unique chocolates. Pets are welcome in the resort's guesthouses, but they're likely to be spoiled with dog bones served on silver trays.
261 rooms. Restaurant, bar. Pool. Pets accepted. $351 and up

WHERE TO EAT

★★★CETRELLA BISTRO & CAFÉ

845 Main St., Half Moon Bay, 650-726-4090; www.cetrella.com

With a dedication to fresh, local and seasonal ingredients, this restaurant serves flavorful yet simple Mediterranean-inspired food. Executive chef Sylvain Montassier confidently creates dishes such as wood oven baked grouper with wild mushroom rice and broth, or honey-glazed Berkshire pork chop with brussel sprouts fricassée, lentils and bacon broth. With over 400 wines to choose from, the friendly staff can suggest the perfect wine to accompany your meal.

Mediterranean. Dinner, Sunday brunch. Closed January-April. $16-35

★★★NAVIO

The Ritz-Carlton, Half Moon Bay, 1 Miramontes Point Road, Half Moon Bay, 650-712-7000; www.ritzcarlton.com

A classic and romantic dining room with views of the ocean, this restaurant inside the Ritz-Carlton, Half Moon Bay serves California cuisine with a focus on fresh seafood. In order to provide the freshest catch, the menu changes daily. Dishes may include local butterfish with braised Shiitake mushrooms, baby bok choy and Shiitake broth; crispy salmon with melted cabbage, caramelized apples and fried celery root; or herb roasted beef tenderloin with yukon gold potato gratin, spinach, oyster mushrooms and red wine sauce. The Sunday brunch is a local favorite.

American, seafood. Breakfast, lunch, dinner, Sunday brunch. $36-85

SPAS

★★★★THE RITZ-CARLTON SPA, HALF-MOON BAY

The Ritz-Carlton, Half Moon Bay, 1 Miramontes Point Road, Half Moon Bay, 650-712-7040,800-241-3333; www.ritzcarlton.com

Golfers will be taken in by the 36-hole oceanfront course at this resort, but its 16,000-square-foot spa is equally impressive. Wind down with a co-ed, candlelit Roman mineral bath, lounge in the oceanfront Jacuzzi or enjoy the steam and sauna facilities. The signature pumpkin body peel delivers the nourishing benefits of this local treat. The well-equipped fitness center overlooks the ocean and the gazebo lawn, which also includes a heated yoga studio or you can take a pilates class, water aerobics or Tai-Chi.

HEALDSBURG

See also Bodega Bay, Clear Lake Area, Fort Ross Historic Park, Guerneville, Santa Rosa

In the center of some of Northern California's most esteemed winemaking appellations, including Alexander Valley, Dry Creek, Chalk Hill and Russian River Valley, is the thriving and charming wine town of Healdsburg, where palm trees and 100-year old redwoods shade manicured grounds and benches in the town square. The town of Healdsburg is centrally located with access to more than 100 world class wineries, from the grandest European-style villas to the more rustic, yet no less well-crafted mom-and-pop shops. One of Sonoma County's most famous towns, it's surrounded by plenty of boutiques, upscale restaurants and art galleries.

WHAT TO SEE
BELLA VINEYARDS AND WINE CAVES
9711 W. Dry Creek Road, Healdsburg, 866-572-3552; www.bellawinery.com

It's the classic tale: Girl meets boy. Girl marries boy. Couple moves to wine country and learns how to make wine. Classic or not, few could pull it off like Scott and Lynn Adams, who have earned accolades for producing some of the best wine in the region. Bella harvests a varied crop of wines from its three distinct vineyards in the Dry Creek and Alexander valleys, including zinfandel and syrah. While the wines are top-notch, a big reason for Bella's appeal is its beautiful caves. Entering on the side of a hill underneath an arbor of vines, you'll be given a glimpse into the inner workings of the winery, as well as an underground taste or two. Tastings $5.
Daily 11 a.m.- 4:30 p.m.

CANOE TRIPS
River's Edge Kayak & Canoe Trips, 13840 Healdsburg Ave., Healdsburg, 707-433-7247; www.riversedgekayakandcanoe.com

If you would like to see more of what Healdsburg has to offer besides wine, take a half, one or two day kayak or canoe trip on the Russian River. All trips include paddles, life vests and a shuttle ride. The trips run throughout the year.

LAMBERT BRIDGE WINERY
4085 W. Dry Creek Road, Healdsburg, 707-431-9600; www.lambertbridge.com

This family-run vineyard is located in the heart of the Dry Creek Valley. The manicured grounds and gardens are planted with edible flowers and herbs. Teak tables and chairs offer a good spot for picnics which you can enjoy with a bottle of wine bought at the vineyard. Or join chef Andrea Mugnaini in the outdoor kitchen for a class on wood-fired cooking, before feasting on your creations with wines to match.
Daily 10:30 a.m.-4:30 p.m.

SIMI WINERY
16275 Healdsburg Ave., Healdsburg, 800-746-4880; www.simiwinery.com

This winery dates from the turn-of-the-century when founders Giuseppe and Pietro Simi came to California during the gold Rush from Italy. Simi's vineyards in the Alexander Valley take up almost 600 acres with diverse soils, which produce Bordeaux varietals and cabernet sauvignon. The company also has the 120-acre Goldfields Vineyard in the Russian River Valley, which produces most of their chardonnay. Stop in the visitor center for a guided tour, which take place twice a day followed by a private tasting.
Daily 10 a.m.-5 p.m.

QUIVIRA VINEYARDS
4900 W. Dry Creek Road, Healdsburg, 707-431-8333; www.quivirawine.com

This innovative estate is committed to organic and biodynamic winemaking practices, transforming the once wood and cinder barn into a solar-paneled, high-tech edifice. Reds are the specialty here, with such smooth varietals as the 2006 Steelhead Zinfandel, a robust blend named after the wild trout that spawn in the onsite creek each year. On a hot day, the sauvignon blanc is refreshing, especially under the shade of Quivira's ancient fig trees. Tastings $5. Daily 11 a.m.-5 p.m.

SPECIAL EVENTS
HEALDSBURG HARVEST CENTURY BICYCLE TOUR
217 Healdsburg Ave., Healdsburg, 707-433-6935; www.healdsburg.com
The town of Healdsburg hosts this bicycle tour through Sonoma County wine country each summer. The ride is moderately challenging with narrow and rough-surfaced roads, but can accommodate both road and mountain bikes. The tour goes through the Alexander, Russian River and Dry Creek valleys. Mid-July.

WHERE TO STAY
★★★HOTEL HEALDSBURG
25 Matheson St., Healdsburg, 707-431-2800, 800-889-7188;
www.hotelhealdsburg.com
This striking, contemporary hotel on the historic Town Plaza is a showpiece of minimalist design, from its public spaces to its guest rooms and suites. Rooms have bright walls and neutral goose down duvets, feather beds and Frette linens. Bathrooms have concrete counters, Italian glass Bisazza tile and walk-in showers with the hotel's own organic bathroom amenities. Windows look out over the plaza or toward the hotel's garden and some rooms have French doors and private balconies. Relax out in the pool and jacuzzi or enjoy spa treatments at the hotel's onsite spa. Treatments include massages, facials, manicures, pedicures and body wraps. All of wine country is easily explored from here, but this hotel is a culinary destination in its own right, with noted chef Charlie Palmer's lauded Dry Creek Kitchen onsite.
55 rooms. Restaurant, bar. Complimentary breakfast.. Fitness center. Pool. Spa. $351 and up

★★★★LES MARS HOTEL
27 North St., Healdsburg,707-433-4211; www.lesmarshotel.com
Imagine the thrill of staying with close friends while on vacation. Now take that thought and add a bucolic wine country setting, a classic chateau-style residence and peerless attention to detail. Located on a side street just off the main strip, the hotel boasts 16 rooms individually decorated with antiques, luxurious Italian linens, fireplaces, marble showers and canopied beds. Some rooms have antique armoires, four-poster beds, and a hydrotherapy jet soaking tub. The bathrooms are complemented with Bulgari amenities and a Le Mars monogrammed robe. Located off the lobby is Cyrus, the hotel's exquisite restaurant serves up French- and Asian-inspired cuisine. Choose whether to have a five- or eight-course meal to get a taste of chef Douglas Keane's talent. The hand-carved walnut-panel library offers a tranquil respite after a day of wine tastings, and the complimentary breakfast delivered to your room each morning will make you think twice about ever staying with friends again.
16 rooms. Complimentary breakfast. Pool. $351 and up

★★★MADRONA MANOR
1001 Westside Road, Healdsburg, 707-433-4231, 800-258-4003;
www.madronamanor.com

This Victorian estate in the hills above the Dry Creek Valley has accommodated travelers since 1981. Most of the rooms have fireplaces and some have balconies with views of vineyards, mountains and gardens. While they don't have televisions, rooms do come with antique furniture, pillow-top mattresses, soft linens and a terry cloth robe.
18 rooms. Restaurant, bar. Complimentary breakfast. Pool. No children under 12. $251-350

ALSO RECOMMENDED
DUCHAMP
421 Foss St., Healdsburg, 707-431-1300, 800-431-9341; www.duchamphotel.com

This contemporary hotel consists of six stand-alone villas with king sized beds, down comforters and pillows, an overstocked shower filled with Aveda products and a private terrace. Amenities include flat-screen TVs, CD players, complimentary wireless Internet access and fireplaces. Sip Duchamp's sparkling wine at the source—the Duchamp Estate Winery is nearby.
6 rooms. Pool. Pets accepted. $351 and up

THE HONOR MANSION
14891 Grove St., Healdsburg, 707-433-4277, 800-554-4667; www.honormansion.com

An Italianate Victorian house built in 1883, this inn is surrounded by century-old trees, including a landmark magnolia. The rooms are uniquely decorated, and some have hand-carved antique furniture, fireplaces and large soaking tubs. Guests also receive complimentary access to a local gym. There are plenty of onsite activities to keep you busy from the swimming pool to tennis courts, bocce ball, croquet and a PGA putting green and full golf course.
13 rooms. Complimentary breakfast. Pool. Golf. Tennis. $251-350

WHERE TO EAT
★★BISTRO RALPH
109 Plaza St., Healdsburg, 707-433-1380; www.bistroralph.com

American, French. Lunch, dinner. Closed Sunday. Reservations recommended. Outdoor seating. Bar. $16-35

★★★★CYRUS RESTAURANT
29 North St., Healdsburg, 707-433-3311; www.cyrusrestaurant.com

Visit Les Mars Hotel in downtown Healdsburg for this congenial 65-seat restaurant. Admire some of the luxurious touches—a cloister ceiling, leather banquettes and tables set with fresh flowers—and sample from others—a champagne and caviar cart, 60 pages of spirits, more than 600 wines and a prix fixe menu of three-, four- or five-course that changes daily. Guests can order cocktails before or after dinner at a large bar and lounge area.
Continental. Dinner. Reservations recommended. Bar. $86 and up

★★★DRY CREEK KITCHEN
317 Healdsburg Ave., Healdsburg, 707-431-0330; www.charliepalmer.com

The restaurant, the brainchild of celeb chef Charlie Palmer, is housed in the modern Hotel Healdsburg. Enjoy an exercise in rustic, dressed up comfort food, with down-home dishes and a waitstaff that's all smiles. Entrées include dishes such as pan roasted bass with vegetable basquaise, beluga cous cous, preserved lemon and crispy caperberries; and Angus beef strip loin with caramelized onion and blue cheese gratin. Desserts include caramelized banana and caramel corn, which consists of cinnamon crisps, brown butter-caramel ice cream and popcorn sherbet. The wine list has more than 600 bottles with many from nearby wineries.

American. Lunch (Friday-Sunday), dinner, Friday-Sunday brunch. Reservations recommended. Outdoor seating. Bar. $36-85

★★★MADRONA MANOR
1001 Westside Road, Healdsburg, 707-433-4231, 800-258-4003;
www.madronamanor.com

This romantic restaurant, housed in a restored inn, serves New California cuisine in a classic and elegant setting. Diners can try a seven- or nine-course tasting menu with or without wine pairings, or choose dishes such as roasted duck breast with crispy confit, hazelnuts, summer beans and quinoa; or broiled black cod with braised lettuce, chanterelles, miso and black garlic from the à la carte menu. Regardless of what you choose, find fresh organic fish and produce from an organic garden onsite. An extensive wine list featuring local and global vintners complements the menu.

American, French. Dinner. Closed Monday-Tuesday. Reservations recommended. Outdoor seating. Bar. $36-85

★★MANZANITA RESTAURANT
336 Healdsburg Ave., Healdsburg, 707-433-8111; www.manzanita336.com

American. Dinner, Saturday-Sunday brunch. Closed Sunday-Monday. Reservations recommended. Bar. $86 and up

★★RAVENOUS
420 Center St., Healdsburg, 707-431-1302

American. Lunch, dinner. Closed Monday-Tuesday. Reservations recommended. Outdoor seating. Bar. $36-85

INVERNESS
See also Bodega Bay

Located north of San Francisco in Marin County, the seaside town of Inverness is one of the villages that surrounds the beautifully rugged Point Reyes National Seashore and Tomales Bay. Other villages nearby include Marshall, Muir Beach, Olema, Point Reyes Station, Stinson Beach and Tomales. Inverness is a popular area for hiking and exploring, and the town is filled with quaint restaurants and bed and breakfasts.

WHAT TO SEE
COWGIRL CREAMERY AT TOMALES BAY FOODS
80 Fourth Street, Point Reyes Station, 415-663-9335; www.cowgirlcreamery.com

These cowgirls whip up around 3,000 pounds of their four soft aged cheeses and three fresh cheeses every week from their headquarters in Point Reyes Station. Visit the original creamery in the barn where owners and founders Sue Conley and Peggy Smith first started making their famous cheese in 1997. Taste and purchase cheeses, books, knives, boards and condiments here; watch through a viewing window as the cheeses are made and take a tour which includes a presentation and a tasting of the cheeses. You can also purchase their cheeses at the Cowgirl Creamery at the Ferry Plaza in San Francisco and their new second creamery in Petaluma (among other places).

Admission: $5, Friday 11:30 a.m. Creamery: Wednesday-Sunday 10 a.m.-6 p.m.

HOG ISLAND OYSTER COMPANY FARM
20215 Highway 1, Marshall, 415-663-9218; www.hogislandoysters.com

The Hog Island Oyster Company has farmed top-notch West Coast oysters in the Tomales Bay since 1983. Thanks to the bay's plankton-rich seawater, the beds produce more than 3 million oysters annually. The farm is also a leading advocate of sustainable and responsible aquaculture. Visitors can buy fresh oysters to go or to shuck and slurp onsite. The farm provides waterfront picnic tables, shucking knives and barbecue grills for a small fee and reservations are required for weekends and holidays.

Daily 9 a.m.-5 p.m.

POINT REYES NATIONAL SEASHORE
1 Bear Valley Road, Point Reyes Station, 415-464-5100; www.nps.gov/pore

A 20-mile-long peninsula of pastoral beachfront jutting into the Pacific, Point Reyes National Seashore is a hodgepodge of active ranchland, dramatic sea cliffs, dense forests and pristine beaches. Hiking, backpacking, sea kayaking, biking, whale-watching (January-April), and bird watching (more than 45 percent of all bird species in North America have been sighted here at one time or another). The man-made elements are also worth a look: a lighthouse at the peninsula's northernmost point, Johnson's Oyster Farm (where you can buy fresh oysters to cook on your campfire) and a re-creation of a onetime Point Reyes mainstay—a Miwok Indian community.

Point Reyes Lighthouse: Thursday-Monday 10 a.m.-4:30 p.m. Bear Valley Visitor Center: Monday-Friday 9 a.m.-5 p.m., Saturday-Sunday 8 a.m-5 p.m.

STINSON BEACH
Highway 1, Stinson Beach, 415-868-1444; www.stinsonbeachonline.com

Only 20 miles from San Francisco, Stinson Beach has three and a half miles of sand, and is popular with surfers, swimmers and sunbathers. If you want to surf, there are shops in the area that provide rentals. Lifeguards are on duty from April through September. A park adjacent to the beach has more than 100 picnic tables and some grills, and the area also includes restrooms, showers and a snack bar, which is open during summer months. Daily sunrise-sunset.

TOMALES BAY STATE PARK

1208 Pierce Point Road, Inverness, 415-669-1140; www.parks.ca.gov

Forty miles north of the Golden Gate Bridge, this state park is filled with virgin groves of Bishop pine trees in the Jepson Memorial Grove and more than 300 species of plants which grow on 2,000 acres. You'll also find plenty of wildlife from foxes, raccoons, deer and bobcats to land and sea birds and jellyfish, clams, crabs and even sharks and rays. The four beaches of Tomales Bay are perfect for swimming, fishing, hiking, biking, picnicking as they are surf-free.

WHERE TO STAY

★★★MANKA'S INVERNESS LODGE

30 Callendar Way, Inverness, 415-669-1034; www.mankas.com

Though a fire destroyed much of the main lodge and restaurant in 2006, the lodge has reopened and is as wonderfully quirky and rustic as ever. Surrounded by national park land, this old-time lodge sits in the hills above a small coastal village. Manka's is made up of three different properties offering different types of lodging from individual rooms in the main hunting and fishing lodge to cabins from the early 1900s to the luxurious Boathouse, sitting above Tomales Bay, with private bathrooms, a galley kitchen, a library and more. Regardless of where you stay, rooms are cozy and warm with comfortable bedding, fireplaces, deep reading chairs, oversized baths, and windows that have views of the bay or the woods. The restaurant features fresh seafood and other local ingredients.

18 rooms. Restaurant. Pets accepted. $251-350

ALSO RECOMMENDED

BLACKTHORNE INN

266 Vallejo Ave., Inverness, 415-663-8621; www.blackthorneinn.com

Located in a wooded canyon, this rustic inn resembles a tree house with four levels of decks. Each room is individually decorated; stays come with breakfast served from a large buffet each morning.

5 rooms. Complimentary breakfast. $251-350

OLEMA INN

10000 Sir Francis Drake Blvd., Olema, 415-663-9559; www.theolemainn.com

This country inn, loaded with antiques, was built in 1876. Rooms feature down comforters, Ralph Lauren linens and antique furniture. The onsite restaurant serves local, organic and sustainable ingredients, including oysters, mussels, sea bass, halibut, duck breast and New York steak. The wine list features unique wines from surrounding wineries.

6 rooms. Restaurant, bar. Complimentary breakfast Pets accepted. $151-250

WHERE TO EAT
★★★MANKA'S INVERNESS LODGE
30 Callendar Way, Inverness, 415-669-1034; www.mankas.com

This acclaimed restaurant is back in business after a fire destroyed the dining room in late 2006. Strictly devoted to fresh, local ingredients, the kitchen creates simple California cuisine, with dishes that change nightly but may include lamb grilled in the fireplace and served with duck confit hash. On weekends, a five- or seven- course prix fixe menu is offered; the rest of the week, you can choose a la carte dishes from the menu as well.

California. Dinner. $36-85

★★OLEMA INN
10000 Sir Francis Drake Blvd., Olema, 415-663-9559; www.theolemainn.com

French. Lunch (Saturday-Sunday), dinner. Outdoor seating. $86 and up

★STATION HOUSE CAFÉ
11180 Highway State Route 1, Point Reyes Station, 415-663-1515; www.stationhousecafe.com

American. Breakfast, lunch, dinner. Closed Wednesday. Outdoor seating. Children's menu. Bar. $16-35

LAKE TAHOE AREA
See also Sacramento, Yosemite National Park

One of the most magnificent mountain lakes in the world, Lake Tahoe straddles two states and offers an abundance of wildlife and recreational opportunities. For a spectacular view, drive to the lake's southwestern part where Eagle Creek, one of the thousands of mountain streams that feed the lake, cascades 1,500 feet into Emerald Bay. Swim in public and commercial pools at 29 public beaches. Boat, fish, ski and head over to the Nevada side to try your luck at the casinos. Tahoe City and South Lake Tahoe information is also listed here.

The curved roads circling North America's largest alpine lake require some effort to navigate, but the shoreline's varied activities—historic sites, hiking, skiing and casinos—make Tahoe a good bet.

From the resort center of South Lake Tahoe, take highways 50 and 89 west along the lake's southern shore. From late spring through mid-fall, tour the Tallac Historic Site, a trio of opulent turn-of-the-century estates, and then enjoy a neighboring beach or nature trail. Highway 89 turns north toward Emerald Bay, one of the most photographed sites in the state, and tiny Fannette Island. A steep hiking trail leads a mile down to Vikingsholm, a bayside replica of a medieval Scandinavian castle that is open for tours in summer. Farther north, Tahoe's rustic West Shore looks across the lake toward dramatically rising mountain peaks. Casinos are clustered at Stateline, Nevada, just north of South Lake Tahoe.

Though only 72 miles around, the lake takes at least three hours to navigate; a full day allows for several stops. In winter, choose from an abundance of ski resorts on the three California sides of Tahoe, some located just a few miles from the lake. Four-wheel drive or tire chains may be necessary to negotiate snowy roads.

WHAT TO SEE
ALPINE MEADOWS
2600 Alpine Meadows Road, Tahoe city, 530-583-4232; www.skialpine.com
Best known for its varied terrain, Alpine Meadows consists of 2,400 acres split between six bowls, steep chutes and wide-open glades (25 percent beginner, 40 -percent intermediate and 35 percent advanced). The resort—13 miles south of I-80 at Truckee—has 13 lifts, a pair of snowboarding-oriented terrain parks, and a 600-foot superpipe for serious carvers. The nearest accommodations are in Tahoe City. Mid-November-late May. Lifts: Daily 9 a.m.-4 p.m. Lodge: Daily 8 a.m.-4 p.m.

DESOLATION WILDERNESS AREA
Eldorado National Forest, 100 Forni Road, Placerville, 530-622-5061; www.fs.fed.us
Desolation has Yosemite's natural beauty without the roads and, by extension, traffic. The granite peaks and 130 alpine lakes in this 64,000-acre wilderness southwest of Lake Tahoe still attract backpackers and anglers, but the need for foot and horse travel helps keep crowds out. Glaciers carved and polished the rock here 200,000 years ago. Tree cover and vegetation are limited, but the animal life—including mule deer, black bears, porcupines, badgers and coyotes—is diverse. Fishermen come for the lakes' and streams' steady supply of rainbow and brook trout. Daily fees for campers are collected in order to increase the level of wilderness ranger patrol, maintenance and restoration among other things, and there are zone quotas as to how many people can be in each zone at a time. Reservations are required.

EMERALD BAY STATE PARK
Highway 89, Tahoe City, 530-541-3030; www.parks.ca.gov
Centered on the glacially carved inlet of its name, this park is surrounded by granite peaks and cliffs on the west side of Lake Tahoe. It is home to tiny Fanette Island, a lone chunk of granite that survived the glacial period, and Vikingsholm, a Scandinavian-style castle. Underwater Park is a scuba-diving hotspot, thanks to the presence of numerous shipwrecks dating from the late 1800s, the heyday of the long-gone Emerald Bay Resort. The park also features several nature trails, a 70-site campground, and a beach with swimming access.

HEAVENLY MOUNTAIN RESORT
3860 Saddle Road, South Lake Tahoe, 775-586-7000; www.skiheavenly.com
Straddling the Nevada-California border just south of Lake Tahoe, this Vail Resort gem has a distinct ski area on each side of the line. In California, Heavenly West offers 15 lifts, which take skiers and snowboarders to trails with the state's longest vertical drop—3,500 feet—and a snowboarding half-pipe. On the Nevada side of the mountain, Heavenly North also has 15 lifts, a snowboard cross-trail and a terrain park. Whichever you choose, the snow is clean and plentiful: 360 inches is the average annual snowfall, bolstered by one of the biggest snowmaking operations in the world. A redeveloped village opened in 2002 with a movie multiplex, an ice-skating rink and a host of eateries, nightspots, shops and hotel rooms.

LAKE TAHOE CRUISES

900 Ski Run Blvd., South Lake Tahoe, 775-589-4906, 800-238-2463;
www.laketahoecruises.com

This long-standing operation offers a full slate of cruises—breakfast, brunch, lunch, dinner/dance and sightseeing. The fleet includes a pair of Mississippi River-style paddle wheelers. Cruise year-round on the 151-foot *M.S. Dixie II*, ported in Zephyr Cove. The *Tahoe Queen*, based out of South Lake Tahoe, becomes a ski shuttle/charter vessel during winter.
Daily. Reservations required.

NORTHSTAR-AT-TAHOE RESORT

100 Northstar Drive, Truckee, 530-562-1010, 800-466-6784; www.skinorthstar.com

Two quad, three triple, three double chairlifts, gondola, patrol. Longest run three miles; biggest vertical drop 2,280 feet. Cross-country skiing; rentals. Half-day rates. Summer activities include tennis, 18-hole golf, mountain biking, horseback riding and swimming. November-April,
Daily.

SIERRA-AT-TAHOE

1111 Sierra-at-Tahoe Road, Twin Bridges, 530-659-7453; www.sierraattahoe.com

This large but low-key resort, founded in 1968, has 2,000 acres set against a 2,212-foot vertical rise, with 25 percent beginner, 50 percent intermediate and 25 percent expert slopes. A favorite of snowboarders, the resort features six terrain parks, one half-pipe and a superpipe. There is also a popular tubing hill but no on-mountain lodging. Shuttle bus service is available.
Mid-November-mid-April. Monday-Friday 9 a.m.-4 p.m., Saturday-Sunday 8:30 a.m.-4 p.m.

SQUAW VALLEY USA

1960 Squaw Valley Road, Olympic Valley, 530-583-6955; www.squaw.com

This ski resort hosted the 1960 Winter Olympics. Today, it has five high-speed quad charlifts, eight triple chairlifts, eight double chairlifts, an aerial cable car, a gondola, five surface lifts, and a ski school. The longest run is 3.2 miles with the largest -vertical drop being 2,850 feet. There are 25 miles of cross-country skiing for those interested in something more tame. Take an aerial cable car to the upper mountain where you'll find the Olympic Ice Pavilion for ice skating and amazing panoramic views. Surrounded by the Sierra Mountains, Squaw Valley's swimming lagoon and whirlpool help skiiers relax after a long day. There are plenty of restaurants and bars here to visit when you're not on the slopes. Mid-November-mid-May.
Daily.

TAHOE STATE RECREATION AREA

Highway 28, Tahoe City, 530-583-3074; www.parks.ca.gov

This highly developed, two-campground complex is an ideal place to get away, so long as you're not looking to get away from it all. Less than a mile east of Tahoe City, the campgrounds are near restaurants and retailers. The Lakeside campground is right on the shore, while the Hillside campground is across the highway.

VIKINGSHOLM

Emerald Bay State Park, Tahoe City, 530-525-7277; www.vikingsholm.com

Amid cedar groves at the base of granite cliffs in Emerald Bay State Park stands the Scandinavian-style castle, Vikingsholm. Landowner Lora Knight commissioned her nephew, a Swedish architect, to design the place, and he drew inspiration from Norwegian churches, Swedish castles and traditional wooden homes in both countries. Visitors must hike a steep one-mile trail from the parking lot to get to the castle's doors. Parking is limited.
Admission: adults $5, children 6-17 $3, children under 6 are free. Late-May-late September, Daily 10 a.m.-4 p.m.

SPECIAL EVENTS
AMERICAN CENTURY CELEBRITY GOLF CHAMPIONSHIP

Edgewood Tahoe Golf Course, Lake Parkway and Highway 50, South Lake Tahoe Area, 530-544-5050; www.tahoecelebritygolf.com

More than 80 sports and entertainment celebrities compete for a $600,000 purse. Celebrity players have included Tony Romo, Jack Wagner, Ray Romano, Oscar De La Hoya, Dan Marino, Michael Jordan, Dennis Quaid, Brian Urlacher among many others. Mid-July.

GREAT GATSBY FESTIVAL

Tallac Historic Site, Highways 50 and 89, South Lake Tahoe, 530-544-5227; www.tahoeheritage.org

The Tallac Historic Site revives the Roaring '20s for a weekend every August with period costumes (flapper dresses, boiler hats) conjuring a West Egg atmosphere and an array of old-fashioned events, including an antique car show, a croquet competition, big band concerts and a pie-eating contest. Attendees are encouraged, but not expected, to come in costume.
Admission: Free. Second weekend in August.

LAKE TAHOE MUSIC FESTIVAL

Tahoe City, 530-583-3101; www.tahoemusic.org

A Lake Tahoe tradition since 1982, the program of this highly regarded concert series festival favors classical and choral music but doesn't stop there—practitioners of everything from bluegrass to jazz to poetry also perform. Professional performers-in-residence tutor young artists in the recently introduced Academy Program. The festival takes place at multiple venues in the Tahoe area, including Homewood Mountain Resort, Donner Lake and Old Greenwood Resort. Late-July-early-August.

WHERE TO STAY
★★★CHALET VIEW LODGE

72056 Highway 70, Portola, 530-832-5528; www.chaletviewlodge.com

Staying at this country lodge, located north of Lake Tahoe in the Mohawk Valley, feels like a weekend away at the home of a stylish friend. The cozy lobby has deep leather couches and a fireplace. Rooms feature luxury bedding, Jacuzzi tubs, flat-screen TVs and Starbucks coffee for the coffeemaker. The restaurant serves breakfast, and dinner.
45 rooms. Restaurant, bar. Fitness center. Pool. Spa. $151-250

★★★EMBASSY SUITES LAKE TAHOE HOTEL & SKI RESORT

4130 Lake Tahoe Blvd., South Lake Tahoe, 530-544-5400, 877-497-8483;
www.embassytahoe.com

This hotel is designed with the guest rooms all facing a landscaped inner atrium. Amenities include a restaurant, lounges, several patios, a swimming pool, fitness center, sauna and meeting and banquet facilities. The lodge is within walking distance of all the major casinos and the lake. A free shuttle takes you to the Heavenly and Sierra-at-Tahoe ski resorts.
400 rooms. Restaurant, bar. Complimentary breakfast. Business center. Fitness center. Pool.

★★INN BY THE LAKE

3300 Lake Tahoe Blvd., South Lake Tahoe, 530-542-0330, 800-877-1466;
www.innbythelake.com

100 rooms. Complimentary breakfast. Fitness center. Pool. $61-150

★★★RESORT AT SQUAW CREEK

400 Squaw Creek Road, Olympic Valley, 530-583-6300, 800-327 3353;
www.squawcreek.com

This full-service resort is just minutes by a private chairlift from the challenging peaks and scenic trails of Squaw Valley, site of the 1960 Winter Olympics. The resort is well-known for its terrific 18-hole golf course (designed by Robert Trent Jones, Jr.), spa, tennis courts and hiking and biking trails, as well as its outdoor skating rink, heated pools, hot tubs and multitude of snowbound activities. This family-friendly mountain getaway also has comfortable rooms and suites and five dining outlets.
405 rooms. Restaurant, bar. Spa. $151-250

WHERE TO EAT

★★★EVANS AMERICAN GOURMET CAFÉ

536 Emerald Bay Road, South Lake Tahoe, 530-542-1990; www.evanstahoe.com

This café has a creative menu that includes options such as roast venison loin with pinot noir-dried cherry demi-glace and parsnip mashed potatoes. The extensive wine list emphasizes selections from California and the Northwest. Desserts, including butter pecan bananas foster, créme brulee and frozen white chocolate mousse, are made fresh daily.
American. Dinner. $16-35

★★NEPHELES

1169 Ski Run Blvd., South Lake Tahoe, 530-544-8130; www.nepheles.com
American. Dinner. Bar. $16-35

★★★SWISS CHALETS

2544 Lake Tahoe Blvd., South Lake Tahoe, 530-544-3304; www.tahoeswisschalet.com

This restaurant, which resembles a chalet you would expect to find among the Swiss Alps, has been chef-owned and operated since 1957. Swiss specialties are the focus of the menu. Enjoy fondue as they do in Switzerland, or try one of the specialty dishes such as authentic wienerschnitzel.
Fondue, Swiss. Dinner. Closed Monday. Children's menu. Bar. $16-35

LOS GATOS

See also San Jose, Saratoga

Set in the middle of Silicon Valley, free-roaming wildcats indigenous to the Santa Cruz Mountains inspired the name La Rinconada de Los Gatos, which means "the cat's corner." Today, two 8-foot sculptured cats, Leo and Leona, guard the town entrance at Poet's Canyon. Look for the cats as you head into the small, upscale downtown for some antique shopping. The downtown of Los Gatos acts as a model of what communities should have in a "downtown," and is listed on the National Register of Historic Places.

WHAT TO SEE
BYINGTON VINEYARD AND WINERY

21850 Bear Creek Road, Los Gatos, 408-354-1111; www.byington.com

If you like a good cabernet, Byington Vineyard and Winery is at the top of its game. Perched at the summit overlooking the vast valley below, Byington—with its ivy-covered stone façade, outdoor patio and bocce ball court—looks like it was transported from the European countryside. Enjoy a glass of wine on the second-story terrace as well as the lawn—all have views of the valley below. Before you depart, take a short spiral pathway to Wedding Hill where brides and grooms exchange vows surrounded by jasmine and overlooking vineyards, redwood forests and the Monterey Bay.
Tastings: $5. Daily 11 a.m.-5 p.m.

LOS GATOS CREEK TRAIL

Lexington Reservoir, Los Gatos; www.losgatosca.gov

Covering 10 miles of Los Gatos from Lexington Reservoir to Meridian Avenue in San Jose, this trail takes you through portions of Los Gatos and is a perfect outdoor activity for hikers and bicyclists.
Daily 7 a.m.-half hour after sunset.

OLD TOWN

50 University Ave., Los Gatos; www.losgatoschamber.com

This is the historic downtown area of Los Gatos. Take a walking tour to see sites such as the Lyndon Plaza (where John Steinbeck, John Ford and Charlie Chaplin met for drinks at the Lyndon Hotel); the Los Gatos Theatre, which was a silent movie house when it was built in 1915; Ford's Opera House; Los Gatos Creek Trail; and the Fretwell Building. There are shops, restaurants, art galleries and flowered garden walkways dating back to 1923.

YOUTH SCIENCE INSTITUTE

333 Blossom Hill Road, Los Gatos, 408-356-4945; www.ysi-ca.org

Located in Vasona Lake County Park, this non-profit organization focuses on educating primary and secondary students on life sciences, physical sciences and social sciences in three Science and Nature centers. Each center houses local and native fish, reptiles, mammals, insects, birds and amphibians along with offering hands-on programs. The Viola Anderson Native Plant Trail provides information on native Northern California plants.
Monday-Friday 9 a.m.-4:30 p.m.

SPECIAL EVENTS
FARMER'S MARKET
Town Plaza Park, North Santa Cruz Avenue and Main Street, Los Gatos;
www.losgatosca.gov
Pick up organic and non-organic produce, specialty foods and fresh flowers
from local farmers at this market. There are usually plenty of foods to sample
as you browse. The market takes place rain or shine.
Daily, Sunday 8 a.m.-1 p.m.

JAZZ ON THE PLAZZ
Town Plaza, Los Gatos, www.jazzontheplazz.com
Every Wednesday night during summer, free concerts feature jazz artists,
with a variety of instruments and sounds. Mid-June-late-August.

MUSIC IN THE PARK
Civic Center Lawn, Los Gatos, www.losgatosca.gov
This 10-week concert series is free to the public and features multicultural
and multigenerational music for everyone. The concerts take place Sunday
afternoons and are presented by the Los Gatos Arts Commission. Past concerts have included an Elvis tribute band, an opera ensemble, the San Jose
Wind Symphony, a Beatles tribute band, a Swing band, and other tribute
bands covering music by Fleetwood Mac, the Allman Brothers, Steely Dan
and more.
Late June-late August.

WHERE TO STAY
★★LA HACIENDA INN
18840 Saratoga-Los Gatos Road, Los Gatos, 408-354-9230, 800-235-4570;
www.lahaciendainn.com
20 rooms. Complimentary breakfast. Business center. Pool. $151-250

★★★THE TOLL HOUSE HOTEL
140 S. Santa Cruz Ave., Los Gatos, 408-395-7070, 800-238-6111;
www.tollhousehotel.com
Fine dining is within walking distance of this European-style hotel set among
picturesque low hills. Spacious rooms are appointed with comfortable beds,
complimentary Internet access, a choice of a daily paper and turndown service among other amenities. A business center features everything you would
need to take care of work on the road. Three Degrees Restaurant and Bar provides a menu filled with local, organic fresh produce with seafood, chicken,
pork chops, ribeye, short ribs and more. The Sunday brunch prix fixe menu
offers options such as blueberry white chocolate pancakes, a cajun chicken
omelet and corned beef hash. Enjoy your meal on the large outdoor patio.
115 rooms. Restaurant, bar. Business center. Fitness center. Pets accepted.
$151-250

WHERE TO EAT
★C. B. HANNEGAN'S
208 Bachman Ave., Los Gatos, 408-395-1233; www.cbhannegans.com
International. Lunch, dinner, late-night. Outdoor seating. Bar. $16-35

★★★★MANRESA
320 Village Lane, Los Gatos, 408-354-4330; www.manresarestaurant.com
This intimate restaurant is the showcase for chef David Kinch's daring and inventive French- and northern Spanish-influenced cuisine, which is heavy on local ingredients, many from an exclusive garden in the Santa Cruz mountains. The exquisitely presented dishes are served in a provincial dining room. Guests may choose a three- or four-course meal or the tasting menu. You might start with mussels braised in butter, avocado and smoked bread to roasted monkfish with braised pearl onions with bone marrow and light chervil cream. From there, move on to beef short ribs with roasted shallots, or broccoli romanesco in anchovy vinaigrette. Finish with cherry blossom mousse with toasted almond meringue kisses, chicory ice cream and rhubarb consommé.
French. Dinner. Closed Monday-Tuesday. Bar. $86 and up

MAMMOTH LAKES
See also Yosemite National Park
Volcanoes and glaciers took their time creating this outdoor paradise of rugged peaks, plentiful lakes, streams, waterfalls, alpine meadows and extensive forests. See the spectacular scenery in summer, then come back in winter to ski the slopes and soak in the hot springs.

WHAT TO SEE
DEVILS POSTPILE NATIONAL MONUMENT
Mammoth Lakes, 760-934-2289; www.nps.gov/depo
Southeast of Yosemite National Park and surrounded by Inyo National Forest, this monument is among the finest examples of columnar basalt in the world, formed approximately 100,000 years ago when basalt lava erupted in the area. These columns, which stand 40 to 60 feet high, are a mile hike from the ranger station where you begin your tour. A short, steep trail leads to the top of the formation for a view of the ends of the columns, which have been polished by glaciers. Pumice, porous lava and nearby bubbling soda springs are evidence of recent volcanic activity. At Rainbow Falls, about two miles down the river trail from the Postpile, the San Joaquin River drops 101 feet, where the foam-white water starkly contrasting with the dark cliffs. Look for rainbows in the afternoon. Mid-June-mid-October,
Daily.

HOT CREEK GEOLOGIC SITE
Owens River Road, Mammoth Lakes, 760-924-5500; www.visitmammoth.com
Boiling hot springs warm the waters in Mammoth Creek as geysers gush upwards and fumaroles send up plenty of steam in this river setting surrounded by mountains. For a view of varied volcanic formations, make your way to boardwalks leading through a steep canyon. Fly-fish for trout upstream in the

hot springs. Swimming is not recommended here. Pets allowed.

INYO NATIONAL FOREST
760-873-2400; www.fs.fed.us/r5/inyo
With seven wilderness areas on two million acres of protected land, the Inyo National Forest is distinct for its variety of natural features: Mount Whitney at 14,496 feet and the famous Minarets, a series of jagged, uniquely weathered peaks in the Sierra Nevadas; Devils Postpile National Monument; the Ancient Bristlecone Pine Forest, which is 4,600 years old and has 600-million-year-old fossils and a unique high-elevation alpine desert at 10,000-14,000 feet; Mono Lake and Mammoth Lakes Basin. Whether you're coming to commune with nature or just to play (swimming, boating, riding, pack trips, nordic skiing, snowmobiling) you'll have plenty of places to stay; there are 83 campgrounds.

MAMMOTH MOUNTAIN SKI AREA
1 Minaret Road, Mammoth Lakes, 760-934-2571; www.mammothmountain.com
Blanketed by over 400 inches of snow each year, Mammoth's 3,500 skiable acres culminate much of that snow on the 11,053-foot peak of the mountain itself. The resort encompasses 28 lifts, three terrain parks and three half-pipes popular with snowboarders, a multitude of lodging and dining options, a golf course, cross-country ski area and a summertime mountain biking park. Fly-fishermen also love the area's snowmelt-fed streams and lakes.

WHERE TO STAY
★★★MAMMOTH MOUNTAIN INN
1 Minaret Road, Mammoth Lakes, 760-934-2581, 800-626-6684;
www.mammothmountain.com
The Mammoth Mountain Inn is a great place to base your vacation if you want to wake up on the mountain itself. Steps away from the gondola and Main Lodge, this Inn is the perfect location for those who want to get on the slopes as soon as possible. Choose from basic rooms to condos or suites; Condo units are equipped with a kitchen and dining area and suites come with a refrigerator. All rooms offer Internet access, a telephone and TV/DVD. Head to the Mountainside Grill for California cuisine or to the Dry Creek Bar for cocktails.
213 rooms. Restaurant, bar. Business center. Fitness center. Pool. $251-350

MENDOCINO
See also Fort Bragg
Once a remote lumber port, Mendocino is now home to a thriving colony of environmentally-minded artists, who coined the slogan, "Keep Mendo Green." Only a four-hour drive from San Francisco, it has become a popular vacation destination for Bay Area residents looking to escape for the weekend. The town's 19th-century legacy is reflected by its New England architecture.

WHAT TO SEE
MENDOCINO ART CENTER

45200 Little Lake St., Mendocino, 707-937-5818; www.mendocinoartcenter.org

Overlooking the Pacific Ocean, the Mendocino Art Center was the focal point for the town's revitalization as an artistic community after its logging economy faltered. Exhibits by working artists at four galleries typically change monthly and several artists-in-residence open their studios to the public on a regular basis. While you're visiting, participate in workshops in disciplines ranging from jewelry making to drama, or catch a show by the Mendocino Theatre Company, which also makes its home here. Pop into the gallery gift shop to pick up one-of-a-kind art.

Daily 10 a.m.-5 p.m.

THE PHILO APPLE FARM

18501 Greenwood Road, Philo, 707-895-2333; www.philoapplefarm.com

In early fall, stop by this nearly 2,000-tree orchard about 120 miles north of San Francisco to pick fresh apples from among 80 varieties. The apple stock is typically sold out by mid-November. At the season's height, take a peek into the busy kitchen, where apples become preserves, butters, syrups and cider, which you can purchase at the farm stand. If you're in San Francisco, you can also find the produce at the Farmers' Market on Saturday or inside the Ferry Building at Cowgirl Creamery where some of the farm's jams and chutneys are sold.

VAN DAMME STATE PARK

Highway 1, Mendocino, 707-937-5804; www.parks.ca.gov

The tiny, 6-inch to 8-foot venerable trees of the Pygmy Forest dominate the southeast part of this 2,190-acre park, where poor soil conditions inhibit tree growth. Some trees, nearly 200 years old, have trunks only an inch in diameter. Divers can head to a protected cove in the Little River and hikers can explore the fern canyons. Rent a kayak or take a kayak tour to see all the tide pools and sea caves. There are also camping and picnicking sites here.

SPECIAL EVENTS
CRAB AND WINE DAYS

Mendocino, 707-462-7417, 866-466-3636; www.gomendo.com

In late January and early February, banners celebrating the Dungeness crab wave in the breeze, crab traps line the docks and locals and visitors come fresh crab and great wine. Since 2000, this annual event has attracted top-name chefs, authors and winemakers, as well as dozens of local businesses, including charter boats, restaurants, wineries, galleries and breweries, which team up to offer harbor cruises and fishing trips, cooking classes, crab cake cook-offs, concerts, and, of course, crab dinners and wine-tasting events. Late January.

MENDOCINO WHALE FESTIVAL

Mendocino, 707-961-6300; www.mendowhale.com

This two-day festival features whale-watching walks, wine tastings and chowder tasting. Whale watch from the Point Cabrillo Lighthouse (only three miles north). The cliffs of Mendocino Headlands State Park also offer a great place to watch the whales migrate. Early March.

WHERE TO STAY

★★★ALBION RIVER INN

3790 N. Highway 1, Albion, 707-937-1919, 800-479-7944; www.albionriverinn.com

Set in a historic town on 10 secluded acres, this inn provides complimentary breakfast, wine, binoculars for whale watching and bathrobes. Rooms are spacious and simply decorated with modern furnishings. Many rooms feature private decks, whirlpool tubs and fireplaces. Enjoy the breathtaking views of the ocean bluffs and rugged north coast from your bathtub. The restaurant here provides beautiful views of the ocean while serving fresh local and regional seafood, meats, and organic produce. Choose from a wine list that features more than 500 wines and more than 140 single malts.

22 rooms. Restaurant, bar Complimentary breakfast.. $151-250

★★★THE HARBOR HOUSE INN

5600 S. Highway 1, Elk, 707-877-3203, 800-720-7474; www.theharborhouseinn.com

Serene gardens surround this refurbished 1916 bed and breakfast featuring craftsmen style architecture. Six rooms are located in the main house, which has high ceilings and large windows that look out to the garden and ocean. Each room is decorated with antiques, luxury bedding, a large bath, a fireplace and sitting area. There are also four cottages, which have private bathrooms, fireplaces and private decks. A full breakfast and four-course dinner for two is included with each room and served daily.

10 rooms. Restaurant. Complimentary breakfast. No children under 16. $251-350

★★★HILL HOUSE INN

10701 Palette Drive, Mendocino, 707-937-0554, 800-422-0554; www.hillhouseinn.com

This charming oceanside inn offers beautiful ocean and garden views, lush gardens, and a convenient location to all that Mendocino has to offer. This inn has had famous guests stay here over the years, including Bette Davis. If you're a fan, choose to stay in the Bette Davis Suite or check out the photo gallery in the lobby with signed photographs of her and other celebrities. The television show *Murder, She Wrote* was also filmed in Mendocino.

44 rooms. Restaurant, bar. $61-150

★★★MACCALLUM HOUSE INN

45020 Albion St., Mendocino, 707-937-0289, 800-609-0492;
www.maccallumhouse.com

This artfully landscaped, secluded inn includes several properties, including a hilltop mansion overlooking the Pacific Ocean and an 1882 mansion on Main Street. Inquire about rooms with fireplaces, claw-foot soaking tubs and picturesque ocean views. There are also seven cottages near the main house, most of which include private decks and wood stoves. Thoughtful amenities include a complimentary gourmet breakfast served daily; in-house limousine service and wine tours; rental bikes; an outdoor hot tub; and croquet on the main lawn. The charming MacCallum House Restaurant serves up fresh organic cuisine, much of which is made and prepared in their own kitchen. 32 rooms. Complimentary breakfast. Restaurant. Pets accepted. Beach. $151-250

★★★THE STANFORD INN BY THE SEA
Highway 1 and Comptche Ukiah Road, Mendocino, 707-937-5615, 800-331-8884; www.stanfordinn.com

This inn's organic gardens, farm and rugged coastal beauty complement the comfort of its tastefully decorated rooms, which include wood-burning fireplaces. The lobby, guest rooms and suites have pine and redwood paneling, which warms up the room and also provides rustic charm. The restaurant, Raven's, has won awards for its organic vegetarian (and vegan at dinner) cuisine. The wine list features wines from certified organic vineyards. Canoes and kayaks are also available for rental to take out on the Big River.
33 rooms. Complimentary breakfast. Restaurant. Spa. Pets accepted. $351 and up

ALSO RECOMMENDED
BREWERY GULCH INN
9401 N. Highway 1, Mendocino, 707-937-4752, 800-578-4454; www.brewerygulchinn.com

With a mission to improve and enhance the ecosystem and regenerate the land, Brewery Gulch Inn is constructed of 150 year-old redwood timber and rooms are painted with eco-spec paint and feature fluorescent lighting, gas-burning fireplaces, organic cotton towels and low-flow showerheads. The kitchen features organic and locally-sourced vegetables and herbs that come from the inn's garden. All rooms feature ocean views, gas fireplaces, down comforters and pillows, feather beds, luxurious linens, organic towels and more.
10 rooms. Complimentary breakfast. No children under 12. $151-250

STEVENSWOOD SPA RESORT
8211 N. Highway 1, Little River, 707-937-2810, 800-421-2810; www.stevenswood.com

This secluded hotel features rooms with wood-burning fireplaces, Italian espresso machines, bath butler service, Egyptian cotton linens, down comforters and more. At the Indigo Eco-Spa, you can receive a range of treatments from facials, massages and scrubs to reflexology.
7 rooms. Restaurant, bar. Complimentary breakfast. Fitness center. Spa. $251-350

WHERE TO EAT
★★★ALBION RIVER INN
3790 N. Highway 1, Albion, 707-937-1919, 800-479-7944; www.albionriverinn.com

Dine on an international menu composed of local produce while admiring views of Albion Cove and the Pacific Ocean. Chef Stephen Smith offers fresh coastal cuisine including shellfish, seafood chowder, prawns, sole, short ribs, crab cakes, pork stew and more. The dessert menu is equally as appealing with choices such as chocolate mousse, cheesecake, housemade sorbet and ice cream. A pianist livens up the dining room on the weekends.

International. Dinner. Reservations recommended. Bar. $36-85

★★★CAFE BEAUJOLAIS
961 Ukiah St., Mendocino, 707-937-5614; www.cafebeaujolais.com
Surrounded by antique roses, edible flowers and unusual plants, this café, housed in a Victorian farmhouse, serves cuisine made from locally grown organic produce and freshly baked goods from its onsite bakery, The Brickery. The main dining room features pale green walls, white linens and dark wood floors for a calm, cozy atmosphere. The garden dining room on the enclosed patio overlooks the green gardens. Entrées include roasted acorn squash with wild and brown rice and pomegranate-zinfandel reduction; and pan-roasted California sturgeon fillet with truffle emulsion sauce.
French, American. Lunch, dinner. Bar. $36-85

MENLO PARK
An East Bay suburb, this community has the oldest continually operating train station in California. The town is headquarters to many technology companies, including Google, which was launched here in 1998. Regional lifestyle magazine *Sunset* also has its offices in Menlo Park.

WHAT TO SEE
FILOLI HOUSE AND GARDENS
86 Cañada Road, Woodside, 650-364-8300; www.filoli.org
This 654-acre estate holds a venerable Georgian-style residence, once featured in the television series *Dynasty*, and 16-acre Italian Renaissance-style gardens with terraces, lawns and pools.
House and garden; guided tours mid-February-October, Tuesday-Saturday 10 a.m.-3:30 p.m. Sunday 11 a.m.-3:30 p.m., reservations required; self-guided tours, no reservations required.

STANFORD LINEAR ACCELERATOR CENTER (SLAC)
2575 Sand Hill Road, Menlo Park, 650-926-3300; www.slac.stanford.edu
Take a 2½ hour tour of this 426-acre national facility, which houses a 2-mile-long linear accelerator that generates the highest-energy electron beams in the world.
Limited hours; reservations required.

SUNSET MAGAZINE GARDENS
80 Willow Road, Menlo Park, 650-321-3600; www.sunset.com
These attractive gardens are tended by the publishers of *Sunset* magazine and books.
Self-guided tour of gardens. Monday-Friday.

WHERE TO STAY
★★★★ROSEWOOD SAND HILL
2825 Sand Hill Rd., Menlo Park, 650-561-1500; www.rosewoodhotels.com
This stylish resort, opened in 2009, fills a need for an upscale place to stay, dine and relax in Silicon Valley. The resort, tucked away against the hills off a busy main road in Menlo Park, feels more like it's in secluded wine country than suburban Menlo Park, with its rambling, low buildings, manicured land-

scaping and beautiful views. The contemporary décor is California casual, with an impressive art collection sourced from local galleries. The rooms are supplied with sprawling bathrooms, plush, pillowy mattresses topped with down duvets and Italian linens, flat-screen TVs and Nespresso coffee makers. The polished staff attends to every need with confidence, whether its recommending a local bottle of wine to sip by the outdoor firepits, or delivering extra thick towels to the poolside chaises. The onsite spa is an attractive, sybaritic space for indulging in a full menu of treatments.

123 rooms. Restaurant, bar. Fitness center. Spa. $351 and up

WHERE TO EAT
★★★MADERA
2825 Sand Hill Rd., Menlo Park, 650-561-1540; www.rosewoodhotels.com

With its massive, floor-to-ceiling windows, intriguing open kitchen and cozy fireplaces, this restaurant inside the new Rosewood Sand Hill resort is a beguiling place to take a table and dig into locally sourced, seasonal California cuisine. Chef Peter Rudolph grew up in the Bay Area and worked in led the kitchen at San Francisco's Campton Place before coming to Madera, and brings with him a passion for the flavors and rich resources found in this region. At dinner, dishes might include pan-roasted squab with braised pine nuts, carrots and kumquat confit, or dayboat scallops with roasted chanterelle mushrooms, rapini and apple turnip purée. Sommelier Paul Mekis holds an advanced sommelier designation, and he puts his vast knowledge to good use in selecting a well-rounded wine list that puts a spotlight on star bottles from the region.

California cuisine. Breakfast, lunch, dinner. Bar. $36-85

SPAS
★★★★SENSE, A ROSEWOOD SPA AT ROSEWOOD SAND HILL
2825 Sand Hill Rd., Menlo Park, 650-561-1500; www.rosewoodhotels.com

This attractive spa is a sanctuary where natural wood and stone are used to create a calming environment that makes the most of the beautiful California setting. The 13 treatment rooms and locker areas are light-filled and luxe—the coed relaxation room is a unique, spacious and appealing space with doors that open onto a private open-air courtyard and fountain. Choose from a menu that carries out the California theme, including treatments such as the Forest Sanctuary ($85), which begins with a eucalyptus exfoliation, moves onto an herbal wrap and aromatherapy hot stone massage. Also offered are a range of facials, manicures and pedicures. The spa includes a movement studio, fitness center with cutting-edge equipment and a spa café with outdoor seating in a charming courtyard.

MONTEREY
See also Big Sur, Carmel, Carmel Valley, Pebble Beach

Named in 1602 by a Spanish explorer for the Count of Monterey, this city hid from European eyes for another 168 years, when it was rediscovered by Fray Crespi, Fray Junipero Serra and Gaspar de Portola. The three founded the Presidio and the Mission San Carlos Borromeo de Rio Carmelo. Since then, the city has retained its calm harbor, white-sand beach, Monterey cypress, pine and red-roofed white stucco houses. A mélange of Mexican, New

THE BIG SUR COASTLINE

Hugging the rugged Big Sur coastline, Highway 1 south of Monterey is often called the most scenic roadway in America. Plan to make several stops on this leisurely drive. Hike down to the coast from a handful of state parks (Garrapata, Andrew Molera, Pfeiffer-Big Sur and Julia Pfeiffer Burns).

Big Sur extends for about 90 miles south of Monterey, but if you're making a one-day drive, turn around well before dark at the tiny hamlet of Lucia, about 50 miles south; the winding route is pitch black at night. Those with two days can spend the night at Lucia in a modest lodge or in the town of Cambria, a few miles south of San Simeon, where Hearst Castle is perched high atop a mountain on the southern fringes of Big Sur. If planning to tour Hearst Castle, reserve a time in advance and allow at least two hours. Drivers have the option of returning to Monterey north on Highway 1 or looping back via Highway 101, a longer and less scenic (but potentially speedier) route that runs inland. To follow this option, take Highway 46 east off Highway 1 a few miles south of Cambria, reaching Highway 101 at Paso Robles. Continue north to Salinas and take Highway 68 west to Monterey. Approximately 240 miles

England, sea, mission and ranch makes Monterey uniquely Californian in its culture and history—the first state constitution was written here. Once a whaling and sardine center—inspiring the novels *Cannery Row* and *Sweet Thursday* by John Steinbeck—overfishing depleted the bay of sardines and emptied the canneries. The row is now dominated by an aquarium, gourmet restaurants and art galleries, while Fisherman's Wharf is the launch point for fishing and sightseeing trips and home to the bay's famous sea otters.

WHAT TO SEE
CANNERY ROW

Cannery Row, Monterey, 831-649-6690; www.canneryrow.com
Immortalized in John Steinbeck's 1945 novel of the same name, Cannery Row grew up around the Asian and American companies that established canning and fishing operations in the area at the turn of the 20th century. The World War I boom turned the city into the Sardine Capital of the World, at least until the Monterey Bay sardine population collapsed due to overfishing. The Cannery Row described by Steinbeck followed in its wake, a haven for bums, prostitutes and eccentrics. Locals pushed to revitalize the decaying strip in the 1950s, an initiative that culminated in 1984 when the Monterey Bay Aquarium was opened in a former cannery. Today, Cannery Row is a parade of lavish waterfront hotels, nearly 100 shops and a dizzying array of seafood restaurants and other eateries.

CASA SOBERANES

336 Pacific St., Monterey, 831-649-7118; www.parks.ca.gov
This adobe house was built in 1842 and contains displays of Monterey history from 1840 to 1970. This Mexican Colonial adobe building is an excellent example of adobe construction. The walls are 38 inches thick and it is filled with antique furniture, a collection of local artwork and silver. Part of the Monterey State Historic Park, this house can only be toured with a State Park guide.
Admission: Free. Guided Tours: Friday-Wednesday 11:30 a.m. and 3 p.m.

COLTON HALL MUSEUM

City Hall, Pacific and Madison streets, Monterey, 831-646-5648;
www.monterey.org/museum

Built as a town hall and public school in 1849 by the Reverend Walter Colton, who served as the Chief Magistrate of the Monterey District during the American occupation of California from 1846 to 1849. The architecture of this building is Classic Revival design of stone and adobe mortar. The first constitution of California (in Spanish and English) was written here. The Old Monterey Jail was added to the building in 1854, at which time Colton Hall served as the Monterey County Courthouse.

Admission: Free. Daily 10 a.m.-4 p.m.

COOPER-MOLERA ADOBE

525 Polk St. at Alvarado Street, Monterey, 831-649-7111; www.parks.ca.gov

Built in 1827 by John Rogers Cooper, the half-brother of Thomas Larkin, this was the home to three generations of Coopers. You can get information there today as it acts as a visitor center and a shop. There is also a historic garden to stroll through as well as a barn with farm animals. Part of the Monterey State Historic Park, this house can only be toured with a State Park guide.

Admission: Free. Tours: Friday-Wednesday noon and 3 p.m.

CUSTOM HOUSE

20 Custom House Plaza, Monterey, 831-649-7118; www.parks.ca.gov

The oldest government building in California was a busy trading center in the 1800s. It used to be Mexico's primary port of entry on the coast of California. The building houses exhibits recreating what it looked like in the 1840s. Commodore John Drake Sloat raised the American flag over this adobe building in 1846, bringing 600,000 square miles into the Union.

Daily 10 a.m.-4 p.m.

LARKIN HOUSE

510 Calle Principal, Monterey, 831-649-7118; www.parks.ca.gov

Built by Thomas Larkin, this house is the "prototype" for Monterey Colonial architecture. Larkin was the first and only U.S. consul to Mexican California. Tour the two story home, which is filled with antiques from all over the world. This house can only be toured with a State Park guide.

Admission: Free. Tours: Friday-Wednesday 10 a.m. and noon.

MONTEREY BAY AQUARIUM

886 Cannery Row, Monterey, 831-648-4800; www.mbayaq.org

The preeminent aquarium in the United States, this space attracts nearly 2 million visitors each year. Located in a former Hovden Cannery, which canned squid and sardines until the early 1970s, the facility is now home to 35,000 plants and animals representing some 550 species, with a focus on local sea life. Impressive exhibits include a three-story kelp forest, Outer Bay (a million-gallon indoor ocean with sharks, barracuda, jellyfish, tuna and sea turtles) and a walk-through shorebird aviary. Kids can let loose in Splash Zone, an educational play area with tunnels, clam-shaped chairs, petting pools with bat rays and starfish and a penguin habitat.

Admission: adults $29.95, students and seniors $27.95, children 3-12 $17.95, children under 3 free. Daily 10 a.m.-6 p.m.; May 26-September 1, Daily 9:30 a.m.-6 p.m.; July-September, Saturday-Sunday 9:30 a.m.-8 p.m.

MONTEREY MUSEUM OF ART PACIFIC STREET

559 Pacific St., Monterey, 831-372-5477; www.montereyart.org
The Monterey Museum of Art focuses on American art and displays early Californian paintings, photography, Contemporary art, and American and Asian art. There are also changing exhibitions of major American artists. Docent-guided tour available; see Web site for details.
Admission: adults $5, students and military $2.50, children 12 and under free. Wednesday-Saturday 11 a.m.-5 p.m., Sunday 1-4 p.m.

OLD FISHERMAN'S WHARF

39 Fisherman's Wharf, Monterey; www.montereywharf.com
The fisherman's wharf is filled with restaurants where you can try fresh seafood. There wharf includes tourist shops, galleries, tackle and bait shops as well as a theater that has been in operation since 1976. It's also a tour boat departure point for whale watching cruises, sailing and fishing. You can also see plenty of pelicans, sea otters and seals hanging out by the pier and in the water. Hours vary of restaurants and shops.

"PATH OF HISTORY" TOUR

20 Custom House Plaza, 831-649-7118; www.parks.ca.gov
This self-guided tour is a two-mile look at Old Monterey including adobes, gardens and other sites of interest. There are yellow tiles in the sidewalk that identify distinguished buildings—several of which are open for public viewing—and explain their history and architecture. Buildings covered are the Cooper-Molera House, the Custom House, Larkin House and Casa Soberanes among others. Obtain a map at the Monterey Peninsula Visitor and Convention Bureau, Camino El Estero and Franklin streets.

PRESIDIO OF MONTEREY

360 Patton Ave., Monterey, 831-242-5104; www.monterey.army.mil
This presidio was developed in 1902 as a cantonment for troops returning from the Philippine Insurrection. It is the site of a monument to John Drake Sloat, commander of the American troops that captured Monterey. It is also the home of the Defense Language Institute. There are 12 historic sites and monuments on Presidio Hill to view. Hours vary.

ROBERT LOUIS STEVENSON HOUSE

530 Houston St., Monterey, 831-649-7118; www.parks.ca.gov
This state historic monument has a large collection of Robert Louis Stevenson memorabilia as well as beautiful gardens. Stevenson lived here for four months while visiting his future wife. At that time, the house was a boarding house known as the French Hotel. Part of the Monterey State Historic Park, this house can only be toured with a State Park guide. Tours: Friday-Wednesday 2 p.m.

ROYAL PRESIDIO CHAPEL

500 Church St., Monterey, 831-373-2628; www.sancarloscathedral.net

Founded in 1770 by Father Junipero Serra, this chapel has been in continuous use since 1795, and is the only presidio chapel remaining in California. This National Historic Landmark has a uniquely ornate façade and has a Spanish Colonial style.

Daily.

SPECIAL EVENTS

MONTEREY COUNTY FAIR

Fairgrounds and Exposition Park, 2004 Fairground Road, Monterey, 831-372-5863;
www.montereycountyfair.com

This county fair features a carnival, pony rides, wine tasting and cooking demonstrations, entertainment and food from around the world. Musical acts range from Berlin to Big Bad Voodoo Daddy. There are contests to take part in, a livestock show and a kid's club with activities. August.

MONTEREY JAZZ FESTIVAL

County Fairgrounds, 2000 Fairground Road, Monterey, 925-275-9255;
www.montereyjazzfestival.org

This three-day festival has entertained crowds with a variety of jazz music since 1958. More than 500 artists perform on 9 different stages on 20 acres of fairgrounds. The first festival featured artists such as Dizzy Gillespie, Louis Armstrong, Billie Holiday and others. You can take part in workshops, clinics and panel discussions with the musicians. Third weekend in September.

WHERE TO STAY

★★★HILTON GARDEN INN MONTEREY

1000 Aguajito Road, Monterey, 831-373-6141, 800-234-5697;
www.hiltongardeninn.com

Located a half-mile from the Monterey beaches, this hotel is set on a beautiful garden landscape among Monterey pine and oak trees. Guest rooms feature comfortable beds, complimentary Internet access, microwaves, refrigerators and private patios or balconies. The Pacific Grille features fresh California cuisine for breakfast and dinner. Unwind in the outdoor pool and whirlpool or sunbathe on the large outdoor patio.

204 rooms. Restaurant, bar. Business center. Fitness center. Pool. $151-250

★★★HOTEL PACIFIC

300 Pacific St., Monterey, 831-373-5700, 800-554-5542; www.hotelpacific.com

Just a block from Fisherman's Wharf in downtown Monterey, this Southwest-style boutique hotel has patios with potted plants, fountains and colorful umbrellas. The lobby features hand-tiled floors, original artwork and photos by Helmut Horn. Guest rooms are divided into living and sleeping spaces and include fireplaces, colorful goose-down featherbeds, hardwood floors, original artwork, tree trunk nightstands and private balconies or patios. A complimentary continental breakfast and afternoon snacks are served daily. Baths feature Aveda products and separate tubs and showers.

105 rooms. Complimentary breakfast. $251-350

★★★HYATT REGENCY MONTEREY

1 Old Golf Course Road, Monterey, 831-372-1234, 800-233-1234;
www.hyattregencymonterey.com

Located about a mile from downtown Monterey, this large, rustic resort on 23 acres of pine and cypress trees is adjacent to the Del Monte Golf Course. Rooms are decorated in natural earth tones and feature pillow-top mattresses, flat-screen TVs and iPod docks. Enjoy Tuscan cuisine with fresh ingredients at TusCA Ristorante. The resort's activities include two swimming pools, tennis, golf and bicycle rentals, and a new full-service spa.
550 rooms. Restaurant, bar. Pool. Spa. Pets accepted. Golf. $251-350

★★THE JABBERWOCK BED AND BREAKFAST

598 Laine St., Monterey, 831-372-4777, 888-428-7253; www.jabberwockinn.com

7 rooms. No children under 12. Complimentary breakfast. $151-250

★★THE MONTEREY HOTEL

406 Alvarado St., Monterey, 831-375-3184, 800-966-6490; www.moonstonehotels.com

69 rooms. Complimentary breakfast. $151-250

★★★★MONTEREY PLAZA HOTEL & SPA

400 Cannery Row, Monterey, 831-646-1700, 800-334-3999;
www.montereyplazahotel.com

Guest rooms at this luxuriously appointed, European-style hotel give guests the impression of being on a ship with an ocean-view balcony. Two restaurants provide culinary diversions, and golf, surf shops, kayak rentals and the Monterey Bay Recreation Trail are all nearby. The landscaped pool deck is right on the water and is the place to be at this coastal retreat.
290 rooms. Restaurant, bar. Business center. Fitness center. Pool. Spa. Beach. $251-350

★★OLD MONTEREY INN

500 Martin St., Monterey, 831-375-8284, 800-350-2344; www.oldmontereyinn.com

10 rooms. No children under 12. Complimentary breakfast. Spa. $351 and up

★★★PORTOLA PLAZA HOTEL

2 Portola Plaza, Monterey, 831-649-4511, 866-711-1534; www.portolaplazahotel.com

This hotel is a short walk from Fisherman's Wharf, Pebble Beach and many shops and galleries. Rooms are furnished with pillow-top beds and artwork by local artists, and many have beautiful views of the bay. A host of outdoor activities are available, including golf, bicycling and kayaking. Dine alfresco at Jacks, which serves hearty cuisine and has an extensive wine list, or enjoy a beer and pub grub at Peter B's brewpub.
379 rooms. Restaurant, bar. Business center. Fitness center. Pool. Spa. $251-350

★★SANCTUARY BEACH RESORT

3295 Dunes Drive, Marina, 831-883-9478, 877-944-3863;
www.thesanctuarybeachresort.com

60 rooms. Restaurant, bar. Complimentary breakfast. Pool. Spa. Beach. $151-250

★★★SPINDRIFT INN

652 Cannery Row, Monterey, 831-646-8900, 800-841-1879; www.spindriftinn.com

At high tide, guests of this intimate, European-style inn can stand directly above the ocean to see the waves crashing in onto McAbee beach. Rooms have window seats, wood-burning fireplaces, flat-screen TVs, marble vanities and canopy beds; some offer views of the ocean. The onsite restaurant, Paradiso Trattoria, specializes in fresh seafood and has an oyster bar. Complimentary breakfast is delivered on a silver tray to your room, and a wine and cheese reception featuring wine from the local Ventana Vineyard takes place each evening.

45 rooms. Complimentary breakfast. Beach. $251-350

ALSO RECOMMENDED
MONTEREY BAY INN

242 Cannery Row, Monterey, 831-373-6242, 800-424-6242; www.montereybayinn.com

Although its exterior is industrial looking, this inn has an excellent location overlooking the bay and Fisherman's Wharf, and the rooms are modern, comfortable, clean and well maintained. Rooms have balconies equipped with binoculars, CD players and local photography books. Get pampered at the Serenity Salon and Spa; enjoy a rooftop hot tub with views of the bay and ocean; and wander down to the accessible beach for scuba diving, sunbathing, swimming or just taking photos of the beautiful scenery.

49 rooms. Complimentary breakfast. Spa. Beach. $251-350

WHERE TO EAT
★★CAFE FINA

47 Fisherman's Wharf, Monterey, 831-372-5200, 800-843-3462; www.cafefina.com

Italian, seafood. Lunch, dinner. Reservations recommended. Children's menu. Bar. $16-35

★★CHART HOUSE

444 Cannery Row, Monterey, 831-372-3362; www.chart-house.com

American. Dinner. Reservations recommended. Bar. $36-85

★★★CIBO RISTORANTE ITALIANO

301 Alvarado St., Monterey, 831-649-8151; www.cibo.com

This sleek, downtown restaurant specializes in innovative interpretations of classic Sicilian cooking. You'll find favorites like gnocchi, ravioli, pasta with bolognese sauce, veal cannelloni, risotto, pizzas, seafood, filets, swordfish, pork chops, Italian sausage, lamb chops and more. Start with fried calamari or fresh oysters and then try the Pizza Cibo with thinly sliced green apple, leeks, prosciutto and mozzarella. A large wine list features vintages from Italy and California along with Cibo's own private labeled chardonnay and cabernet sauvignon. You can also hear an eclectic mix of jazz six days a week

at this live music hot spot.
Italian. Dinner. Children's menu. Bar. $36-85

★★DOMENICO'S ON THE WHARF
50 Fisherman's Wharf, Monterey, 831-372-3655; www.domenicosmonterey.com
Italian, seafood. Lunch, dinner. Reservations recommended. Children's menu. Bar. $36-85

★★★THE DUCK CLUB
400 Cannery Row, Monterey, 831-646-1706; www.montereyplazahotel.com
This elegant restaurant tucked away in the Monterey Plaza Hotel features a seasonal menu and wood-roasted dishes prepared in an exhibition-style kitchen from executive chef James Waller. As the name suggests, duck is a specialty; try the Steinbeck's Duck dish with roasted potatoes and caramelized orange sauce. The menu also features fresh local produce and sustainable seafood.
American. Breakfast, dinner. Reservations recommended. Children's menu. Bar. $86 and up

★★★FRESH CREAM RESTAURANT
99 Pacific St., Monterey, 831-375-9798; www.freshcream.com
Lauded by local and national foodies, Fresh Cream serves California-French fare in a historic-looking building overlooking Fisherman's Wharf and Monterey Bay. The dining room is bright and sunny with floor to ceiling windows and skylights so you get a good view of the bay. Try an appetizer such as foie gras pate, capers and onion with brioche toast; lobster raviolis with lobster butter and black and gold caviar; or dungeness crab cakes. Entrées include grilled filet mignon with roasted portabellas and truffle madeira sauce; pan-seared ahi tuna; and broiled lobster tail and grilled prawns with white corn bisque and brioche toast. The wine list features wines from California and France.
French. Dinner. Reservations recommended. Bar. $36-85

★★★JOHN PISTO'S WHALING STATION
763 Wave St., Monterey, 831-373-3778; www.whalingstationmonterey.com
Just two blocks from Cannery Row and Monterey Bay, John Pisto's serves generous portions in a handsome setting, which includes a horseshoe-shaped bar, copper walls, alabaster lamps, beveled glass windows and large French posters. Pick your lobster out of the tank or opt for a tasty sirloin, filet mignon or prime rib. Chef and restaurateur John Pisto, who owns four restaurants, also hosts a TV cooking show, *Monterey's Cookin' Pisto Style*, but you still might be able to catch him working in the kitchen.
American, steak. Dinner. Children's menu. Bar. $36-85

★★★MONTRIO BISTRO
414 Calle Principal, Monterey, 831-648-8880; www.montrio.com
Housed in an old brick firehouse, this bistro's downtown Monterey dining room has soft sculptures suspended from the ceiling to muffle sound and track lighting made from fine metalwork twisted into the shape of grapevines. House specialties include crab cakes with spicy remoulade, rotisserie

chicken over roasted garlic whipped potatoes and oven-roasted portobello mushrooms. For dessert, try the decadent flourless chocolate cake with port swirl ice cream.
American, Mediterranean. Dinner. Children's menu. Bar. $16-35

★★RAPPA'S SEAFOOD RESTAURANT
101 Fisherman's Wharf, Monterey, 831-372-7562; www.rappas.com
Seafood. Lunch, dinner. Reservations recommended. Children's menu. Bar. $16-35

★★★SARDINE FACTORY
701 Wave St., Monterey, 831-373-3775; www.sardinefactory.com
Known as the flagship of Cannery Row, this restaurant serves New American cuisine in several elegant dining rooms, including the Captain's Room and the Conservatory, a glassed-in space. Start out with a cocktail in the Lounge where a pianist plays Tuesday through Saturday, before heading to dinner. The menu consists of fresh fish, shellfish, meat and locally grown produce including dishes such as prawns with black truffle risotto and lemon caper sauce.
Seafood. Dinner. Reservations recommended. Children's menu. Bar. $36-85

★★★STOKES RESTAURANT & BAR
500 Hartnell St., Monterey, 831-373-1110; www.stokesrestaurant.com
Housed in a historic pink adobe building dating to 1833, this downtown restaurant has several dining rooms and a mix of contemporary and early California décor, including Mexican tile and chairs and a wood-burning oven. The dining rooms feature large tables and wooden booths and banquettes with stencil designs and colorful paintings on the wall. The Mediterranean-inspired cuisine is made with regional produce, meats, fish and cheeses. Enjoy their housemade organic sourdough bread that's baked fresh Daily. Try the pork shoulder with broccoli rabe, crispy polenta and star anise jus; or vegetarian crêpes with spinach béchamel, spring vegetables and aged Gruyère.
American, Mediterranean. Dinner. Bar. $16-35

★★★TARPY'S ROADHOUSE
2999 Monterey Salinas Highway, Monterey, 831-647-1444; www.tarpys.com
From a historic 1917 hacienda on Salinas Highway, Tarpy's serves innovative American country fare—steaks, wild game and seafood. Dishes include grilled ribeye with herb au jus and horseradish sour cream on mashed potatoes; meatloaf with marsala-mushroom gravy on roasted garlic whipped potatoes; and grilled tiger shrimp on rice pilaf with citrus salsa and lemon beurre blanc.
American. Lunch, dinner, Sunday brunch. Outdoor seating. Children's menu. Bar. $36-85

MOUNT SHASTA

See also Chico

Less than nine miles from the volcano that shares its name, Mount Shasta is a good base for fishing in nearby lakes and streams and year-round outdoor activities in the surrounding area. City water from a nearby spring is so pure that it is untreated.

WHAT TO SEE

LAKE SISKIYOU AND LAKE SISKIYOU CAMP-RESORT

4239 W. A. Barr Road, Mount Shasta, 888-926-2618; www.lakesis.com

This 430-acre lake is ideal for fishing and swimming. There is a marina and boat ramp as well as boat, kayak and canoe rentals. Adjacent to the lake is a campsite where there are tent and RV sites.
April-October, Daily.

MOUNT SHASTA

www.shastahome.com

This perpetually snow-covered double-peak volcano towers to 14,162 feet. Five glaciers persist on the slopes, feeding the McCloud and Sacramento rivers. A scenic drive on the Everitt Memorial Highway climbs from the city of Mount Shasta up the slope 7,840 feet for a magnificent view. White pine, the famous Shasta lily and majestic stands of red fir are found at various elevations.

MOUNT SHASTA SKI PARK

104 Siskiyou Ave., Mount Shasta, 530-926-8610; www.skipark.com

This ski park covers 425 acres with 32 trails, with the longest run at 1.75 miles and the biggest vertical drop at 1,390 feet. There are three triple chairlifts, one surface lift, patrol enforced zones, a ski school, and rentals. There is also night skiing available on 14 trails (check Web site for details).
Mid-December-mid-April, Friday-Saturday 9 a.m.-9 p.m., Sunday-Thursday 9 a.m.-4 p.m.

SHASTA DAM AND POWER PLANT

Shasta Dam Blvd., Shasta Lake, 530-275-4463; www.shastalake.com/shastadam

The second largest dam in the U.S. and three times as high as Niagara Falls, Shasta Dam measures in at 602 feet high and 3,460 feet long. Waters of three rivers back up to form Shasta Lake, which is 35 miles long with a 365-mile shoreline. House boating is popular here; boats are available for rent at several local marinas.
Visitor Center: Daily 8 a.m.-4:30 p.m.

SHASTA STATE HISTORIC PARK

Highway 299 West, Shasta, 530-243-8194; www.parks.ca.gov

This 13-acre park includes the remains of the old Gold Rush town, Shasta City, with several well-preserved original buildings, a historical museum and an art gallery.
Museum: Wednesday-Sunday 10 a.m.-5 p.m.

SHASTA-TRINITY NATIONAL FOREST

Shasta Lake Visitor Center, 14225 Holiday Road, Redding, 530-275-1589;
www.fs.fed.us/r5/shastatrinity/

More than two million acres of forest, five wilderness areas, hundreds of mountain lakes, streams and rivers make up this national forest. It is the meeting point of the Trinity Alps Wilderness, Mount Shasta Wilderness, Castle Crags Wilderness, Chanchelulla Wilderness and the Yolla Bolly-Middle Eel Wilderness areas.

Visitor Center Hours: Memorial Day-Labor Day, Wednesday-Sunday 8 a.m.-4:30 p.m.

WHERE TO STAY

★★BEST WESTERN TREE HOUSE MOTOR INN

111 Morgan Way, Mount Shasta, 530-926-3101, 800-545-7164; www.bestwestern.com

98 rooms. Complimentary breakfast. Pool. Pets accepted. $61-150

★★MOUNT SHASTA RESORT

1000 Siskiyou Lake Blvd., Mount Shasta, 530-926-3030, 800-958-3363;
www.mountshastaresort.com

65 rooms. Restaurant, bar. Spa.. $151-250

★★BEST WESTERN HILLTOP INN

2300 Hilltop Drive, Redding, 530-221-6100, 800-971-6905; www.thehilltopinn.com

114 rooms. Complimentary breakfast. Restaurant, bar. Pool. $61-150

WHERE TO EAT

★★★CAFÉ MADDALENA

5801 Sacramento Ave., Dunsmuir, 530-235-2725; www.cafemaddalena.com

Locals come to this wood-paneled, bistro-style restaurant for its innovative menu of Spanish, Italian and Provençal cuisine and Mediterranean wines. Chef Brett LaMott creates his menu based on the quality and freshness of seasonal ingredients and cooks in an open kitchen, which overlooks the sunlit and cozy dining room. Typical dishes include grilled flatbread with fresh chorizo, spinach, garlic and chickpeas; scallops and prawns with snap peas and pea shoots; confit of duck leg; and vermicelli with pancetta, garlic, peas and mint. In summer, outdoor seating is available in the garden.

Mediterranean. Dinner. Closed Monday-Wednesday from January-early February. Outdoor seating. $16-35

★★THE HIGHLAND HOUSE RESTAURANT

Mount Shasta Resort, 1000 Siskiyou Lake Blvd., Mount Shasta, 800-958-3363;
www.mountshastaresort.com

American. Dinner, Sunday brunch. Outdoor seating. $36-85

MOUNTAIN VIEW

See also Palo Alto, Santa Clara

This charming Bay Area suburb, located south of San Francisco, is now internationally famous for being the world headquarters of search engine phenomenon Google, Inc. It's also home to many other Silicon Valley businesses, including Microsoft and AOL. The main downtown area is filled with shops, cafés and restaurants. There is also a superb farmers' market that is open all year.

WHAT TO SEE
SHORELINE AT MOUNTAIN VIEW

3070 N. Shoreline Blvd., Mountain View; www.ci.mtnview.ca.us
Part of the Shoreline Regional Wildlife and Recreation Area, this park offers plenty to see and do. The Shoreline Amphitheatre, operated by Live Nation, hosts different types of musical acts for outdoor concerts (the majority of the amphitheatre is covered but the outdoor lawn seats are better to lounge and dance under the stars). Tour the oldest house in Mountain View, the Rengstorff House, built in 1867. There are large wildlife habitats at Shoreline where you can hike along ponds, marshland and hills to spot a variety of animals. Bike, jog or hike through one of Shoreline's seven miles of trails that wind through the area. Rent pedalboats, rowboats, canoes or kayaks to take out on Shoreline Lake or take a windsurfing, sailing or kayaking lesson. Or spend the day on the 18 hole golf course, and stop in afterwards for a meal at Michael's, the clubhouse for Shoreline Golf Links.

WHERE TO EAT
★★★CHEZ TJ

938 Villa St., Mountain View, 650-964-7466; www.cheztj.com
After experiencing an elegant meal at Chez TJ—courtesy of award-winning chef Bruno Chemel—you won't believe that the restaurant has such humble roots. Once the residence of town council member Julius Weilheimer, the green-painted Victorian-style house is now home to fans of fine dining looking for upscale California cuisine. With four different dining rooms, you'll also find an intimate setting. Chez TJ supports local farms and producers getting much of their ingredients at local markets. The wine list boasts the bounty of Mountain View's neighboring vineyards, with each selection carefully chosen to pair with dishes on the menu. Chemel features a tasting menu for $120, with wine pairings for $195.
American. Dinner. Closed Sunday-Monday. Reservations recommended. $86 and up

NAPA

See also Calistoga, Rutherford, Sonoma, St. Helena, Yountville
In recent years, Napa has undergone a transition that has seen new shops, restaurants and upscale hotels move into its historic downtown, making what was once a pass-through town on the way to the valley's vineyards a destination in its own right. There are more than 300 wineries in the Napa Valley, most of which are open to the public. But wine is only the beginning of this area's treasures.

WHAT TO SEE
ARTESA VINEYARD & WINERY

1345 Henry Road, Napa, 707-224-1668; www.artesawinery.com
A striking contrast with the restored historic vineyards so common to Napa Valley, this winery has sleek modernist architecture and its own artist in

residence. Built by the Codorníu family, Spain's largest makers of sparkling wine, the vineyard started with sparkling varieties but has since expanded to quality still wines.
Daily 10 a.m.-5 p.m.

BOTHE-NAPA VALLEY STATE PARK

3801 St. Helena Highway N., Calistoga, 707-942-4575; www.parks.ca.gov
Flush with pine and redwood groves, this 1,800-acre state park has camp-grounds, picnic areas, a swimming pool, a horseshoe pit and more than 10 miles of rugged hiking and horseback riding trails. Some areas reach elevations as high as 2,000 feet.
Daily. Swimming Pool: Memorial Day weekend-mid-June, Saturday-Sunday noon-6 p.m.; mid-June-Labor Day, Daily noon-6 p.m.

BOUCHAINE VINEYARDS

1075 Buchli Station Road, Napa, 707-252-9065, 800-654-9463; www.bouchaine.com
Best known for its pinot noir, a grape that thrives in the cool Carneros Valley, Bouchaine is the oldest continually operating winery in the region. Renovated extensively in 1995, the winery received numerous local architectural and historic awards, due in part to its use of recycled materials. The end result is a fireplace-warmed tasting room, as well as a deck and terrace with hill views, which makes for cozy wine tasting. Tours by appointment.
Daily 10:30 a.m.-4 p.m.

DARIOUSH

4240 Silverado Trail, Napa, 707-257-2345; www.darioush.com
A visit to Darioush is more akin to a journey to ancient Persia than Napa Valley. From the 16 monumental freestanding columns greeting visitors as they enter to the richly textured travertine stone surrounding the entire compound and the amphitheater used for special events and performances, this vineyard is an experience in itself. Proprietor Darioush Khaledi grew up in Iran's Shiraz region, bringing his international expertise to California's famous wine country in 1997. The results are chardonnays, viogniers and cabernet sauvignons that are smooth and well balanced. The large tasting bar resembles something of an extravagant hafla (an Arabic dance party)—it can get packed and quite lively.
Daily 10:30 a.m.-5 p.m.

DI ROSA PRESERVE

5200 Sonoma Highway, Napa, 707-226-5991; www.dirosapreserve.org
Set on 217 acres with a 35-acre lake, this preserve houses the largest collection of contemporary California Bay Area art in the world, including nearly 2,000 works by approximately 800 artists. On the grounds are four gallery buildings, a sculpture meadow, gardens and a meditation chapel. The Gatehouse Gallery is open to the public; however, to see the other galleries, sculpture meadow, and di Rosa residence, you'll have to schedule a tour.
Admission (to Gatehouse Gallery): Free. Wednesday-Friday 9:30 a.m.-3 p.m.; tour times vary, call or visit Web site for schedule.

DOMAINE CARNEROS

1240 Duhig Road, Napa, 800-716-2788; www.domaine.com

Those looking to embrace the essence of France without flying across the Atlantic need go no further than Domaine Carneros. The property occupies prime real estate in the heart of Napa and its apex, the majestic Domaine Carneros chateau, was modeled after an historic 18th-century mansion owned by the Taittinger family in Champagne, France. The winery specializes in sparkling wines including brut, brut rosé and blanc de blancs; and pinot noir; and uses only locally grown grapes to gain the perfect delicate balance of flavors. In lieu of a traditional tasting, Domaine offers flights, as well as full glass or bottle table service in the main chateau or along the back terrace. Caviar and other savory hors d'oeuvres are also available, set to match the bottles of bubbly.

Daily 10 a.m.-6 p.m. (Last tasting is at 5:45 p.m.) Tours: 11 a.m., 1 p.m. and 3 p.m.

DOWNTOWN NAPA

Napa Valley Visitor Bureau, 1310 Napa Town Center, Napa, 707-266-7459; www.napavalley.com

Ride a free downtown trolley that passes through several Victorian neighborhoods—the city has more pre-1906 Victorians than anywhere else in Northern California, an area that was hit by the big earthquake the same year. The trolley makes stops at the Napa Premium Outlets and Oxbow Public Market among other places. Napa County Landmarks periodically conducts 90-minute guided walking tours (see Web site for more information, www.napacountylandmarks.org).

GETAWAY ADVENTURES

2228 Northpoint Parkway, Santa Rosa, 707-568-3040, 800-499-2453; www.getawayadventures.com

Tour the Napa Valley on two wheels. Several shops in neighboring towns rent bikes if you'd like to plan your own itinerary or opt for an all-out luxury tour with a small group. Getaway's Best of Napa and Sonoma weekend tours span two days and two nights, and the price includes bikes and equipment, gourmet meals, stays in small luxury hotels or bed and breakfasts, a support van, tours of wineries and elegant picnic lunches. Longer tours are available, as are specialty trips such as spa and holiday weekend packages.

Daily.

THE HESS COLLECTION

4411 Redwood Road, Napa, 707-255-1144, 877-707-4377; www.hesscollection.com

Owner Donald Hess found a way to merge his two passions—traditional winemaking and contemporary art—at this unusual winery and gallery. The wine, always flowing in the tasting room, has a reputation for being high quality and is available for purchase at the vineyard store. Take a tour of the Museum and then taste three current release wines paired with culinary creations ($35 per person Thursday; $40 per person Friday and Saturday). Tastings: $10. Daily 10 a.m.-5 p.m.

HOT AIR BALLOONING

Balloons Above the Valley, 603 California Blvd., Napa, 707-253-2222, 800-464-6824; www.balloonrides.com

See the beauty of Napa Valley from up high, between 1,000 to 3,000 feet high. These hot air balloon trips (approximately an hour in the air) are narrated and include a champagne brunch overlooking the Napa River. You'll leave just before sunrise when the weather is cooler and the wine is calm. The schedules fill up quickly, so call ahead to make a reservation.

Admission: $210 (internet booking specials tend to be cheaper).

JOHN F. KENNEDY PARK

955 School St., Napa, 707-257-9529; www.cityofnapa.org

This inviting and popular city park has tables and barbecue pits for picnicking, softball, baseball and soccer fields, a volleyball court, boat launch on the Napa River, children's playground and the Napa Golf Course.

Daily.

LAKE BERRYESSA

Visitor Center, 5520 Knoxville Road, Napa, 707-966-2111; www.usbr.gov

Created in 1957, this artificial lake is one of the largest fresh water bodies in California. With 165 miles of shoreline, it has become a year-round recreation favorite of locals who come to boat, swim, fish, hike, camp, bike and picnic. The lake has seven resorts, popular with boaters, and abundant birdlife including eagles, hawks, songbirds, great blue herons, pelicans, ducks and geese.

Daily. Visitor Center: Saturday-Sunday 10 a.m.-4 p.m.

LUNA VINEYARDS

2921 Silverado Trail, Napa, 707-255-5862; www.lunavineyards.com

Although it hasn't been around for long, this vineyard has the feel of a centuries-old Italian villa, complete with olive trees. Luna specializes in Italian wines: pinot grigio, sangiovese, merlot and their proprietary wine, Canto.

Daily 10 a.m.-5 p.m.

NAPA VALLEY OPERA HOUSE

1030 Main St., Napa, 707-226-7372; www.napavalleyoperahouse.org

Built in 1879, the Opera House is not only one of Napa's most significant historic landmarks but also a venue for the performing arts, including jazz, classical, world music, dance, comedy and theater. Closed for almost a century, it recently reopened following a partial restoration. Performances are being staged only in the first floor Café Theatre. Hours and ticket prices vary with performance.

Box Office: Monday-Friday 10 a.m.-5 p.m., Saturday noon-4 p.m. (and one hour before shows).

NAPA VALLEY WINE TRAIN

1275 McKinstry St., Napa, 707-253-2111, 800-427-4124; www.winetrain.com

Take a scenic trip aboard a turn-of-the-century Pullman or a 1950s diesel Streamliner. Typically a three-hour ride, the train travels a 36-mile route from

Napa through St. Helena, passing dozens of vineyards. A variety of packages are available—standard lunch and dinner rides, which can include tasting in the wine tasting car and stops at various vineyards, as well as gourmet and champagne meals, a Sunday dinner and concert series and a murder mystery dinner theater.
Daily.

OAKVILLE GROCERY

7856 St. Helena Highway, Oakville, 707-944-8802; www.oakvillegrocery.com
Frequented by tour buses and carloads, this grocery may resemble a quaint, old country store but inside lies an astonishing array of gourmet foods, cheeses, Northern California wines, fresh produce, pastries, breads and local specialty items, perfect for gifts, picnics and cooking. Stop here to pack a picnic before heading out to vineyards.
Daily 8 a.m.-6 p.m. The espresso bar opens at 7 a.m.

OXBOW PUBLIC MARKET

610 First St., Napa, 707-226-6529; www.oxbowpublicmarket.com
After a day of vineyard hopping, you'll no doubt be hungry. If you're looking for more of a DIY dinner option, head to Oxbow Public Market, a one-stop artisanal food and wine shop located in Napa's up-and-coming Oxbow District. Grab a cup of made-to-order coffee from San Francisco's own Ritual Coffee Roasters, pick up a bottle of local wine from Oxbow Wine Merchant, or opt for the fresh-baked bread, house cured meats or newly shucked oysters. Whatever you grab, you can be assured it'll be local, and tasty.

PINE RIDGE WINERY

5901 Silverado Trail, Napa, 707-253-7500, 800-486-0503; www.pineridgewinery.com
This elegant winery, founded in 1978, has an array of award-winning wines and a new reserve tasting room. Stroll the estate gardens, tour the vast cabernet caves, which are 130 feet underground, and participate in barrel tasting (special tasting by appointment only). Experience a gourmet multi-course dinner with wine pairings in the beautiful wine cave.
Daily 10:30 a.m.-4:30 p.m. Tours: 10 a.m., noon, 2 p.m., by appointment only.

REGUSCI WINERY

5584 Silverado Trail, Napa, 707-254-0403; www.regusciwinery.com
This winery goes way back. In fact, it's one of the few "ghost wineries," a term given to those wineries that were around before 1900. During the 1890s, many vineyards were wiped out because of a phylloxera infestation. However, a few were folded into more modern facilities, one of which was located on the Regusci ranch. In 1932, Gaetano Regusci bought the historic property, at first farming other crops, and it has been a family business ever since. Today, the family only farms grapes, having established the winery in 1996. You'll find cabernet sauvignon as well as merlot, zinfandel and chardonnay. Tastings and tours by appointment only.

SILVERADO TRAIL

www.silveradotrail.com

This 29-mile drive, the first permanent road to be built between Napa and Calistoga in 1852, is said to afford travelers a glimpse of the nation's foremost wine region as it looked 30 years ago. The leisurely drive connects more than 40 of the area's smaller wineries, and many of their wines are only available directly from the winery. It can take less than an hour to follow the trail or you can opt for a full day's exploration.
Daily.

SKYLINE WILDERNESS PARK

2201 Imola Ave., Napa, 707-252-0481; www.ncfaa.com/skyline/skyline_park.htm

A well-maintained park with some trails dedicated to hiking, others to horseback riding and mountain biking, and several camping areas as well as picnic grounds, gardens, disc golf and an archery range. A great day hike is the Marie Creek Trail, which leads to an overlook above Lake Marie.
Daily.

WILLIAM HILL WINERY

1761 Atlas Peak Road, Napa, 707-265-3024; www.williamhillestate.com

Specializing in cabernet sauvignon, William Hill is a small, elegant winery in southern Napa. General tastings run $10-20, but it's worth the $40 fee to reserve a spot in the William Hill Estate Experience Tour, where visitors take a tour of the vineyard and learn about winemaking, then taste a selection of wines with local artisan foods as well as some reserve wines. Seating is limited, and dates and times vary, so call ahead or appointments.
Daily 10 a.m.-5 p.m.

SPECIAL EVENTS
CHEFS' MARKET

First Street and Napa Town Center, Napa, 707-257-0322; www.napadowntown.com

Not only does this free Thursday night market have outstanding farm-fresh produce and gourmet specialty items, but it also features artisans, cooking demonstrations, beer and wine gardens, children's activities and live entertainment.
Late-May-July, Thursday 5-9 p.m.

MUSIC IN THE VINEYARDS: NAPA VALLEY CHAMBER MUSIC FESTIVAL

707-258-5559; www.napavalleymusic.com

Come for the music, stay for the intermission wine tasting at these vineyard performances. The intimacy of the settings makes them ideal for chamber music, and the music festival is a favorite with locals. Performances are on Saturday and Sunday during August, and midweek events include concerts, recitals, lecture demonstrations and open rehearsals that are free to the public.
Early to mid-August.

NAPA VALLEY MUSTARD FESTIVAL

707-938-1133; www.mustardfestival.org

This celebration was first conceived to enliven the valley during the typically slow winter months. But there's nothing particularly wintry about the area in February and March—in fact, the festival is so named because much of the valley is covered in brilliant yellow wild mustard flowers. The now popular celebration includes grand dinners, jazz concerts, art exhibitions, a photography contest and wine tasting. For the current year's schedule of events, check out the Web site. Late-January-March.

WHERE TO STAY

★★★THE CARNEROS INN

4048 Sonoma Highway, Napa, 707-299-4900, 888-400-9000; www.thecarnerosinn.com

Between Napa and Sonoma and surrounded by vineyards, this all-cottage hotel offers spacious accommodations with an array of modern amenities—heated slate floors in the bathrooms, flatscreen televisions and spa treatments enhanced by the use of local herbs and fruits. Fine dining is just a few steps away at the Hilltop Dining Room while the Boon Fly Café is a good place to begin the day, order lunch to go or taste local wines.
86 rooms. Restaurant, bar. Business center. Fitness center. Pool. $351 and up

★★EMBASSY SUITES

1075 California Blvd., Napa, 707-253-9540; www.embassysuites.com

205 rooms. Restaurant, bar. Complimentary breakfast. Pool. Pets accepted. $151-250

★★HILTON GARDEN INN NAPA

3585 Solano Ave., Napa, 707-252-0444; www.hiltongardeninn.com

80 rooms. Restaurant, bar. Fitness center. Pool. $151-250

★★★LA RESIDENCE

4066 Howard Lane, Napa, 707-253-0337, 800-253-9203; www.laresidence.com

This secluded 1870 Gothic Revival mansion combines the charm of Napa Valley with the style of the French countryside. Minutes from the region's vineyards, the hotel is set among two acres of gardens, vineyards, redwoods and fountains. Rooms feature charming antique furniture, original artwork and many have fireplaces. Amenities include Frette bathrobes, luxurious Mascioni and Sferra linens, Matouk towels and Molton Brown bath products. A complimentary gourmet breakfast is served each morning. Leafy trees shade guests relaxing by the pool and jacuzzi during the day, and wine and hors d'oeuvres are served by the fire or outside on the terrace each evening. 25 rooms. Complimentary breakfast. Pool. $251-350

★★★MARRIOTT NAPA VALLEY HOTEL & SPA

3425 Solano Ave., Napa, 707-253-8600, 800-228-9290; www.napavalleymarriott.com

The largest hotel in the Napa Valley, this sprawling complex of two-story, beige stucco wings has a luxurious spa, salon and fitness facility, a large outdoor pool, two restaurants and a sports bar and proximity to wine country.

Handsome guest rooms have pillow-top mattresses, bolster pillows, duvet-topped beds, and large, practical work desks. Other amenities include a flat-screen TV, delivery of Daily newspaper and Internet access. Enjoy a complimentary wine tasting and then pamper yourself at Amadeus Spa.

274 rooms. Restaurant, bar. Business center. Fitness center. Pool. Spa. $151-250

★★★MERITAGE NAPA RESORT

875 Bordeaux Way, Napa, 707-251-1900; www.themeritageresort.com

Got a hankering for more than a quaint bed and breakfast while cruising through Napa Valley? Meritage Napa Resort provides that extra bit of lavish elegance on your trip. The resort's wine namesake reflects its proximity to Sonoma and Napa Valley, and traces of it are evident everywhere. From the cave-like Spa Terra (located entirely underground) to the Trinitas wine-tasting room, Meritage Napa redefines the meaning of wine-cellar chic. Tuscany-inspired Siena Restaurant adds the final touch to the resort.

158 rooms. Restaurant, bar. Business center. Fitness center. Pool. Spa. $251-350

★★★MILLIKEN CREEK INN & SPA

1815 Silverado Trail, Napa, 707-255-1197, 800-835-6112; www.millikencreekinn.com

Located on the Silverado Trail, this posh hideaway is minutes from the valley's acclaimed wineries, yet its gentle pace and riverside setting tempt guests to stick around for massages and terrace dining. The Asian-influenced rooms have fireplaces and fresh flowers, and many offer private decks or patios. Beds are fitted with Frette linens, piled high for extra comfort.

12 rooms. Complimentary breakfast. Pool. Spa. No children under 18. $351 and up

★★★NAPA RIVER INN

500 Main St., Napa, 707-251-8500, 877-251-8500; www.napariverinn.com

Located along the Napa River, this boutique hotel, consisting of three buildings, has spacious guest rooms that are smartly decorated with canopy beds, elegant brocade duvets and fireplaces. Some rooms have river views with balconies. Each morning, guests receive a complimentary breakfast of fresh baked breads, pies and pastries from a bakery next door. Afternoon wine tastings enhance the relaxed atmosphere and to really pamper yourself, make an appointment for an in-room spa treatment. If you're looking for more space, book the Captain Hatt Suite, which offers a separate living area, fireplace and wet bar.

66 rooms. Restaurant, bar. Complimentary breakfast. Pets accepted. $251-350

★★★SILVERADO RESORT

1600 Atlas Peak Road, Napa, 707-257-0200, 800-532-0500; www.silveradoresort.com

With two 18-hole, Robert Trent Jones-designed courses and 17 tennis courts, the 200-acre Silverado Resort attracts sports enthusiasts from across Northern California. Though most come to play golf and to use the state-of-the-art 16,000 square foot spa, many come to relax in the comfortable rooms. They come complete with thick robes, Egyptian cotton linens, and wood-burning fireplaces. Spacious one- and two-bedroom suites are perfect for families. There are also two restaurants and a lounge to enjoy a juicy steak and a glass of wine after a long day of golf.

280 rooms. Restaurant, bar. Fitness center. Pool. Spa. $251-350

WHERE TO EAT
★★★BISTRO DON GIOVANNI
4110 Howard Lane, Napa, 707-224-3300; www.bistrodongiovanni.com

With a heated outdoor terrace, manicured gardens and an open kitchen with a wood-burning oven, this quaint stucco bistro has all the charm of dining in the Tuscan countryside. Most of the produce is from the restaurant's own garden and homemade olive oil from olive trees can be purchased. Start out with carpaccio or chickpea and olive fritters, and then dig into risotto with chanterelles, artichokes, thyme, pancetta and fontina val d'aosta. Or sample something from the wood oven, like roasted Sonoma duck or Napa Valley lamb. If you have room for dessert, the hazelnut crème brûlée is rich and satisfying.

Italian, French. Lunch, dinner. Reservations recommended. Outdoor seating. $36-85

★★CELADON
500 Main St., Napa, 707-254-9690; www.celadonnapa.com

International. Lunch, dinner. Outdoor seating. Bar. $36-85

★★★CUVÉE
1650 Soscol Ave., Napa, 707-224-2330; www.cuveenapa.com

After a day exploring Napa Valley, head to Cuvée for what locals deem the town's best happy hour. Local wines and snacks supplemented by an easy-going vibe make this place popular. Bar menu favorites include a skillfully fried calamari and Napa cheesesteak sandwich.

American. Lunch (Monday-Friday), dinner. Reservations recommended. Outdoor seating. Bar. $36-85

★★★NAPA VALLEY WINE TRAIN
1275 McKinstry St., Napa, 707-253-2111, 800-427-4124; www.winetrain.com

Ride the "Gourmet Express" for a well-crafted culinary and wine experience, with a three- or four-course meal. Chef Kelly Macdonald creates cuisine using fresh organic produce, meats and fish. This unusual three-hour tour will take you through the heart of the Napa Valley in meticulously restored 1915-1917 Pullman dining cars with luxurious interiors or 1950 Vista Dome cars for an elevated scenic view. There are also winery tours, which start with a three-course lunch and then take you on private winery tours and tastings to some of Napa's best wineries.

American, French. Lunch, dinner. Reservations recommended. Children's menu. Bar. $16-35

★★★UBUNTU
1140 Main St., Napa, 707-251-5656; www.ubuntunapa.com

Though you'll find no meat on the menu, the focus at Ubuntu is less on depravity than fresh, innovative cuisine from local community gardens. Named after the Zulu term for "humanity toward others," the space functions as both a vegetarian restaurant and a yoga studio. The open kitchen serves up such succulent dishes as coq au vin with spring vegetables, a deep-fried egg and Lion's Run Cabernet, and toasted bread dumplings with courgettes and basil. Executive chef Jeremy Fox grows most of the restaurant's food on its own biodynamic farm and prepares an eclectic menu of items sure to please even the most stubborn carnivore. And lest you forget you're in Napa Valley: Wine pairings are offered to compliment the nightly garden menu.

Vegetarian. Lunch (Friday-Sunday), dinner. Outdoor seating. Bar. $16-35

SPAS
★★★★THE SPA AT THE CARNEROS INN
The Carneros Inn, 4048 Sonoma Highway, Napa, 707-299-4850;
www.thecarnerosinn.com

Napa Valley's Carneros Inn takes the country farmhouse and turns it on its head with clean lines and simple sophistication. The sun-filled, mood-lifting spa perfectly complements this resort's laid-back attitude. The inviting space pampers guests with a themed treatment menu that includes regional inspiration from the harvests, farms, cellars, minerals and creeks of the Carneros Valley. Therapies include selections such as honeydew exfoliations, chardonnay facials, goat butter body wraps, grape seed and guava body scrubs, and lemongrass and ginger sea mineral body wraps. Before or after your treatment, enjoy the swimming pool, hot pool, rosemary-infused steam room and dry sauna. For those guests who prefer to remain within the confines of their private cottages, the spa offers a menu of in-room treatments, including organic garden wraps and couples' massages.

★★★SPA TERRA
Meritage Napa Resort, 875 Bordeaux Way, Napa, 707-251-3000; www.spaterra.com

The concept of a spa in a serene, underground grotto is just what Spa Terra achieves. Located at the Meritage Napa Resort, it is literally housed in the earth—40 feet underground—inside the Estate Cave, where the Trinitas Tasting Room also resides. The spa takes full advantage of local ingredients such as grape seed, olives and citrus, which are used in many of the body and facial treatments. One of its signature treatment packages, the Solo Vino, indulges spa-goers with a grape seed scrub and jet shower rinse, followed by a Wine Cave Mud body wrap and finished off with a 50-minute massage.

OAKHURST
See also Yosemite National Park

Near the south entrance of Yosemite National Park, this community derives much of its economy from tourists who come to explore the park. Located along Highway 49, the Gold Chain Highway, the area is filled with historic structures dating to the Gold Rush.

WHERE TO STAY
★★BEST WESTERN YOSEMITE GATEWAY INN
40530 Highway 41, Oakhurst, 559-683-2378, 888-256-8042;
www.yosemitegatewayinn.com

122 rooms. Restaurant, bar. Fitness center. Pool. $61-150

★★★★★CHATEAU DU SUREAU
48688 Victoria Lane, Oakhurst, 559-683-6860; www.chateausureau.com

Tucked away in the heart of the Sierra Nevada forest is a lovely hideaway known as Chateau du Sureau. Foodies have been coming to the Elderberry House restaurant since 1984 for its haute cuisine, and the restaurant did so well that owner Erna Kubin-Clanin opened an inn to accommodate her guests. This charming Provençal castle features quaint balconies and a dramatic round fieldstone tower. The grounds are planted with manicured topiaries and the stucco walls are dotted with Elderberry bushes that cover the castle's rolling grounds. Inside, chambermaids wearing black with white-linen aprons deliver baskets of goodies and tea. There is no front desk, no check-in formalities. The 10 unique bedrooms, nearly all of which have fire-places, include canopy and sleigh beds, cathedral ceilings and views of the Sierra Nevada Mountains and there are no televisions, so you can truly relax. There is a swimming pool, bocce ball court and life-size chess set to keep guests busy; or enjoy a spa treatment at the Spa Sureau.

10 rooms. Closed two weeks in January. Complimentary breakfast. Restaurant, bar. Pool. Spa. $351 and up

WHERE TO EAT
★★★★ERNA'S ELDERBERRY HOUSE
Chateau Du Sureau, 48688 Victoria Lane, Oakhurst, 559-683-6800;
www.chateausureau.com

This charming restaurant, with three dining areas, offers an exquisite seasonal menu of California cuisine served in a setting decorated with antique French provincial furnishings, brocade tapestries and original oil paintings. Since 1984, Erna Kubin-Clanin has guided the kitchen toward farm-raised meats and local produce. Prix fixe menus change daily and consist of five courses paired with three or four California or international wines; or choose a meal off the a la carte menu with options such as wienerschnitzel or braised rabbit. The 725-bottle wine list is overseen by Erna's daughter Renee and includes several rare and cult California wines as well as many Austrian selections, in honor of Erna's birthplace.

American, French. Dinner, Sunday brunch. Closed first two weeks in January. Reservations recommended. Outdoor seating. Bar. $86 and up

SPAS
★★★★SPA DU SUREAU
48688 Victoria Lane, Oakhurst, 559-683-6193; www.chateausureau.com

Decorated throughout in charming Art Deco style, there are only three treatment rooms (all with iPod docks) and one wet room at this petite spa. The star, however, is the decadent double treatment room with its black marble fireplace, two massage tables separated by translucent drapes, lounge chairs and Jacuzzi. The spa also features a Hydrostorm shower system—one of only a handful in the country—that uses aroma and color therapy aquatics. The treatment menu includes European Kur baths which feature marine hydrotherapy and use only top-notch ingredients, such as moor mud from the Czech Republic, touted for its high concentration of vitamins and minerals.

OAKLAND

See also Berkeley, San Francisco, San Jose, San Mateo

Once part of the Rancho San Antonio, a 48,000-acre domain of former Spanish cavalry sergeant Luis Maria Peralta, Oakland was acquired as a town site by Horace W. Carpentier, who named it for the evergreen oaks that marked the landscape. The city also has abundant parks, shops and museums. Just across the bay from San Francisco, Oakland will send you there via ferry or the Bay Area Rapid Transit system (BART), which links suburban areas and Oakland with San Francisco.

WHAT TO SEE

ANTHONY CHABOT REGIONAL PARK & LAKE CHABOT

9999 Redwood Road, Castro Valley, 510-569-0213, 888-327-2757; www.ebparks.org

This East Bay regional park covers over 5,000 acres of land for hiking and horseback riding, biking, camping and golf. There are 31 miles of hiking trails along the East Bay Skyline National Trail. Not too far away is the Willow Park 18-hole Golf Course and restaurant. A perfect camp to pitch a tent is Chabot Family Campground, which overlooks Lake Chabot, where there are fishing and boating facilities, bicycle trails and picnic areas.
Daily 7 a.m.-10 p.m.

CAMRON-STANFORD HOUSE

1418 Lakeside Drive, Oakland, 510-874-7802; www.cshouse.org

This house, built in 1876, now serves as a museum with authentic period furnishings, sculpture and paintings. Once home to the notable Camron and Stanford families, the building served as the Oakland Public Museum from 1910 to 1967. Guided tours.
Admission: adults $5, seniors $4, children 12-18 $3, children 11 and under free. Third Wednesday afternoon of each month from 1-5 p.m., also by appointment.

CHABOT SPACE AND SCIENCE CENTER

10000 Skyline Blvd., Oakland, 510-336-7300; www.chabotspace.org

Built in 1883, this 86,000-square-foot complex includes the nation's largest public refracting telescope, a state-of-the-art planetarium, a MegaDome theater and hands-on science exhibits. There are other telescopes, including the Meridian Transit, funded by Anthony Chabot in 1885. It also has a six-acre environmental education area and a nature trail.
Admission: adults $14.95, seniors & students $11.95, children 3-12 $10.95. Wednesday-Thursday 10 a.m.-5 p.m., Friday-Saturday 10 a.m.-10 p.m., Sunday 11 a.m.-5 p.m.; call or visit the Web site for telescope viewing and holiday hours.

CHILDREN'S FAIRYLAND

Lakeside Park, 699 Bellevue Ave., Oakland, 510-452-2259; www.fairyland.org

This 10 acre park contains a child-sized fairyland, with tiny buildings depicting various fairy tales. Kids can play on sets of their favorite fairytales and stories. Many play areas contain live animals and birds. The grounds include a carousel, Ferris wheel, train and trolley rides, children's bumper boats and a puppet theater.

Admission: $7, children under 1 free. Hours change seasonally; check Web site for information.

JACK LONDON SQUARE

311 Broadway, Oakland; www.jacklondonsquare.com

This famous square is surrounded by Clay Street, Franklin Street, Embarcadero and the Oakland Estuary. Jack London lived and worked in this colorful waterfront area, spending most of his time writing his most famous novels in the still-operating Heinold's First and Last Chance Saloon at the foot of Webster Street. Several restaurants and the reconstructed cabin in which the author weathered the Klondike winter of 1898 reflect characters and situations from his life and books. Adjacent is Jack London Village at the foot of Alice Street, which has shops, restaurants and a marina area.
Daily.

JOAQUIN MILLER PARK

3300 Joaquin Miller Road, Oakland, 510-238-3187;
www.oaklandnet.com/JoaquinMillerPark/

This 500 acre park contains the 68 acres of estate that once belonged to author Joaquin Miller, otherwise known as the "Poet of the Sierras." He had monuments built, some of which are on display, and managed the planting of 75,000 trees in an effort to create an artist's retreat. One of these structures is the Abbey, which was built in 1889 by Miller and today is a Registered National Historic Landmark. The park is also the site of Woodminster Amphitheater, the setting for the Woodminster Summer Musicals. There are hiking and picnic areas, community centers and the Sequoia Horse Arena.
Daily.

LAKESIDE PARK, LAKE MERRITT AND LAKE MERRIT WILDLIFE REFUGE

Bellevue and Grand avenues, Oakland, 510-238-2196; www.oaklandnet.com

Lakeside Park, located in downtown Oakland, welcomes visitors who come to see the many amenities this park has to offer including gardens, bandstands, a nature center, the Children's Fairyland and more. Within Lakeside Park is Lake Merritt, the largest city-bound natural body of saltwater in the world, surrounded by drives and handsome buildings and is also known as "the jewel of Oakland." The Wildlife Refuge located here is North America's oldest wildlife refuge and is a National Historic Landmark. It features nature and conservation exhibits; native birds; illustrated lectures and walks; and an animal feeding area; a boating center with kayak rentals, tennis courts, a golf course and plenty of hiking and walking trails.
Daily.

OAKLAND-ALAMEDA COUNTY COLISEUM

7000 Coliseum Way, Oakland, 510-569-2121; www.coliseum.com

Oakland's professional baseball team, the Athletics, otherwise known as the "A's," play ball in the Oakland-Alameda County Coliseum. It's also home to the professional football team, the Oakland Raiders. The A's were led by Frank Thomas in 2006 to reach the American League Championship for the first time since 1992. The A's have featured plenty of all-stars over the years including Tony LaRussa, Mark McGwire, Jose Conseco and Jason Giambi.

OAKLAND MUSEUM OF CALIFORNIA

1000 Oak St., Oakland, 510-238-2200; www.museumca.org

The only museum dedicated exclusively to California's history, art and natural sciences, the Gallery of California Art traces the work of California artists from the 1800s to today. The museum features several temporary exhibitions each year, ranging in subject matter from fashion to photography to archaeology.

Admission: adults $8, seniors and students $5, children under 6 free.

Wednesday-Saturday 10 a.m.-5 p.m., Sunday noon-5 p.m.

OAKLAND ZOO

9777 Golf Links Road, Oakland, 510-632-9525; www.oaklandzoo.org

Situated on 525 acres, the zoo houses 440 native and exotic animals, a children's petting zoo and a lion habitat with a pride of six lions, along with an African Savannah filled with animals native to Africa, among much more. Also here are children's rides and picnic areas.

Admission: adults $10.50, seniors and children 2-14 $7, children under 2 free. Daily 10 a.m.-4 p.m.

PARAMOUNT THEATRE

2025 Broadway, Oakland, 510-465-6400; www.paramounttheatre.com

A restored 1931 Art Deco movie palace, designed by architect Timothy L. Pflueger, is now home to the Oakland Ballet, the Oakland Symphony and a variety of musical performances. Tour

Admission: $5. Tours take place the first and third Saturday of each month and start at 10 a.m. at the Box Office entrance. Box Office Hours: Tuesday-Friday 11 a.m.-5:30 p.m., Saturday 11 a.m.-3 p.m.

USS POTOMAC

Franklin D. Roosevelt Pier, Jack London Square, 540 Water St., Oakland, 510-627-1215; www.usspotomac.org

Once Franklin D. Roosevelt's "Floating White House" and now a fully restored, floating museum, the 165-foot steel vessel was built in 1934 as the Coast Guard cutter *Electra*. There are narrated two-hour educational cruises around San Francisco Bay from May through November.

Dockside tours: Mid-January-mid-December, Wednesday, Friday, Sunday; groups by appointment only. Reservations are required for cruises; see Web site for information.

SPECIAL EVENTS
LAKEFEST ART & WINE FESTIVAL
Lakeshore Avenue Business District, Oakland, 510-645-1034;www.oaklandlakefest.com
This annual fest features live music, artisans, wine, food, a children's carnival and more.
Early August.

WHERE TO STAY
★★THE INN AT JACK LONDON SQUARE
233 Broadway, Oakland, 510-452-4565, 800-633-5973; www.innatthesquare.com
100 rooms. Complimentary breakfast. Business Center. Fitness center. Pool. $61-150

★★★WATERFRONT PLAZA HOTEL
10 Washington St., Oakland, 510-836-3800, 800 729-3038, 888-842-5333;
www.waterfrontplaza.com
Having recently undergone a renovation, this hotel offers upgraded guestrooms, a new restaurant and more. Just a short ferry ride from San Francisco and blocks from shops and entertainment, the hotel sits in Jack London Square on the Oakland Harbor. Settle into a suite and take in the water views from a private balcony. The onsite restaurant, Miss Pearl's Jam House, features island cuisine (jerk chicken, sweet fried plantains) and Caribbean-inspired cocktails.
145 rooms. Restaurant, bar. Fitness center. Pool. $151-250

WHERE TO EAT
★★★BAY WOLF
3853 Piedmont Ave., Oakland, 510-655-6004; www.baywolf.com
Thriving since 1975 in an early 1900s Victorian, Bay Wolf serves food influenced by the food of Tuscany, Provence and the Basque country with a California twist. Dine on the heated veranda or in one of two small dining rooms. The menu changes regularly but may include salt-baked duck breast; housemade herbed ravioli with spring vegetables and wild mushroom broth; or cumin-crusted roasted rack of pork with grilled asparagus and sherry. The wine list also features regional wines from the Mediterranean.
American, Mediterranean. Lunch, dinner. Reservations recommended. Outdoor seating. Bar. $16-35

★★BISTRO SOIZIC
300 Broadway, Oakland, 510-251-8100; www.soizicbistro.com
French. Lunch, dinner. Closed Sunday. Reservations recommended. Bar. $16-35

★★IL PESCATORE RISTORANTE
57 Jack London Square, Oakland, 510-465-2188; www.ilpescatoreristorante.com
Italian, seafood. Lunch, dinner, Saturday-Sunday brunch. Reservations recommended. Outdoor seating. Bar. $36-85

★★★OLIVETO CAFÉ & RESTAURANT
5655 College Ave., Oakland, 510-547-5356; www.oliveto.com

Known for its authentic Italian cuisine, Oliveto specializes in organic house-made pastas, and serves fresh-milled corn polenta, a selection of housemade salumi and fresh baked desserts and pastries. The menu changes almost daily, but you'll find dishes such as pappardelle with braised rabbit; ravioli filled with wild nettles, green garlic and new potatoes; fresh-milled polenta with spring vegetables and chanterelle mushrooms; spit-roasted leg of lamb with fried asparagus and young onions; and wild striped bass with spinach, potatoes and artichoke-Morrocan olive relish. The simple and sleek restaurant features artwork from local artists, garden flowers, and plenty of windows. A downstairs café is available for more casual dining.
Italian. Lunch (Monday-Friday), dinner. Bar. $36-85

★★SCOTT'S SEAFOOD
2 Broadway, Oakland, 510-444-3456; www.scottseastbay.com

Located in the center of Jack London Square, the menu here features fresh seafood such as Dungeness crab, ahi tuna, swordfish, halibut, grilled sole, baked scallops and vegetable risotto. Stop in on Sunday for the New Orleans-inspired champagne jazz brunch, when you can sit outside and listen to a live jazz trio.
Seafood. Lunch, dinner, Sunday brunch. Outdoor seating. Bar. $16-35

PALO ALTO
See also Mountain View, Santa Clara, Saratoga

Spanish explorers took note of the tall, ancient, two-trucked redwood tree that still stands at the city's northwest entrance. The city that bears its name, El Palo Alto ("tall tree"), has flourished in the last two centuries. It's home to Stanford University and one of the nation's most important electronics development and research centers.

WHAT TO SEE
JUNIOR MUSEUM & ZOO
1451 Middlefield Road, Palo Alto, 650-329-2111; www.cityofpaloalto.org

The Palo Alto Junior Museum and Zoo features displays that encourage children's interest in art, science, history and anthropology through a variety of media with hands-on exhibits and workshops. The zoo features more than 50 exotic and native animals. There is a creek habitat, which covers 15 cubic meters of San Francisquito Creek, which has a cross-sectional view of that last remaining natural creek which runs through Palo Alto.
Admission: $3 (suggested donation). Tuesday-Saturday 10 a.m.-5 p.m., Sunday 1-4 p.m.

HOOVER TOWER
434 Serra Mall Stanford, Stanford, 650-723-2053; www.stanford.edu

Part of the Hoover Institution on War, Revolution and Peace research center, which was founded by President Herbert Hoover during World War I, the Hoover Tower is a landmark of Stanford. Hoover was part of the graduating class at Stanford in 1895 and as an alumnus, he gave a gift to build and start this institution. Ride the elevator up to the 14th floor of this 250-feet tower for a panoramic view of campus and the peninsula from the carillon platform.

Admission: adults $2, seniors and children 12 and under $1. Daily 10 a.m.-4:30 p.m. (closed during finals and academic breaks).

STANFORD SHOPPING CENTER

680 Stanford Shopping Center, Palo Alto, 650-617-8200; www.stanfordshop.com

One of the largest malls in Northern California, this open-air facility is home to more than 140 tenants, including top-tier department stores Bloomingdales and Nordstrom and a variety of restaurants and specialty stores—including an upscale supermarket, an open-air farmers' market and several cafés and bakeries. In summer, come on Thursday evenings for a jazz concert series. Monday-Friday 10 a.m.-8 p.m., Saturday 10 a m.-7 p.m., Sunday 11 a.m.-6 p.m.

STANFORD UNIVERSITY

450 Serra Mall, Stanford, 650-723-2300; www.stanford.edu

Located in the center of Silicon Valley, between San Francisco and San Jose, the world-renowned Stanford was founded in 1891 by Senator and Mrs. Leland Stanford in memory of their only son who died at 15 of typhoid fever. It is said that the Stanfords hoped that "the children of California shall be our children." Designed by Frederick Law Olmsted, Stanford has become one of the world's leading universities with students who have produced influential companies such as Google, Hewlett-Packard and Yahoo!

THOMAS WELTON STANFORD ART GALLERY

419 Lasuen Mall, Stanford, 650-723-2842; art.stanford.edu

This gallery is used as a venue for Stanford and Bay Area communities as well as a teaching resource for the Department of Art and Art History. Changing exhibits feature artwork from students in the M.F.A. program and focuses on contemporary art.

Admission: Free. Tuesday-Friday 10 a.m.-5 p.m., Saturday-Sunday 1-5 p.m.

WINTER LODGE

3009 Middlefield Road, Palo Alto, 650-493-4566; www.winterlodge.com

The only outdoor ice rink in the U.S. located west of the Sierra Nevada Mountains, Winter Lodge offers daily public skate sessions as well as group lessons and hosts private parties. There are also skate rentals and an outdoor picnic area. Check Web site for updated schedule information.

Admission: $8. Skate Rental: $3. Late September-mid-April, Monday 3-5 p.m.; Tuesday and Thursday 8-10 a.m., 3-5 p.m.; Wednesday and Friday 8-10 a.m., 3-5 p.m., 8-10 p.m.; Saturday 3-5 p.m., 8-10 p.m.; Sunday 3-5 p.m., 5:30-7:30 p.m.

WHERE TO STAY
★★★DINAH'S GARDEN HOTEL
4261 El Camino Real, Palo Alto, 650-493-2844, 800-227-8220; www.dinahshotel.com

This tranquil oasis in the midst of Silicon Valley is richly appointed with eight acres of gardens featuring lagoons, waterfalls and art sculptures. Guest rooms are decorated uniquely with influences from all over the world. For larger more private rooms, rent the Asian Sunset Signature Suite which has two bedrooms, two and a half baths, a dining table as well as a kitchen with granite countertop, dishwasher, utensils and dishware. The hotel features two swimming pools, a fitness center with a sauna, and Trader Vic's restaurant, which has an international menu with Polynesian décor.

148 rooms. Restaurant, bar. Complimentary breakfast. Business center. Fitness center. Pool. $61-150

★★★★FOUR SEASONS HOTEL SILICON VALLEY AT EAST PALO ALTO
2050 University Ave., East Palo Alto, 650-566-1200; www.fourseasons.com

Built in 2006, this 10-story, 190,000-square-foot luxury hotel's contemporary rooms have marble bathrooms with deep-soaking tubs, separate glass-enclosed showers, flat-screen TVs, DVD/CD players, a spacious work area with desk and floor-to-ceiling windows. Work out in the state-of-the-art fitness center—exercise machines have their own audiovisual monitors and wireless headsets—or pick up a map of nearby jogging and biking trails. Enjoy the rooftop pool and whirlpool and have lunch in private poolside cabana with umbrellas and lounge chairs. You can even get some work done while by the pool—the area has a television, telephones and Internet access. Relax with a spa treatment at the full-service spa, which has seven treatment rooms. The hotel's contemporary dining room Quattro serves up Italian-influenced California cuisine and a wine list of international vintages. The hotel's sophisticated bar is the perfect place to have a cocktail.

200 rooms. Restaurant, bar. Business center. Fitness center. Pool. Spa. $351 and up

★★★GARDEN COURT HOTEL
520 Cowper St., Palo Alto, 650-322-9000, 800-824-9028; www.gardencourt.com

This hotel is located in the heart of Silicon Valley near Stanford University, shopping and restaurants. Sunlit rooms overlook a courtyard full of flowers and have four-poster beds, down comforters and cotton terry robes, BOSE radio and CD player and Aveda bath products. Most guest rooms also feature either a whirlpool, fireplace, breakfast nook or private balconies. Complimentary coffee and tea service and breakfast pastries are available in the lobby a long with fresh fruit in the common areas and an evening port and cookies. This hotel is committed to being a green business and is part of the Palo Alto Green, a renewable energy power program.

62 rooms. Complimentary breakfast. Fitness center. Pets accepted. $251-350

★★★SHERATON PALO ALTO HOTEL

625 El Camino Real, Palo Alto, 650-328-2800, 888-625-5144; www.sheraton.com

Surrounded by flower gardens, koi ponds and fountains, this resort-like hotel stands at the entrance to Stanford University, near the Stanford Shopping Center. Guest rooms have Sheraton Sweet Sleeper beds (and dog beds area available too), bathrobes, flat-screen televisions, and generous workstations with ergonomic chairs. An outdoor heated pool, fitness facility and in-room massage treatments from the hotel's Thermae Spa, are available to aid in fitness and relaxation. The Cardinal Club Lounge is a great place to grab a cocktail and the Poolside Grill serves a delicious breakfast buffet and a lunch and dinner menu with California cuisine.

346 rooms. Restaurant, bar. Complimentary breakfast. Business center. Fitness center. Pool. Pets accepted. $151-250

★★★THE WESTIN PALO ALTO

675 El Camino Real, Palo Alto, 650-321-4422, 800-937-8461; www.westin.com/paloalto

Located near Stanford University, this contemporary hotel is spread over five Mediterranean-style buildings. Comfortable rooms have luxury bedding and bathrooms, as well as modern touches such as CD players, flat-screen televisions, an iPod docking station and wireless Internet access. Restaurant Soleil features Californian and Mediterranean cuisine and serves breakfast, lunch and dinner. Luna Lounge is a great spot to sip a martini after dinner. There is an outdoor heated pool and whirlpool to enjoy and a fitness center to get in a workout. Pick up a map jogging/walking map to take advantage of the surrounding Palo Alto area.

184 rooms. Restaurant, bar. Business center. Fitness center. Pool. Pets accepted. $151-250

WHERE TO EAT

★★★EVVIA ESTIATORIO

420 Emerson St., Palo Alto, 650-326-0983; www.evvia.net

This warm, rustic restaurant has a fireplace, wood floors, hand-made pottery, and copper pots and pans that hang all around that carry the Mediterranean tone throughout the restaurant. There is an open kitchen, which adds excitement to the atmosphere. The menu takes its cues from the Greek islands, with classic dishes such as saghanaki, moussaka and souvlaki. Other entrées include braised lamb shank with aromatic spices on orzo and myzithra cheese; and lemon-oregano chicken with roasted sweet onions and potatoes. For dessert, there's traditional baklava to enjoy with Greek coffee. Dishes are made with fresh and seasonal local ingredients.

Greek. Lunch (Monday-Friday), dinner. Bar. $16-35

★★SCOTT'S SEAFOOD

Town and Country Village Mall, 855 El Camino Real, Palo Alto, 650-323-1555; www.scottsseafoodpa.com

Seafood, steak. Breakfast (Monday-Friday), lunch (Monday-Friday), dinner, Saturday-Sunday brunch. Reservations recommended. Outdoor seating. Bar. $36-85

★★★TAMARINE
546 University Ave., Palo Alto, 650-325-8500; www.tamarinerestaurant.com

Small plates are the standard at this contemporary, vegetarian-friendly Vietnamese restaurant, which encourages sharing. Entrées such as seared scallops with green curry and lemongrass bass are mixed with a choice of seven different types of rice, from jasmine to coconut to black and short grain rice with citrus butter. Specialty cocktails, including the Tamarine Mojito and Gingermint martini, win raves. Designed by a top design firm, the walls of the restaurant are covered in rich colors and fine art from Vietnam. Emerging artists from Vietnam exhibit their artwork in the restaurant's gallery.
Vietnamese. Lunch, dinner. Reservations recommended. Bar. $16-35

★★★★THE VILLAGE PUB
2967 Woodside Road, Woodside, 650-851-9888; www.thevillagepub.net

About 30 minutes from San Francisco and San Jose, this upscale pub emphasizes the use of local artisanal and organic ingredients, including produce cultivated at the restaurant's partner farm in the nearby Santa Cruz Mountains. The two dining rooms are quaint yet charming and there is an outdoor veranda for private parties. The seasonal menus feature contemporary American dishes with French and Mediterranean influences such as bacon wrapped trout with braised sauerkraut and riesling butter sauce; and seared duck breast with huckleberry duck jus, braised leeks and scarlet turnips. Diners craving more traditional pub fare will find burgers, steaks and fries as well. Desserts feature decadent options such as walnut cake with marscarpone mousse and fruit; and opera cake with mocha buttercream and chocolate ganache. The ample wine list includes a number of reasonably priced selections along with half-bottles and a variety of by-the-glass options.
American. Lunch (Monday-Friday), dinner. Reservations recommended. Bar. $36-85

★★ZIBIBBO
430 Kipling St., Palo Alto, 650-328-6722; www.restaurantlulu.com

Mediterranean. Lunch, dinner, brunch. Outdoor seating. Bar. $16-35

SPAS
★★★THE SPA AT FOUR SEASONS SILICON VALLEY AT EAST PALO ALTO
The Four Seasons Silicon Valley at East Palo Alto, 2050 University Ave., East Palo Alto, 650-566-1200; www.fourseasons.com

Located inside East Palo Alto's Four Seasons hotel, this contemporary spa has seven treatment rooms and offers everything from Thai massage to shiatsu. Facials include the Bergamot and Chamomile Hydration treatment, which quenches parched skin, and the Acai and Willow Bark Detoxifying facial to help adult acne and rosacea. Pedicures take place in secluded individual stations and include a relaxing foot massage. Try the Four Seasons Hot Stone Therapy, which places warm stones on your body to open energy channels before the massage. Guests of the spa can use the steam rooms, whirlpool and outdoor pool before or after treatments. Poolside or in-room massages are also available.

PEBBLE BEACH

See also Carmel, Monterey

This small town is known for its scenic beauty, the palatial houses of its residences and, most of all, its golf courses, where the annual National Pro-Amateur Golf Championship and other prestigious tournaments are held. It's also known for being the scenery along 17-Mile Drive from Carmel to Monterey.

WHAT TO SEE
17-MILE DRIVE

Pebble Beach; www.pebblebeach.com
Stretching from Carmel to Monterey, along the Pacific and through the Del Monte Forest, this toll road is one of the most scenic coastal drives in the world. The winding road will take you past the Lodge at Pebble Beach; the ocean coast; the Spyglass Hill Golf Course; The Inn and Links at Spanish Bay; the trademark of Pebble Beach, the Lone Cypress tree; and through an exclusive neighborhood and many other points of interest. Stop for lunch along the way at the Seal Rock picnic area or visit one of the points on the ocean to watch for sea otters, seals and sea lions

PEBBLE BEACH GOLF LINKS

1700 Seventeen Mile Drive, Pebble Beach, 831-644-7960; www.pebblebeach.com
Although it's quite a drive from San Francisco, an opportunity to play on one of the nation's most exclusive courses is irresistible. To get a tee time, call well in advance (at least a month) and be prepared to spend more than $400 per person. The course goes over the Pacific Ocean at times, and the sound and sight of waves lapping at the edges of the course is exhilerating.

WHERE TO STAY
★★★★CASA PALMERO AT PEBBLE BEACH

1518 Cypress Drive, Pebble Beach, 831-622-6650, 800-654-9300; www.pebblebeach.com
This grand Mediterranean-style estate overlooks the first and second fairways of Pebble Beach Golf Links and provides a pampering get-away. The guest rooms echo the resort's sophistication with their overstuffed furniture and neutral tones. In each room, you'll find a wood-burning fireplace, fresh flowers, a luxurious robe and slippers and oversized soaking tubs. The Spa Rooms are on the ground floor and feature a private patio with a whirlpool. If you're looking for more space, book a Palmero Suite with a living room and fireplace, wet bar, oversized bath, four-poster bed and an outdoor courtyard with a whirlpool. Enjoy the serene pool area or take advantage of the larger Pebble Beach complex's many restaurants, shops, private tennis club, yoga classes, spa and, of course, world-renowned golf. Guests also enjoy a breakfast basket and complimentary refreshments at the bar and lounge every evening.
24 rooms. Complimentary breakfast. Bar. Fitness center. Pool. Spa. Golf. Tennis. $351 and up

★★★★THE INN AT SPANISH BAY

2700 Seventeen Mile Drive, Pebble Beach, 831-647-7500, 800-654-9300;
www.pebblebeach.com

Direct access to the revered links at Pebble Beach makes this inn popular with golfers, while the splendid natural setting overlooking the Pacific Ocean and Spanish Bay has universal appeal. Views of the Del Monte Forest, famed golf course and ocean are striking, especially when enjoyed from the privacy of a guest room or suite. With nine different types of guest rooms to choose from, you can decide whether you want a view of the Del Monte Forest, the ocean, the golf course, or the courtyard. Some rooms come with fireplaces, outdoor patios or balconies, deep soaking whirlpool tubs, sitting and dining areas, and even a grand piano, if you choose. A gallery of shops showcases fine sportswear and resort apparel along with tennis and golf equipment. From an expertly staffed tennis and fitness facility to the outdoor pool, the amenities are top notch. Four distinctive dining establishments tease taste buds with an array of offerings.

269 rooms. Restaurant, bar. Business center. Fitness center. Pool. Spa. Golf. Tennis. $351 and up

★★★★THE LODGE AT PEBBLE BEACH

1700 Seventeen Mile Drive, Pebble Beach, 831-647-7500, 800-654-9300;
www.pebblebeach.com

Distinguished by its impressive architecture and spectacular ocean side setting, the Lodge at Pebble Beach is the jewel in the crown of the world-class Pebble Beach resort. The traditionally styled rooms are spacious, and most include a wood-burning fireplace and patio or balcony with views of flowering gardens or oceanside fairways. Spa rooms have a private garden with outdoor whirlpools. For a panoramic view of the ocean, book an Ocean View room, which also has a view of the 18th hole/fairway and Stillwater Cove and a patio or balcony. Unwind by the pool or play tennis in the resort's state-of-the-art tennis facility. The four restaurants also offer a variety of elegant settings, and run the gamut from casual American fare and succulent seafood to updated, lightened versions of French classics. The Lodge's spa celebrates the diversity of natural resources indigenous to the Monterey Peninsula in its treatments and therapies.

161 rooms. Restaurant, bar. Fitness center. Spa. Golf. Tennis. $351 and up

WHERE TO EAT

★★★CLUB XIX

1700 Seventeen Mile Drive, Pebble Beach, 831-625-8519; www.pebblebeach.com

Located in the Lodge at Pebble Beach on the lower level of the main building, just off the famous 18th green of the championship Pebble Beach Golf Links, this luxurious restaurant has beautiful views of Carmel Bay. Enjoy seasonal fare, prepared in the contemporary French style, in the intimate inside dining room or outdoors on the patio, which has two fireplaces. During the day, you'll find a more Parisian café-like atmosphere with lighter fare. In the evening, you'll find an elegant and romantic setting with a chef's tasting menu or an a la carte menu featuring items such as foie gras, seared salmon, and veal chop.

American, French. Dinner. Outdoor seating. Bar. $86 and up

SPAS
★★★★THE SPA AT PEBBLE BEACH
1700 Seventeen Mile Drive, Pebble Beach, 831-649-7615, 888-565-7615;
www.pebblebeach.com

Blending California's Spanish-colonial heritage with Pebble Beach's gloriously rugged natural setting, the Spa at Pebble Beach is a perfect blend of exotic elegance, with its terra-cotta-hued exterior and in-room fireplaces. Water rituals revive, replenish and restore, and body treatments nourish the skin with grape seed and sea salt scrubs. The spa's signature treatments are worth noting, including the Palmero, which uses a papaya-pineapple enzyme scrub, then a hydrating wrap, a scalp massage with warm coconut oil and a coconut moisturizer. After a long day on the golf course, try the Par-Four Massage, with two therapists performing a massage at the same time. The spa features other holistic healing methods including acupuncture, energy balancing and shiatsu, reiki, reflexology, and thai massages. With a full salon, the Spa also offers facials, waxing, haircuts and coloring, manicures and pedicures.

RUTHERFORD
See also Calistoga, Napa, Santa Rosa, St. Helena, Yountville

A little more than four miles south of St. Helena on Route 29 is the small hamlet of Rutherford, home to acclaimed restaurants and some of biggest and best wineries in the area due to the dry soil and year-round sunshine.

WHAT TO SEE
LAKE HENNESSEY RECREATIONAL AREA
Sage Canyon Road, Rutherford, 707-226-7455; www.napachamber.com

A soothing counterpoint to the bacchanalia of gourmet food and fine wines, this recreation area is also close to the action when you're ready to dive back in. It's a prime destination for area anglers, who fish the waters for large- and small-mouth bass, trout and crappies. No motorboats are allowed on the lake, which makes it especially peaceful.
Daily.

PEJU PROVINCE WINERY
8466 St. Helena Highway, Rutherford, 707-963-3600; www.peju.com

Though many come for the wine, they often stay for the entertainment. This exquisite estate, replete with a unique castle-like copper-topped tower, a reflecting pool, fountains and beautifully landscaped gardens, appeals to all the senses with tastings, cooking classes, art exhibits and more. The wines aren't too shabby, either. In fact, Peju's Reserve 2004 Cabernet Sauvignon is one of the best in the region.
Daily 10 a.m.-6 p.m.

ROBERT MONDAVI WINERY
7801 St. Helena Highway (Highway 29), Oakville, 888-766-6328;
www.robertmondaviwinery.com

Since 1966, Robert Mondavi has produced some of the finest wines in the valley and has been an innovative spirit in the winemaking process. Housed in a graceful, mission-style building, tours at the winery are available Tues-

day through Sunday (at 10 a.m.), which educate guests about wine tasting. Reservations are recommended.
Daily 10 a.m.-5 p.m.

ROUND POND OLIVE MILL

886 Rutherford Road, Rutherford,, 888-302-2575; www.roundpond.com

Round Pond Olive Mill produces some of the valley's finest gourmet olive oils. You could easily spend an entire afternoon here. For the full experience, make reservations for the alfresco lunch, tour the olive mill and learn about the meticulous cold-press process behind Round Pond's four signature oils: Italian varietal, Spanish varietal, blood orange and Meyer lemon. A guide will lead you through tastings of each paired with vinegars (also made here), fresh organic produce and gourmet bread. The afternoon is topped off with a family-style lunch of local cheeses, meats, fruits and olive oil cake for dessert. On the third Saturday of every month from noon to 4 p.m., purchase fresh olive oil straight from the spigot. They also make wine at the charming vineyard across the street. Estate Tastings: $25.
Daily 11 a.m.-4 p.m., by appointment. Guided tours and tastings: $35.
Daily 11 a.m., 1 p.m., 3 p.m., by appointment. Olive oil tour and tasting: $25, appointment only.

RUBICON ESTATE

1991 St. Helena Highway, Rutherford, 707-968-1161; www.rubiconestate.com

If you take one winery tour while visiting Napa, make it Rubicon. The knowledgeable and engaging tour guides will fill you in on how Francis Ford Coppola came to own this winery, and how he brought it full circle. It's the kind of story that makes movie magic, but this vineyard has no Hollywood flash. While you can easily envision Coppola sitting at one of the outside tables puffing on a stogie, the vineyard, which looks like it was transported from Italy, is where the famous director quietly raised his family outside of the spotlight, and where he and his wife still reside. You may also be surprised by how good the wines are, particularly the Rutherford Edizione Pennino Zinfandel (the label has a picture of Italy and the Statue of Liberty, a homage to Francis' grandfather) and the Rutherford Cabernet Sauvignon, a tribute to the stylized cabernets of the previous owner.
Admission: $25 (includes tasting, Legacy historical tour, access to the historic Chateau, the Estate Wine Library and the Centennial Museum). Daily 10 a.m.-5 p.m.

ST. SUPÉRY VINEYARDS AND WINERY

8440 St. Helena Highway, Rutherford, 707-963-4507, 800-942-0809;
www.stsupery.com

This center provides a hands-on lesson in grape growing and winemaking—from planting through bottling. Its "SmellaVision" course enables you to deconstruct a wine's bouquet. You can take a free self-guided tour or sign up for a one-hour guided tour, held daily at 1 p.m. and 3 p.m., and participate in tastings and sampling the small-production wines in the reserve tasting library.
Daily 10 a.m.-5 p.m.

STAGLIN FAMILY VINEYARD

1570 Bella Oaks Lane, Rutherford, 707-944-0477; www.staglinfamily.com

Located behind its more famous neighbor, Robert Mondavi Vineyards, Staglin Family is a true family-run, locally-loved vineyard. This by-appointment only winery produces some of the area's most highly regarded cabernet sauvignon in the valley. The tour ends in the underground wine caves, as you're invited to pull up a chair at the grand dining room table and taste the fruits of their labor—literally. Tour and Tasting: $50.

Monday-Friday 11 a.m.-3 p.m.; reservations required.

SPECIAL EVENTS
ROBERT MONDAVI WINERY SUMMER CONCERT SERIES

7801 St. Helena Highway (Highway 29), Oakville, 888-769-5299;
www.robertmondaviwinery.com

Since the summer of 1969, locals have lined up to watch top pop, jazz and R&B performers—from Cassandra Wilson and Ella Fitzgerald to Boz Skaggs and Patti LaBelle—at this outdoor music festival. This year's lineup includes Natalie Cole, Smokey Robinson, the B-52's and more. Picnic on the lawn, listen to music and enjoy a summer night against the backdrop of historic vineyards. Late June-August.

WHERE TO STAY
★★★AUBERGE DU SOLEIL

180 Rutherford Hill Road, Rutherford, 707-963-1211, 800-348-5406;
www.aubergedusoleil.com

Mediterranean in spirit and appearance, this wine country retreat opened in 1981 as a restaurant. Today, the kitchen continues to win praise for its inventive wine country dishes. The rooms recall a Provençal farmhouse, and balconies open out to enchanting views of the countryside. Luxurious touches include Frette linens, flat-screen TVs, wet bars with Sub Zero refrigerators (full size in suites), CD players with a choice of CDs, wine, fruit and a personal welcome note. Between the tranquil setting, the shimmering pool and the sensational spa, which uses grape seeds in many of its treatments, relaxation is guaranteed.

50 rooms. Restaurant, bar. Business center. Fitness center. Pool. Spa. No children under16. Tennis. $351 and up

★★RANCHO CAYMUS INN

1140 Rutherford Road, Rutherford, 707-963-1777, 800-845-1777;
www.ranchocaymus.com

26 rooms. Restaurant, bar. Complimentary breakfast. $251-350

WHERE TO EAT
★★★★AUBERGE DU SOLEIL RESTAURANT

180 Rutherford Hill Road, Rutherford, 707-963-1211, 800-348-5406;
www.aubergedusoleil.com

French-born San Francisco restaurateur Claude Rouas set out to create a Provence-like destination restaurant in Northern California with his 1981 fine dining room, Auberge du Soleil. Diners liked it so much they demanded overnight accommodations—and received them four years later. The dining room offers a warm setting with a large fireplace, wood furnishings and colorful art. The seasonal French-California menu features artisanal ingredients and products from local farms, spotlighted in dishes such as Meyer lemon risotto with artichokes, parmesan and yuzu emulsion; and spiced local lamb with fingerling potatoes, dates and picholine olives. Don't miss the local cheese selections for dessert. The six-course tasting menu comes with wines to match from the large, locally strong list. There is also a four-course vegetarian tasting menu. If you're touring the valley by car, consider it for a lunch stop where you can enjoy the panoramic views from the terrace or for a romantic dinner.

American, French. Breakfast, lunch, dinner. Bar. $86 and up

SPAS

★★★★THE AUBERGE SPA
180 Rutherford Hill Road, Rutherford, 707-963-1211, 866-228-2490;
www.aubergedusoleil.com

The glorious Napa Valley surroundings have inspired this spa's philosophy, with vineyard, garden and valley themes dominating the treatment menu. Nutrient-rich grape seed and locally grown herbs and flowers are the foundation for the vineyard's massages, body treatments and facials. Try unique massage techniques, such as the Rhythmic Water Massage which takes place in water while your therapist guides you through stretches and massage. Seasonal treatments are also a highlight of a visit to this spa, where a couples mustard bath is featured in spring, a luscious peaches and cream body mask is available in summer, a harvest-inspired cleanse or body glaze in fall and a peppermint and eucalyptus body treatment in winter. You can schedule personal fitness classes from yoga to pilates. If you're spending the weekend with a significant other or just a group of friends, you can schedule treatments in the Melisse Suite, which can accommodate four people, featuring a fireplace, private tanning deck and heated pool.

SACRAMENTO

See also Oakland

From its humble origins, Sacramento has always been a fortune seeker's city. Captain John A. Sutter first built a small business empire here in New Helvetia, a colony for his Swiss compatriots, only to see his workers desert him and his dream collapse with the discovery of gold at Coloma in 1848. Sutter's son, however, took advantage of the situation when he laid out Sacramento City on family-deeded land near the boat line terminus. At the entrance to Gold Rush country, the city's population rocketed to 10,000 within seven months and became California's capital in 1854.

Transportation was important in the city's growth. In 1860, the Pony Express made Sacramento its western terminus. Later, Sacramento's "Big Four"—Mark Hopkins, Charles Crocker, Collis P. Huntington and Leland Stanford—financed the building of the Central Pacific Railroad over the Sierras. Deepwater ships reach the city via a 43-mile-long channel from Suisun Bay. Sacramento's new port facilities handle an average of 20 ships a month, carrying import and export cargo from major ports around the world. The city may flex its industrial muscles but to flower-lovers, it's simply the Camellia Capital of the world.

WHAT TO SEE
CALIFORNIA INDIAN HERITAGE CENTER
2618 K St., Sacramento, 916-324-8112; www.cihc.parks.ca.gov

Indians of California are recognized and honored at this heritage center. It preserves their traditions and culture and tells the stories of their past. Displays, exhibits and galleries include dugout canoes, weapons, pottery and basketry. The grounds and heritage center are restored to the natural state in which California Indians would use the land for living, ceremonial purposes and traditional gatherings.
Daily 10 a.m.-5 p.m.

THE CALIFORNIA MUSEUM
1020 O St., Sacramento, 916-653-7524; www.californiamuseum.org

This museum pays tribute to the great state of California providing exhibits on state history with an emphasis on California's inspirational people, places and events. Governor Schwarzenegger and First Lady, Maria Shriver, act as honorary co-chairs to the museum. Shriver established an exhibit focusing on the contributions of women on California called "California's Remarkable Women," and the permanent exhibit, California Hall of Fame, which honors those people who have left a mark on California.
Admission: adults $8.50, students and seniors $7, children 6-13 $6, children 5 and under free. Monday-Saturday 10 a.m.-5 p.m., Sunday noon-5 p.m.

CALIFORNIA STATE CAPITOL MUSEUM
10th and L streets, Sacramento, 916-324-0333; www.capitolmuseum.ca.gov

A working museum and a fixture in California's state park system, this lavish Roman-inspired 1874 structure is surrounded by 40 lush acres with international flora, including California natives such as redwoods and fan palms. The building's domed rotunda straddles the two houses of the Legislature, with many of the meticulously restored rooms—including the former governor's office, decorated to match its 1906 appearance—accessible to the public. In-depth guided tours cover the lawmaking process and California's often-turbulent political history.
Admission: Free. Daily 9 a.m.-5 p.m. Tours: Daily 9 a.m.-4 p.m. (every hour).

DISCOVERY MUSEUM SCIENCE & SPACE CENTER
3615 Auburn Blvd., Sacramento, 916-575-3941; www.thediscovery.org

A modern touch in Old Sacramento, this non-profit center organizes engaging exhibits on history, science, space and technology to all ages. Artifacts from the city's history are enshrined in a replica of the 1854 City Hall, but the broader historical focus is on the California Gold Rush, depicted through a re-created mineshaft and other displays. There is a planetarium to learn about the night sky and 20-minute star shows. The Challenger Learning Center, also located here, explores space travel.
Admission: adults $5, seniors and children 13-17 $4, children 4-12 $3, children 3 and under free. September-June, Tuesday-Friday noon-4:30 p.m., Saturday-Sunday 10 a.m.-4:30 a.m.; July-August, Daily 10 a.m.-5 p.m.

FAIRYTALE TOWN

3901 Land Park Drive, Sacramento, 916-808-7462; www.fairytaletown.org

A city-owned, nonprofit kids' park that opened in 1959, Fairytale Town livens up classic children's stories and rhymes with 25 fantastic play sets. Don't expect big-budget, Disney-style rides, but rather a fun, low-tech experience that allows kids to climb up (and tumble down) Jack and Jill's hill, jump Jack-be-Nimble's candlestick and play on the Beanstalk Giant's foot in the span of an afternoon. Adjacent to the Sacramento Zoo, the town also has a puppet theater, snack bars and petting zoo. Unless accompanied by a child, adults are not permitted.

Admission: adults and children 3-12 $4 ($4.50 Saturday-Sunday), children 2 and under free. November-February, Thursday-Sunday 10 a.m.-4 p.m.; March-October, Daily 9 a.m.-4 p.m.

GOVERNOR'S MANSION STATE HISTORIC SITE

1526 H St., Sacramento, 916-323-3047; www.parks.ca.gov

Built by a hardware tycoon in 1877, this majestic Second Empire-Italianate mansion in downtown Sacramento served as California's executive mansion from 1903 to 1967, which was the end of Ronald Reagan's term as state governor. The lavish house is now a historic museum, offering guided tours on the hour (which is the only way to catch a glimpse of the inside of this mansion).

Admission: adults $4, children 6-17 $2, children 5 and under free. Daily 10 a.m.-5 p.m.

MIDTOWN SACRAMENTO SHOPPING DISTRICT

Alhambra Boulevard and C Street, Sacramento

Similar to shopping districts in San Francisco and Seattle, Midtown's J and K streets have independently-owned sidewalk cafés, coffee shops, boutiques, art galleries and interesting home and garden merchants. Among the area's stalwarts are Mixed Bag (2405 K St.), jam-packed with a diverse inventory of jewelry, kitchenware and gifts; and Tasha's the Uncommon Shop (1005 22nd St. at J Street), specializing in imports ranging from batik dresses to Middle Eastern décor.

OLD SACRAMENTO

1004 Second St., Sacramento, www.oldsacramento.com

A slum by the 1960s, this area of Sacramento revived itself by looking back on its early days. Locals set out to simultaneously preserve and revitalize the district, and it soon became a National Landmark and a State Historic Park full of shops, eateries, nightclubs and museums, which includes a railroad museum and the Discovery Museum History Center, many of them housed in historic buildings. The area now known as Old Sacramento is the setting for numerous special events, including the renowned Jazz Jubilee music festival and Gold Rush Days, where the entire district dresses up 1850s style.

SACRAMENTO ZOO

3930 W. Land Park Drive, Sacramento, 916-808-5888; www.saczoo.com

Opened in 1927, this zoo features expanses that re-create natural habitats and fully realized ecosystems. Among the dozens of endangered animals are orangutans, chimpanzees, tigers and cheetahs. Of special note is the Claire Mower Red Panda Forest, a mixed-species environment with a breeding pair of endangered red pandas living alongside Asian birds, fish and reptiles. In 2006, the Dr. Murray E. Fowler Veterinary Hospital opened.

Admission: adults $9, seniors $8.25, children 3-12 $6.50, children under 3 free. February-October, Daily 9 a.m.-4 p.m.; November-January, Daily 10 a.m.-4 p.m.

SIERRA NEVADA BREWING COMPANY

1075 E. 20th St., Chico, 530-896-2198; www.sierranevada.com

One of the largest and best-known microbreweries in the United States (to the point where the micro prefix almost no longer applies), the Sierra Nevada Brewing Company's headquarters in Chico is a must-visit for beer aficionados. A free tour takes visitors from the brew house through the bottling plant, showcasing the brewery's European methods, which utilize only four ingredients: water, hops, yeast and barley malts. While the tour does not include complimentary samples, there is a retail store and a taproom/restaurant. Many come just for the wide variety of tasty brews, including the renowned Sierra Nevada Pale Ale as well as some Sierra Nevada brews available only on draft. Check the Big Room's full-calendar of rock and blues concerts.

Taproom and Restaurant: Tuesday-Thursday 11 a.m.-9 p.m., Friday-Saturday 11 a.m.-10 p.m., Sunday 11 a.m.-9 p.m. Guided Brewery Tours: Monday-Friday 2:30 p.m., Saturday noon-3 p.m., Sunday 2:30 p.m. Gift Shop: Daily 10 a.m.-6 p.m.

WILLIAM LAND PARK

3800 Land Park Drive, Sacramento, 916-277-6060; www.cityofsacramento.org

This downtown park is full of beautiful trees and picnic areas. There is a wading pool, basketball court, playground, softball fields, soccer fields, lakes, a rock garden, jogging path and more. William Land Golf Course is also located here; it's the city's oldest golf course, with 9-holes, a barbecue area and Mulligan's Café. Funderland, an amusement park for kids, is onsite and admission is free (however, you have to pay for tickets for rides individually). Daily.

SPECIAL EVENTS
BOCKBIERFEST

3349 J St., Sacramento, 916-442-7360; www.sacramentoturnverein.com

Held annually at downtown's Turner Hall in early April, the Sacramento Turn Verein's Bockbierfest is a one-night celebration of German dance, music, food and of course, plenty of beer. Expect plenty of sausages, polka bands, folk dancing and bockbier, the dark, rich and potent Bavarian brew.

Early April.

CALIFORNIA STATE FAIR

1600 Exposition Blvd., Sacramento, 916-263-3247; www.bigfun.org

This fair has been an annual event since 1854 and draws in almost a million people. The fair includes exhibits, livestock competitions, a talent show, carnival food and entertainment on more than 10 stages, thoroughbred racing, freestyle motocross performances, a dachshund derby and one-mile monorail. Past concerts have included performances by artists such as Smash Mouth, Jessica Simpson, Natasha Bedingfield, Air Supply and Gary Allan. Every Tuesday is Kids' Day, when all children under 12 are free. Mid-August-early September.

SACRAMENTO JAZZ JUBILEE

Old Sacramento, 916-372-5277; www.sacjazz.com
Every Memorial Day weekend since 1974, the top jazz festival in the West has featured a lineup including more than 600 jazz artists and 60 bands from all over the country and all over the stylistic map: traditional jazz, blues, Western, swing, ragtime, salsa, zydeco, barbershop and many more. The weekend kicks off Friday with a parade and there's a gospel service on Sunday. Free shuttles transport concertgoers between the events' many venues. May.

WHERE TO STAY

★★★HILTON SACRAMENTO ARDEN WEST

2200 Harvard St., Sacramento, 916-922-4700; www.sacramentoardenwest.hilton.com
This contemporary hotel in Sacramento's Point West area is close to the Cal Expo State Fairgrounds and minutes from the Capitol Rotunda. The guest rooms' soft camel-colored walls, earth tone bedding and country pine furniture create a cozy atmosphere. Amenities include flat-screen televisions, luxury linens and pillow-top beds. Enjoy comfort foods at the onsite Harvard Street Grille and martinis at the Cameo Lounge.
331 rooms. Restaurant, bar. Business center. Fitness center. Pool. $151-250

★★HOLIDAY INN CAPITOL PLAZA–SACRAMENTO

300 J St., Sacramento, 916-446-0100, 800-465-4329; www.sacramentohi.com
359 rooms. Restaurant, bar. Business center. Fitness room. Pool. $251-350

★★★HYATT REGENCY SACRAMENTO

1209 L St., Sacramento, 916-443-1234, 800-633-7313; www.sacramento.hyatt.com
Directly across from the State Capitol and Capitol Park, this hotel is adjacent to the Sacramento Convention Center and Community Theater. Rooms have large working desks, leather ergonomic chairs, marble bathrooms and black-and-white photography. Dawson's steakhouse features creative dishes such as grilled salmon with fennel and leak ragout; and pan roasted Muscovy duck with madeira and orange glaze. Enjoy a drink at one of two bars, Dawson's Bar or Amourath 1819 bar, which also has an outdoor patio.
503 rooms. Restaurant, bar. Business center. Fitness center. Pool. $251-350

★★RED LION HOTEL SACRAMENTO AT ARDEN VILLAGE

1401 Arden Way, Sacramento, 916-922-8041, 800-733-5466; www.redlion.com
270 rooms. Restaurant, bar. Fitness center. Pool. Spa. Pets accepted. $61-150

★★★SHERATON GRAND SACRAMENTO HOTEL

1230 J St., Sacramento, 916-447-1700, 800-325-3535; www.sheraton.com

Just a block from the State Capitol, this hotel has a historic setting in the restored 1923 Public Market Building. The modern guest rooms offer the Sheraton Sweet Sleeper bed, flat-screen TVs, Internet access, oversized desks and views of the skyline or city. There's a large 24-hour fitness center, a heated outdoor pool and nearby golf course. The three restaurants include Morgan's Central Valley Bistro, the more casual Glides Market and the Public Market Bar.

503 rooms. Restaurant, bar. Business center. Fitness center. Pool. Pets accepted. $151-250

★★★THE STERLING HOTEL

1300 H St., Sacramento, 916-448-1300, 800-365-7660; www.sterlinghotel.com

This charming Victorian mansion set on landscaped gardens feels like a countryside retreat, yet it is only a few blocks from the city's downtown shopping plaza, the State Capitol and the convention center. The rooms have period furnishings, Italian marble bathrooms and jacuzzi tubs. Enjoy a gourmet lunch and dinner at the hotel's Chanterelle restaurant, which features steaks, chicken, seafood along with vegetarian and vegan dishes. The restaurant has an outdoor patio where you can sample dishes such as butternut squash ravioli, a peppercorn crushed filet or a Black Angus burger with chanterelles.

17 rooms. Complimentary breakfast. Restaurant. Business center. $151-250

WHERE TO EAT

★★★BIBA

2801 Capitol Ave., Sacramento, 916-455-2422; www.biba-restaurant.com

Since it opened in 1986, chef and owner Biba Caggiano's restaurant has offered a carefully crafted menu of Italian cuisine, an impressive wine list and a relaxed, contemporary atmosphere. Dishes include housemade pasta including gnocchi and fettuccine, grilled lamb chops and steak, veal cutlets and seared tuna. A prix fixe menu is also available during the week. Desserts feature a daily homemade gelato, cherry tarts, tiramisu and rich Italian chocolate mousse.

Italian. Lunch (Monday-Friday), dinner. Closed Sunday. Bar. $36-85

★★★CHANTERELLE

1300 H St., Sacramento, 916-442-0451; www.sterlinghotel.com

This 35-seat restaurant in the Sterling Hotel's four-story Victorian mansion is known for its regional organic California cuisine and quaint setting. Lunch and dinner entrées include grilled Australian lamb rack with pear-pearl onion and bacon mushroom hash, fig and apricot chutney; and porcini-crusted veal medallions with roasted mushrooms, mashed potatoes and veal demi glaze. Daily soups are homemade and there are always options for vegetarians and vegans, like the butternut squash ravioli with brown butter sage sauce, pine nuts and sautéed spinach or three cheese lasagna withe eggplant, wild mushroom, spinach, zucchini, yellow squash and marinara sauce. Sunday brunch is served in the hotel's stunning ballroom.

American. Lunch, dinner, Sunday brunch. Outdoor seating. $36-85

★★★THE FIREHOUSE
1112 Second St., Sacramento, 916-442-4772; www.firehouseoldsac.com

A Sacramento institution, this fine-dining destination has been in business since 1960. With fine artwork, chandeliers and formally-attired waitstaff, this restored 1853 firehouse is a good choice for celebratory dinners. Entrées include a Tuscan pork shank braised with tomatoes, white wine and herbs, garlic mashed potatoes, rainbow chard, wild mushrooms and lemon gremolata; pancetta-wrapped sea scallops with fennel-pear chutney and walnut-arugula risotto croquette. There is also a changing monthly tasting menu.
American. Lunch (Monday-Friday), dinner. Bar. Reservations recommended. Outdoor seating. Bar. $36-85

★★FRANK FAT'S
806 L St., Sacramento, 916-442-7092; www.fatsrestaurants.com

Chinese. Lunch, dinner. Reservations recommended. Bar. $16-35

★★★LEMON GRASS ASIAN GRILL & NOODLE BAR
601 Munroe St., Sacramento, 916-486-4891; www.lemongrassrestaurant.com

Chef and owner Mai Pham's food is inspired by that found on the streets and in the markets of Asia. Sample dishes include Bangkok beef with broccoli, mushrooms, onions and tomatoes stir fried with garlic, Thai basil and chilies; and monk's curry which includes tofu, broccoli, tomatoes, kabocha squash and seasonal vegetables simmering in a yellow curry-coconut milk.
Thai, Vietnamese. Lunch (Monday-Friday), dinner. Closed Sunday. Reservations recommended. Outdoor seating. Bar $16-35

★★★MORTON'S, THE STEAKHOUSE
621 Capitol Mall, Sacramento, 916-442-5091; www.mortons.com

This steakhouse chain, which originated in Chicago in 1978, calls out to serious meat-lovers. If you have trouble choosing between a selection of hearty carnivorous delights—such as a 24-ounce porterhouse (the house specialty), fresh fish, lobster or chicken entrées—Morton's tableside menu presentation (with display cart) will help you decide. There are also sides such as macaroni and cheese, hashbrown potatoes and sautéed fresh spinach and mushrooms. Desserts include double chocolate mousse, carrot cake and a legendary hot chocolate cake.
American. Lunch (Monday-Friday), dinner. Reservations recommended.. Bar. $36-85

★★PIATTI RISTORANTE & BAR
571 Pavillions Lane, Sacramento, 916-649-8885; www.piatti.com

Italian. Lunch, dinner. Sunday brunch Reservations recommended. Outdoor seating. Bar. $16-35

★★PILOTHOUSE
1000 Front St., Sacramento, 916-441-4440, 800-825-5464; www.deltaking.com

Seafood. Breakfast, lunch, dinner, Sunday brunch. Reservations recommended. Outdoor seating. Bar. $16-35

★RICK'S DESSERT DINER
2322 K St., Sacramento, 916-444-0969; www.ricksdessertdiner.com
Dessert. Outdoor seating. $15 and under

SAN FRANCISCO
See also Berkeley, Oakland

With hills, parks, cable cars, a bustling waterfront, a startlingly diverse population, an abundance of sights, shops, restaurants and attractions, San Francisco is the true capital of the West. Author and raconteur Gene Fowler once said, "Every man should be allowed to love two cities—his own and San Francisco."

A city of precipitous hills, San Francisco stretches 7 miles across in each direction and embraces a bay that is one of the planet's most perfect natural harbors. Indeed, the city itself is mostly water—out of 129.4 total square miles, only about 46 are land. San Francisco's unique geography and its temperate climate—warm in winter, cool in summer, often pleasantly sunny or beautifully shrouded in fog—have led people from every country on Earth and every state in the Union to make the city home. The leading national groups are Italian, German, Irish, Chinese, English, Russian, Latin American, Japanese, Korean and Filipino.

The city takes its name from a mission erected in 1776 and dedicated to St. Francis of Assisi. American troops overthrew Mexican rule in 1846, and two years later, a torrent of people flooded into the city to seek their fortunes. An average of 50 sailing ships a month anchored in San Francisco Bay; many left empty when crews abandoned them to look for gold. As businessmen began to build today's venerable shopping empires and the railroad marched into town—with the help of Chinese labor—the city evolved and prospered until 1906. The fire that followed that year's infamous 8.6 earthquake raged unchecked for three days and wiped out the entire business district, killing 2,500 people and causing $350 million in damages. With the ashes still warm, the city started rebuilding; a little more than a decade later, it made a full recovery. In 1945, international delegates assembled here to found the United Nations.

Hellenic in its setting and climate, European in its intellectual and cultural scope, American in its vigor and informality and Asian in its stateliness in tranquility, this cosmopolitan metropolis has no rival besides New York City. A car isn't absolutely necessary to get around—public transportation includes cable cars, streetcars, subway trains and buses—but it will enable the greatest range of exploration. For an overview of the city, take the scenic "49-Mile Drive," marked with blue and white seagull signs. This drive begins at City Hall in the Civic Center (Van Ness Avenue and McAllister Street) and twists around the city, taking you past many of its landmarks. You can pick up this route and follow its signs at any point or obtain a map of the drive from the San Francisco Visitor Information Center, lower level of Hallidie Plaza, Powell and Market Streets. The San Francisco hills are not for faint-hearted drivers, but they're not as bad as they look. Be sure to turn your wheels toward the curb and set your brake when parking. In this way alone, San Francisco is like any other city: a runaway vehicle won't improve the trip.

WHAT TO SEE
ALCATRAZ ISLAND
The Embarcadero near Bay Street, Pier 33, Golden Gate National Recreation Area, SanFrancisco, 415-981-7625; www.nps.gov/alcatraz

Escape to Alcatraz and explore the prison cells that once held some of America's most notorious criminals, including Al "Scarface" Capone, kidnapper George "Machine Gun" Kelly, Bonnie and Clyde's accomplice Floyd Hamilton and Robert "Birdman" Stroud. Surrounded by the Bay's treacherous waters, the reputedly "escape-proof" prison witnessed 14 breakout attempts. Although no successful prison breaks were ever confirmed, five escapees remain missing and are presumed drowned. Among Alcatraz's more interesting artifacts are the dummy heads created by three would-be escapees. Made from used toilet paper, cardboard, cement chips, and hair scraps from the barbershop floor, they're a testament to captive creativity. A penitentiary from 1934 to 1963, "The Rock" now provides sanctuary for thousands of seabirds.
Admission: adults $26 day tours, $33 night tours; children 12-17 $26 day tours, $32 night tours; children 5-11 $16 day tours, $19.50 night tour; children under 5 free; seniors $24.50 day tours, $34.50 night tour. Hours vary.

AMERICAN CONSERVATORY THEATER
415 Geary St., San Francisco, 415-749-2228; www.act-sf.org
★
★★★
★★★
★★★
★★

Home to the nationally acclaimed conservatory (alumni include Danny Glover, Annette Bening and Denzel Washington) and theater company of the same name, this gilded palace of Corinthian columns was built as part of the post-1906 earthquake reconstruction. Known for both its cutting-edge productions, such as David Mamet's controversial *Oleanna* and Tony Kushner's Pulitzer Prize-winning *Angels in America*, and its Victorian-era architecture, the ornate building ranks on the U.S. Department of the Interior's National Register of Historic Places. Not satisfied to rest on the laurels of its lush surroundings or on the annual success of classics like *A Christmas Carol*, the company has cultivated relationships with contemporary masters, among them Tom Stoppard and Mamet.
Performances are at 8 p.m., with some 2 p.m. matinees; no performances on Monday.

ANGEL ISLAND STATE PARK
The Embarcadero at Beach Street, Pier 39, Angel Island, 415-435-1915; www.angelisland.org

For beautiful vistas of San Francisco, the Marin Headlands and Mount Tamalpais, head to Angel Island, a small state park just off the coast of Tiburon. The 1.2-mile isle, which is filled with lush flora, also provides spectacular hiking and biking. The island has had many uses over the years—from a cattle ranch to an Army garrison to a controversial immigrant-processing station known as "The Ellis Island of the West"—before being converted into a national park in 1954. Now, the island offers volleyball and baseball, manicured picnic grounds, historical tours and a café serving barbecued oysters. Roller skates, scooters and Segways are forbidden.
Ferries depart daily from San Francisco, Oakland and Tiburon. Daily 8 a.m.-sunset.

AQUARIUM OF THE BAY

Pier 39, The Embarcadero and Beach street, San Francisco, 415-623-5300;
www.aquariumofthebay.com

Go on an underwater adventure without getting wet. The aquarium's three exhibits immerse you in the rich local marine life. A moving walkway glides through two 300-foot-long acrylic tunnels surrounded by 700,000 gallons of water and more than 20,000 aquatic animals, including swarming schools of anchovies, bright sea stars and angel sharks. If Jaws gave you nightmares, watch out—the aquarium is also home to a nearly 10-foot sevengill shark, the largest in captivity. Get up close with the softer side of the Bay at the last exhibit, where you can pet live bat rays, leopard sharks, sea cucumbers (which are related to starfish and sea urchins, but are shaped more like, well, cucumbers) and other tide pool critters.

Admission: adults $15.95, seniors and children 3-11 $8. Hours may vary so check the Web site. Behind the Scenes Tour: adults $21.95, children 5-11 and seniors $14.

ASIAN ART MUSEUM OF SAN FRANCISCO

200 Larkin St., San Francisco, 415-581-3500; www.asianart.org

Beginning as a wing in the M. H. de Young, this museum has since blossomed into the largest collection of Asian art in the U.S., housing more than 17,000 pieces in the city's former Main Library (stunningly renovated by Gae Aulenti, designer of Paris' Musée d'Orsay.) Trek through three floors of history and culture spanning 6,000 years and covering seven geographic regions. While the museum is rich in relics—it is home to the oldest known Chinese Buddha in the world—it also regularly exhibits contemporary artwork, including manga (the popular Japanese-style comics) and Japanese haute couture from the Kyoto Costume Institute.

Admission: adults $12, seniors $8, students and children 13-17 $7, children under 12 free. Thursday after 5 p.m. $5. Tuesday-Wednesday, Friday-Sunday 10 a.m.-5 p.m., Thursday 10 a.m.-9 p.m. Daily gallery and architectural tours free with admission. Free first Sunday of every month.

BAKER BEACH

Lincoln Boulevard and Bowley Street, Pacific Heights, 415-561-4300; www.nps.gov

San Francisco isn't known for its beaches, mostly because it's just too cold or cloudy to use them most of the year. There are, however, a handful of sweltering, clear-as-crystal days in the summer that demand that you grab your towel and sunblock and head to Baker Beach. During these times, the mile stretch of golden sand becomes a microcosm of San Francisco, featuring a rollicking mix of college students, slackers, businessmen playing hooky, parents, dog walkers and, down at the north-most end by the Golden Gate Bridge, nudists (who flock to the beach no matter what the conditions are). It's an eclectic group, which might explain why the original Burning Man Festival (the annual art event dedicated to radical self-expression now held in Nevada's Black Rock Desert) was launched here back in 1986.

BARBARY COAST TRAIL

Mission and Fifth streets, San Francisco, 415-454-2355; www.barbarycoasttrail.org

From the birthplace of the Gold Rush to the beginning of the Beats, this fascinating walking tour takes you through San Francisco's storied past. Wild and rowdy tales of shanghaied sailors, streetwalkers and Pony Express riders accompany your every step as you wind your way through 3.8 miles of the city's rich history. Less scandalous highlights include the first Asian temple in the U.S. as well as the oldest Catholic cathedral west of the Rockies. Like bronze bread crumbs, 170 medallions and arrows embedded in the sidewalk mark the trail's path. Download one of the three themed audio tours from the Web site, purchase the printed guide online or at several local bookstores and set out on your own, or arrange for a guided tour with author and trail creator Daniel Bacon. For a varied and fascinating look at San Francisco's history, fuel up with an espresso at North Beach's beatnik hot spot Vesuvio Café and then follow along to the beat of the "Poets, Paesanos and Windjammers" audio tour.

Admission: $22. Guided tours are available by appointment only.

THE BEAT MUSEUM

540 Broadway, San Francisco, 800-537-6822; www.thebeatmuseum.org

The Beat Museum gives a lesson in America's counter-culture revolution that you won't read about in history class. Open since early 2006, the small space tells the tales behind the lives of Jack Kerouac, Allen Ginsberg, Neal Cassady and other bohemian icons of the '50s and '60s movement. Just around the corner from Lawrence Ferlinghetti's City Lights Bookstore and Jack Kerouac Alley, the shop features everything from commemorative bobblehead dolls and yo-yos to personal correspondence to long out-of-print books, providing ample illustration of how the Beats changed the way people think about poetry and fiction.

Tuesday-Thursday noon-10 p.m., Friday-Sunday 10 a.m.-10 p.m. Closed Monday.

CABLE CAR MUSEUM

1201 Mason St., San Francisco, 415-474-1887; www.cablecarmuseum.com

Housed in the historic Washington/Mason cable car barn and powerhouse, San Francisco's oldest and hardest-working icon is celebrated in this informative museum. After witnessing the brutal death of horses that slipped on slick cobblestone streets while struggling to pull streetcars, Andrew Smith Hallidie was inspired to invent an alternative mode of transportation. A godsend to humans and horses alike, the first cable car was successfully tested in 1873. It quickly caught on and an extensive network of 53 miles of track eventually crisscrossed the city. More than just a monument to a bygone era, the museum overlooks the engines and whirring wheels that power and pull the Powell-Mason, Powell-Hyde and California Street lines. Downstairs, you can view the sheaves and cable lines entering the building through their underground channel.

Admission: free. April-September, Daily 10 a.m.-6 p.m.; October-March, Daily 10 a.m.-5 p.m.

CALIFORNIA ACADEMY OF SCIENCES

55 Music Concourse Drive, Golden Gate Park, San Francisco, 415-379-8000; www.calacademy.org

From the rolling green hills of its "living roof" to its 25-foot-deep coral reef aquarium, the California Academy of Sciences' new home (opened in September 2008) brims with life. Wander through the rainforest dome as free-flying birds and butterflies swoop and flutter around you. Take a trip below the flooded forest and hang out with the anacondas and piranhas while gazing up through a 25-foot-long acrylic tunnel. Or ditch the earthly environs altogether and embark on a virtual space odyssey with real-time NASA feeds of shuttle launches and missions in the planetarium. Old favorites have also returned, including a rare white alligator and the Tusher African Center's ridiculously cute colony of South African penguins.

Admission: adults $24.95, seniors and teens 12-17 $19.95, children under 7 free. Monday-Saturday 9:30 a.m.-5 p.m., Sunday 11 a.m.-5 p.m. Free every third Wednesday of the month.

THE CANNERY

2801 Leavenworth St., San Francisco, 415-771-3112; www.thecannery.com

Overlooking the San Francisco Bay, this popular complex of shops, restaurants and markets is housed in one of Del Monte's old fruit-processing factory in 1907. Similar to what you might find in Europe, among shops, galleries and restaurants, you'll find entertainment from comedians and musicians performing in the courtyard.

Shops open daily at 10 a.m.

CARTOON ART MUSEUM

655 Mission St., San Francisco, 415-227-8666; www.cartoonart.org

With a generous donation in 1987 from *Peanuts* creator Charles Schultz, the Cartoon Art Museum become the only museum in the United States devoted to preserving cartoon art. In addition to displaying close to 6,000 original pieces—some dating back to the 18th century—the museum organizes seven major exhibits each year and has a cartoon art classroom and bookstore.

Admission: adults $6, seniors and students $4, children 6-12 $2, children under 5 free. Tuesday-Sunday 11 a.m.-5 p.m.

CHINATOWN

Grant Avenue and Stockton Street; www.sanfranciscochinatown.com

Chinatown buzzes with quaint trinket shops, steaming dim sum parlors and green grocers overflowing with tropical produce, but its history is rather scandalous. Back in 1906, when much of the community was destroyed in the legendary earthquake and fire, city officials tried to move the entire northeastern neighborhood south to Hunters Point. When Chinese officials and American merchants balked, they came upon a compromise, rebuilding the area as a tourist destination, complete with vague notions of what China is "really" like. Today, most of the actual Chinese community lives in the Richmond or Sunset neighborhoods, far removed from the toyshops and angled rooftops of Chinatown. Despite its manufactured past, there's no denying the area's vibrant mercantile present: Exotic delicacies such as armadillos and pigs' noses press up against store windows while fish wriggle in ice buckets on the sidewalk.

CITY LIGHTS BOOKSTORE

261 Columbus Ave., San Francisco, 415-362-8193; www.citylights.com

Browse three floors of tightly packed stacks at this Beat Generation bookshop. A must-see for all literature lovers, City Lights Bookstore was co-founded by poet Lawrence Ferlinghetti in 1953 as the country's first all-paperback bookseller. In 1955, Ferlinghetti started City Lights Publishers, perhaps best known for publishing Allen Ginsberg's groundbreaking Howl & Other Poems in 1956, which led to Ferlinghetti's arrest on obscenity charges. The shop now carries a wide range of both paper and hardback titles. Reflecting the free-speech interests of its founders, it caters to those outside-the-mainstream voices, with books on progressive politics and social issues, works from small presses and an entire room devoted to poetry.

Daily 10 a.m.-midnight.

CLIFF HOUSE, SEAL ROCKS AND SUTRO BATHS

1090 Point Lobos, San Francisco, 415-386-3330; www.cliffhouse.com

There are two restaurants at the neoclassical Cliff House: the Bistro, which was restored in 2004 has an older vibe with photos of celebrities of eras past hanging on the wall; beautiful views of the ocean, the Marin Coast to the north, Ocean Beach and Seal Rocks habitat of sea lions; and an elegant-diner like feel. The food is fantastic but the warm popovers they serve you beforehand steal the show. The other restaurant, Sutro's, is a bit more stylish with floor-to-ceiling windows, which give a panoramic view of the ocean. It's housed in the newer wing of the building and the menu is filled with fresh seafood and organic produce. Right next to the Cliff House is the Sutro Bath ruins, which used to be the lavish Sutro Baths built by Adolph Sutro. In 1896, the baths opened as classic Greek freshwater tanks for swimming and there were slides, springboards and high dives for people to enjoy. Today, you can see what is left of these once-famous baths.

COIT TOWER

1 Telegraph Hill Blvd., San Francisco, 415-362-0808

No longer one of the tallest buildings in San Francisco, Coit Tower's Telegraph Hill location still offers spectacular 360-degree panoramas of downtown and the Bay from its observation deck. Rescued as a child from a fire, wealthy eccentric Lillie Hitchcock Coit put a third of her fortune toward the construction of the 210-foot tower—a monument to honor the city she loved and its volunteer firemen. However, contrary to popular belief, the fluted column is not meant to resemble a fire hose nozzle. You can check out the lobby's Diego Rivera-inspired WPA murals for free, but the elevator ride to the top costs a few bucks. Avoid the traffic jam on Telegraph Hill Boulevard (which leads to the parking lot) and take the steep Filbert Steps to the top instead; the cute garden cottages and intermittent views make the climb more than worthwhile (the tower functions as a lookout today).

Admission: adults $4.50, seniors $3.50 children 6-12 $2, children under 6 free. Daily 10 a.m.-5 p.m.

COW HOLLOW AND MARINA DISTRICT
Union Street and Van Ness Avenue, San Francisco
Two of San Francisco's tiniest neighborhoods, the adjacent Marina District and Cow Hollow, both come from relatively humble beginnings. Originally tidal marshlands, the Marina District rose from the rubble of the 1906 earthquake, when the area was used as a dumping ground for debris; Cow Hollow takes its name from the dairy bovines that once grazed here. Today, these districts are home to yacht clubs, gorgeous Art Deco buildings and Victorian houses. Hit these neighborhoods to hang with wealthy, beautiful and carefree 20- and 30-somethings. Boutiques, art galleries, antique shops, restaurants and bars catering to this trendy clientele line the parallel Chestnut Street (Marina) and Union Street (Cow Hollow). During the day, the Marina Green and Crissy Field provide the area's fit young residents with ample space for jogging, rollerblading, kite flying, Frisbee throwing or simply spreading out on a picnic blanket alongside the waterfront.

EMBARCADERO CENTER
1 Embarcadero Center, San Francisco, 415-772-0700; www.embarcaderocenter.com
A city within a city, the center spans six blocks—from Clay and Sacramento streets between Drumm and Battery streets in San Francisco's Commercial District. A former shipping dock nicknamed the Barbary Coast, it was known as a raucous district of saloons, prostitution and thievery in the 1840s. It has since evolved into five office towers with three interconnected shopping levels—four in the historic former Federal Reserve Bank Building Center—housing a vast complex of entertainment options, including more than 125 retail shops and restaurants, a five-screen cinema, wine and music festivals, concerts, garden shows and even an ice rink.
Monday-Friday 10 a.m.-7 p.m., Saturday 10 a.m.-6 p.m., Sunday noon-5 p.m.

THE EXPLORATORIUM

3601 Lyon St., San Francisco, 415-561-0360; www.exploratorium.edu
Kids can channel their inner mad scientists at the Exploratorium, one of the most entertaining science museums in the country. Children come to use the acoustic parabolic dishes, which allow them to hear mom and dad whispering from across the noisy room. But the fun exhibit has a purpose other than spying on your parents: It's one of the more than 400 works that illuminate the mysteries of visual perception, sound and touch. Housed in the Palace of Fine Arts, the interactive museum was built in 1969 by Manhattan Project physicist Frank Oppenheimer. Be sure to try your own experiments with the Wave Organ, which is built from pipes and concrete and juts into the nearby ocean, and the Tactile Dome, a pitch-black maze of chutes and ladders and all sorts of touchy-feely textures beloved by children and teenagers alike.
Admission: adults $14, students, seniors and children 13-17 $11, children 4-12 $9, children under 4 free. Tuesday-Sunday 10 a.m.-5 p.m.

FERRY BUILDING MARKETPLACE
1 Ferry Building, San Francisco, 415-983-8000; www.ferrybuildingmarketplace.com
Built in 1898, the Ferry Building was once a lively transportation hub, wel-

coming train travelers from the East and ferryboat passengers from across the Bay. Now a popular stop for foodies, the renovated landmark offers some of the Bay Area's best restaurants and specialty food shops, including Ferry Plaza Wine Merchant, which offers a unique selection of wines from smaller producers and a wine bar where customers can sit and sip the merchandise, and the nationally acclaimed Vietnamese restaurant Slanted Door, which features a wall of windows overlooking the Bay. Take in the tastes of California while wandering through the building's three-story-high, sunlit hall. Head toward the iconic 240-foot tall clock tower on Saturday and Tuesday mornings for the Ferry Plaza Farmers Market and pick up a farm-fresh breakfast of locally grown organic produce and artisanal breads, cheeses and preserves. Saturday's market regularly draws 10,000 to 15,000 happily munching shoppers, making it a great place to people-watch while enjoying your meal on one of the waterfront benches.

Monday-Friday 10 a.m.-6 p.m., Saturday 9 a.m.-6 p.m., Sunday 11 a.m.-5 p.m. Ferry Plaza Farmers Market: Tuesday 10 a.m.-2 p.m., Saturday 8 a.m.-2 p.m.

THE FILLMORE

1805 Geary Blvd., San Francisco, 415-346-6000; www.thefillmore.com

Rock history was made here. At the height of the '60s counter-culture revolution, rock promoter Bill Graham lit the stage with performances by the likes of Janis Joplin, the Grateful Dead and Jimi Hendrix—all of it catalogued in the famed psychedelic concert posters that now adorn the venue's walls. A holdover from its hippie heritage, a bucket of free apples still welcomes you at the top of the stairs. Inside, the one-time dance hall, with its glittering chandeliers and wooden floor, now hosts a mix of musical talent, from rock to hip hop to the occasional country crooner. For a clear view of the stage, arrive early for a seat at one of the balcony tables.

Box office: Sunday 10 a.m.-4 p.m. and 30 minutes before the doors open until 10 p.m. on show nights.

FISHERMAN'S WHARF

Taylor Street and the Embarcadero, San Francisco, 415-674-7503;
www.fishermanswharf.org

While a few fishing boats still set sail from here, much of the wharf's maritime past has been overwhelmed by its present-day resemblance to a shopping mall. If you're searching for that perfect sweatshirt, keychain or shot glass with San Francisco boldly printed on it, you'll find plenty of choices in the kitschy shops that stretch from Ghirardelli Square to Pier 39. While you're here, drop a few coins at Musee Mecanique, home to the mechanical (some say maniacal) Laffing Sal and a collection of other mechanized contraptions, antique arcade games and player pianos. But it won't cost you a dime to see the real stars of the wharf: Some 900 barking and brawling sea lions have set up camp on Pier 39's floating docks, and it's the best show around. The food isn't all bad, either. Get a taste of the Dungeness crab from one of the seafood street vendors. Or grab some clam chowder in a bread bowl from Boudin Bakery; its been pulling sourdough bread out of the oven in San Francisco since 1849.

FORT MASON CENTER

Golden Gate National Recreation Area, Marina Boulevard and Buchanan Street, San Francisco, 415-345-7500; www.fortmason.org

This multicultural complex located in what was once the Army's western headquarters, takes up 13 acres across the waterfront. With nine buildings, this center has galleries, offices, a conference center, classrooms and other meeting spaces. There are theaters; the San Francisco Museum of Modern Art Artists Gallery; the Museo ItaloAmericano, which is dedicated to researching, collecting and showcasing the works of Italian and Italian-American artists; a gourmet vegetarian restaurant; a radio station; a bookstore and more. A national historic landmark, Fort Mason Center boasts spectacular views of the Golden Gate Bridge and the hills of Marin.

Daily 8 a.m.-midnight

FORT POINT NATIONAL HISTORIC SITE

End of Marine Drive on the Presidio, Presidio/Golden Gate National Recreation Area, 415-556-1693; www.nps.gov

Located under the narrows of the Golden Gate, the fort affords some of the most awe-inspiring views of the bridge's massive orange-vermillion beams and the bay below. Built between 1853 and 1861, the three-tiered brick fortress was armed with 102 cannons at its greatest strength, but never fired a single shot in battle. However, it was almost attacked by a Confederate raider, the CSS Shenandoah; the ship was sailing toward the harbor when it learned that the war had ended. This National Historic Site's exhibits focus on Civil War-era history, including the role of African- American soldiers and women in the military. A cannon-loading demonstration will show you how to fire one off like a Civil War artilleryman—you never know when that skill will come in handy.

Friday-Sunday 10 a.m.-5 p.m. Pier crabbing demonstration: March-October, Saturday 10 a.m.-noon. Candlelight tour: November-February, Saturday.

GHIRARDELLI SQUARE

900 North Point St., Fisherman's Wharf, 415-775-5500; www.ghirardellisq.com

Ghirardelli Square has been a major tourist attraction since 1964, when local businessman William Roth bought the old chocolate factory and transformed it into shops and offices. Added to the National Register of Historic Places in 1982, the square has recently undergone another redesign, with the upper offices being converted into a high-end residence club run by the Fairmont hotel chain. Hit the original Ghirardelli Ice Cream and Chocolate Shop for a traditional hot fudge sundae (you'll need two spoons and a partner to finish one), and a look at manufacturing equipment from the 1852 factory.

GOLDEN GATE BRIDGE

Highway 101, San Francisco, 415-921-5858; www.goldengate.org

One of the country's most recognized and beloved landmarks, this bridge stretches across the chilly, choppy waters of the Golden Gate Strait, linking San Francisco to the south and Marin County to the north. When engineer Joseph Strauss (and architects Irving and Gertrude Morrow) set out to create the bridge in 1930 many skeptics predicted that it would never be completed or that it would be unable to withstand the fierce winds generated by the

Pacific Ocean to its immediate west. The first cars drove across the bridge seven years later, after Strauss finished under budget and ahead of schedule. The bridge's main span extends 4,200 feet, which was a record at the time of its construction. Each of its towers weighs 44,400 tons and stretches 746 feet above sea level. Walk or bike (1.7 miles) across the bridge and take time to admire its timeless design as well as the view. Architect Irving Morrow chose to paint the bridge "international orange," a striking hue that blends remarkably well with the scenic natural surroundings. Vehicles crossing the bridge from the north must pay a toll.

GOLDEN GATE NATIONAL RECREATION AREA

Fort Mason, San Francisco, 415-561-4700; www.nps.gov/goga

Within 75,000 acres of recreation area—connected by the Golden Gate Bridge—are 28 miles of San Francisco's shoreline with many beaches, lagoons, rugged headlands, meadows, picnic facilities and 100 miles of trails, countryside that extends 20 miles north into Marin County and 1,047 acres of San Mateo County to the south. The most popular visitor areas are the former penitentiary on Alcatraz Island, the historic Cliff House, Fort Point National Historic Site, Muir Woods National Monument and the Cultural Entertainment Center, Fort Mason. Congress designated the area in 1972 as one of the first urban national parks. Nearby Muir Woods National Monument, in Muir Beach, is Slide Ranch (www.slideranch.com), a dairy farm since the 19th century where you can learn about sustainable agriculture, which the Bay Area so passionately embraces. Hours vary, but most areas are open Daily.

GOLDEN GATE PARK

Fulton at 36th Avenue and Lincoln at 41st Avenue, San Francisco, 415-831-2700; www.parks.sfgov.org

Larger than New York City's Central Park, this 1,017-acre recreation area is packed with more outdoor fun than you can throw a Frisbee at—from rollerblading along John F. Kennedy Drive on Sunday to sharpening your marksmanship skills at the archery range to simply pondering whether a rose by any other name would smell as sweet in the Shakespeare Garden. There are almost too many ways to enjoy a day at this park. Among the seemingly endless possibilities are 21 tennis courts, four soccer fields, three lawn-bowling greens and swing dancing lessons in the street. Built atop ocean dunes in the 1870s, this verdant rectangle teems with plant and animal life, too, including duck-filled lakes, some of the best fly-casting pools in the country and even a bison paddock. Plus, the gorgeous domed Conservatory of Flowers (one of the oldest wood-and-glass-pane greenhouses in the world) contains more than 10,000 plants from around the globe. Home of the California Academy of Sciences and the de Young Museum, the park also offers plenty of indoor entertainment. If all this activity leaves you breathless, sit for a spell and sip some tea in the lovely Japanese Tea Garden, one of the most popular tourist attractions at the park.

HAIGHT-ASHBURY

Haight and Ashbury streets, San Francisco

Thanks to 1967's "Summer of Love" (and the ensuing inflammatory media coverage), the Haight-Ashbury neighborhood has become synonymous with the hippie ideal. While the concepts of peace, love and psychedelic drugs remain, for the most part, these days the houses are full of yuppies instead of musicians. In fact, the Haight has become more of a shopping mecca than a counter-cultural breeding ground—albeit one that sells everything from rock posters to roach clips to used records. Get lost in the seemingly endless rows of CDs and vinyl at Amoeba Records or search for hipster castaways and vintage treasures at Wasteland (1660 Haight St., 415-863-3150; www.wasteland.com), a popular second-hand clothing store.

HARRY DENTON'S STARLIGHT ROOM
Sir Francis Drake Hotel, 450 Powell St., San Francisco, 415-395-8595;
www.harrydenton.com
Although it's more of a tourist trap than a local hangout, the Starlight Room's 21st floor perch in the Sir Francis Drake Hotel offers an undeniably gorgeous 360-degree view. With its plush red and gold banquettes, chandeliers and silk drapery, the place itself isn't so shabby, either. And thanks to the dress code (no caps, sportswear, casual jeans or sneakers), it's also the rare bar where you can show off your glitziest cocktail dress without feeling out of place in the perennially casual Bay Area. Bartenders in white tuxedoes pour martinis and cosmos as a crowd of young and old gets down to the band's Motown classics and the DJ's mix of Top 40 hits from the '70s, '80s, '90s and today. Tuesday-Saturday 6 p.m.-2 a.m. Sunday shows at noon and 2:30 p.m. Table reservations recommended.

JAPANTOWN
1625 Post St., San Francisco; www.sfjapantown.org
Japantown (or, as it's known to locals, "Nihonmachi") grew out of the Earthquake of 1906, after which Japanese people settled in the Western Addition neighborhood, opening Nipponese restaurants and stores. But the area didn't come into its own as a tourist destination until 1968, when several international conglomerates erected Japan Center, three malls on five acres devoted to Japanese cateries, bookstores, grocery stores, hotels, shops and even a spa. One of only three remaining Japantowns in the continental U.S., Nihonmachi hosts both the spring Cherry Blossom Festival, a street fair featuring a parade, traditional cuisine, crafts and taiko drummers, and the boundary-pushing San Francisco International Asian American Film Festival, offering a place where tradition meets technology and progress coexists with the past.

LITTLE ITALY AND NORTH BEACH
Between Columbus Avenue and Telegraph Hill, Broadway and Bay Street, San
Francisco; www.sfnorthbeach.org
Originally settled by Italians, this community in the North Beach neighborhood still feels like the motherland, with its old-world delis, cafés, gelato parlors and Italian restaurants. For many, it is best known as a center of bohemian life and the 1950s home of the Beats, a group of writers and poets that included Jack Kerouac and Allen Gingsberg. The neighborhood is also home to the City Lights Bookstore—owned by Beat poet Lawrence Ferlinghetti—which published Ginsberg's Howl & Other Poems. Other Beatnik landmarks located here are Kerouac Alley, Vesuvio Café and the Beat Museum.

LOMBARD STREET

1000 block of Lombard Street, between Hyde and Leavenworth streets, San Francisco

Lombard is known as "The Crookedest Street in the World." This designation doesn't stem from any illegal deeds or wrongful actions committed there; rather, the title comes from one block of the throughway between Hyde and Leavenworth streets, in which the avenue takes eight sharp turns. (The switchbacks were added in 1922, when they were deemed necessary for people to navigate the sharp decline.) Nowadays, tourists go out of their way to traverse the strip, which features vibrant flowers and a speed limit of 5 miles per hour. Shutterbugs can't resist the postcard-perfect red cobblestone and dense green shrubbery, making it one of the world's most photographed streets as well.

MISSION DISTRICT MURALS

Precita Eyes, 2981 24th St., San Francisco, www.precitaeyes.org

San Francisco is a city of local color—both literally and figuratively. There are about 1,500 murals painted on various walls and buildings throughout the city, each telling different tales of fallen comrades, mythological heroes and abstract thoughts. The Mission District houses a large concentration of the city's murals, thanks in part to groups like the now defunct Mujeres Muralistas, the Chicano art mural movement of the '70s, and the current Precita Eyes Mural Arts Center. The organization also hosts classes on mural painting, as well as offers walking and biking tours of the 80-plus pieces near its storefront. The Mission murals prove that art can be both evocative and instructive, and they offer a nice alternative to a museum on a beautiful day.

Admission for tours: adults $12, students $8, children under 17 and seniors $5, children under 12 $2. Saturday-Sunday 11 a.m., 1:30 p.m.

MISSION DOLORES

3321 16th St., San Francisco, 415-621-8203; www.missiondolores.org

Constructed by Spanish settlers in 1776, Mission Dolores is the oldest remaining structure in San Francisco. Not surprisingly, the original log-and-thatch building has undergone many renovations over the years, most notably during the California Gold Rush, when parts of it were leased or sold as saloons and gambling facilities, and after the 1906 earthquake, during which much of the surrounding areas were scorched. Around 1913, the larger, grander Mission Dolores Basilica was erected next door. Since then, patrons and tourists have flocked to witness the chapel's sleek adobe elegance, with its mesmerizing painted ceiling beams (the design was inspired by the Ohlone tribe's face paint) and the elaborate golden altars brought from Mexico around the turn of the 19th century. The Basilica's ornate Catholic grandeur, is spectacular, resplendent with intricate tile work, stunning stained-glass windows and a wide domed ceiling. If the sheer beauty isn't enough for you, maybe the opportunity to see one of Alfred Hitchcock's locations from the classic film *Vertigo* will convince you.

Suggested donation: adults $5, seniors and students $3. May-October, Daily 9 a.m.-4:30 p.m.; November-April, Daily 9 a.m.-4 p.m.

MUSEUM OF CRAFT AND FOLK ART

51 Yerba Buena Lane, San Francisco, 415-227-4888; www.mocfa.org

From exhibits featuring the work of four generations of African-American quilt makers to the intricate needlework of contemporary tattoo artists, this museum has woven together traditional and contemporary crafts and folk art from around the world for more than 25 years. Given its focus, the place begs involvement. Explore your creative side in one of its hands-on workshops. If you have kids, keep an eye out for the family activity days led by the museum's school program staff. After being inspired by all the fine craftsmanship, you can pick up a handcrafted item, like a blown-glass vase shaped like a splashing droplet or a whimsical ceramic tea set perfect for a Mad Hatter's party; the museum's gift shop represents more than 50 established and emerging artists.

Admission: adults $5, children under 18 free, seniors $4. Free on Tuesday. Monday-Friday 11 a.m.-6 p.m., Saturday-Sunday 11 a.m.-5 p.m. Closed Wednesday.

PAINTED LADIES/ALAMO SQUARE

712-720 Steiner St., San Francisco

Contrary to their name, the Painted Ladies aren't overly rouged harlots. Rather, they're narrow, Victorian-style buildings drenched in vibrantly colored paints. Approximately 48,000 homes were built in this style around the turn of the 20th century, though many of the houses were covered in gray Army surplus stock during the two world wars. In the '60s and '70s, the colorist movement took hold, and many homeowners revived the bright lemon yellow, bubble-gum pink and periwinkle hues of the past. Elizabeth Pomada and Michael Larsen brought national attention to the houses with their 1978 book, Painted Ladies: San Francisco's Resplendent Victorians, and nowadays people flock to Alamo Square to snap shots of one particular row of sunstruck beauties.

PALACE OF FINE ARTS

3301 Lyon St., San Francisco, 415-567-6642; www.palaceoffinearts.org

The Palace of Fine Arts is one of the most popular spots for snapping wedding photos in San Francisco. Where else can you pose before a Roman-style rotunda with giant columns, a lagoon full of ducks and geese and a bevy of lush Monterey cypresses? The palace was originally constructed as part of the 1915 Panama-Pacific International Exposition, which celebrated the completion of the Panama Canal and San Francisco's resurrection following the 1906 earthquake. Built to look like a ruin, the palace's eight domed structures eventually fell into actual disrepair, until they were bulldozed in the mid-'60s. One dome and the rotunda were immediately reconstructed—right down to the famed weeping women who adorn the top of the colonnades—and the Exploratorium science museum and a 1,000-seat theater were built next door. Today, along with the bride and groom, you'll find everyone from locals and tourists to film crews (the site has been used for scenes in *The Rock*, *Time After Time* and *Vertigo*) utilizing the romantic setting.

MARIN COUNTY

Allow a full day to drive down and hike along the Pacific coastline where you can admire redwood forests, spy elephant seals and migrating whales at Tomales Bay and soak up the superb Point Reyes National Seashore.

Cross the Golden Gate Bridge to the Marin Headlands, where Conzelman Road runs along the cliff sides and offers a spectacular look back at the San Francisco skyline. Follow the roadway as it loops back to Highway 101, then head north past Sausalito continuing on Highway 1 toward the coast. Your first stop is Muir Woods, the state's most popular and accessible growth of virgin redwoods. Short trails lead through the main groves.

Continue north to Mount Tamalpais, and follow signs toward East Peak for picnic areas and dramatic panoramas of the entire Bay Area. Farther north, just off Highway 1, the hiking trails of Point Reyes National Seashore begin near the Bear Valley Visitor Center. For a more complete tour of the park, go north about 22 miles on Sir Francis Drake Highway through the resort town of Inverness, continuing along the peninsula, which is lined with rolling grasslands, forests flush with wildlife, estuaries and oft-deserted beaches. At the peninsula's tip, you'll find a lighthouse perched high over the Pacific, a top whale-watching site in winter; you may have to park and ride a shuttle bus at peak times on weekends.

On the return trip, dig into a meal at one of Point Reyes Station's restaurants, then follow the Point Reyes Petaluma road (and directional signs) across the rolling countryside to either Petaluma or Novato, where you'll head south on Highway 101 to San Francisco. Approximately 90-120 miles.

PRESIDIO

Golden Gate National Recreation Area, San Francisco, 415-561-4323; www.nps.gov

What used to be an army post for 218 years, the Presidio is now part of the Golden Gate National Recreation Area on 1,450 acres. The present Officer's Club, which is also the Visitor Center, contains sections of the first building to be erected in San Francisco. Markers indicate points of historical interest, like Crissy Airfield, Fort Scott, San Francisco National Cemetery and nature sites like Baker Beach, Mountain Lake, Presidio Forest and Presidio Golf Course and Clubhouse.

Visitor Center: 9 a.m.-5 p.m.

PRESIDIO GOLF COURSE & CLUBHOUSE

300 Finley Road, San Francisco, 415-561-4661; www.presidiogolf.com

Back in the day, only military leaders like Teddy Roosevelt and Dwight Eisenhower could marvel at the greens of the Presidio Golf Course. But in 1995, when the Army facilities were converted to a national park, these illustrious fairways became open to the public. Now, you too can play with military precision, winding your way through eucalyptus tree groves and nefarious sand traps, all the while soaking in the breathtaking Bay scenery. Conveniently located 10 minutes from downtown San Francisco, the course is overseen by Arnold Palmer Golf Management, which knows a thing or two about winning tough battles. See Web site for prices.

Daily.

SAN FRANCISCO 49ERS (NFL)

Candlestick Park, 490 Jamestown Ave., Candlestick Point, 415-656-4900;
www.sf49ers.com

The 49ers' record five Super Bowl wins makes them one of the most successful franchises in NFL history. However, their last title came in 1994, and
recent years have been mediocre at best. While the faithful still turn out in
red and gold to support or chastise the team, most of the drama has been hap-
pening off field. Following the city's inability to come up with a feasible plan
to replace the worn-down Candlestick Park, the 49ers brass indicated they
would move the team south to Santa Clara in 2012. Counter plans have been
offered, but nothing has been agreed upon—leaving gridiron fans gnashing
their teeth about more than missed field goals.

SAN FRANCISCO BALLET

War Memorial Opera House, 301 Van Ness Ave., San Francisco, 415-861-5600;
www.sfballet.org

Founded in 1933, this is the country's oldest professional ballet company
and one of its largest. Under the direction of Helgi Tomasson (a longtime
lead dancer for legendary choreographer George Balanchine) for 20-plus
years, the San Francisco Ballet has risen from a regional troupe to one of
the world's premier companies. While firmly grounded in the classical ballet
tradition, the company is known for pioneering newly commissioned works
and innovative spins on classics. Its annual Nutcracker production in December is nothing shy of magical. You'll leave dancing like a sugarplum fairy, or
rather wishing you could. The regular repertory season runs from the end of
January through May in the War Memorial Opera House.

SAN FRANCISCO GIANTS (MLB)

AT&T Park, 24 Willie Mays Plaza, San Francisco, 415-972-2000; www.sfgiants.com

Following the loss of Barry Bonds, there's been a marked lack of excitement surrounding the Giants. Pitcher Tim Lincecum—of the 99-mile-per-
hour fastball and unorthodox delivery—is a budding superstar, but he only
plays every five days. Nowadays, the biggest attraction may be the park itself,
which has gone through more name changes than P. Diddy, but is currently
known as AT&T Park. Even if you don't paddle a kayak into McCovey Cove
to catch homers, you're sure to enjoy the stadium's stunning views, idiosyn-
cratic layout, intense garlic fries and gorgeous brick wall (complete with
viewing areas for fans who can't afford a ticket). One or two more brawny
hitters, and the Giants will chase the ring again.

SAN FRANCISCO MUSEUM OF MODERN ART

151 Third St., San Francisco, 415-357-4000; www.sfmoma.org

Designed by noted Swiss architect Mario Botta, SFMOMA's burnt-sienna
brick exterior and iconic black-and-white central cylinder stand in stark contrast to the surrounding glass and steel towers. The museum's world-class
collection of more than 25,000 works of modern and contemporary art
ranges from Henri Matisse's 1905 masterpiece Femme au chapeau (Woman
with a Hat) to Jeremy Blake's 21st-century digital animation. Along with
its impressive catalogue of painting, sculpture, architecture, and design and
media art, the museum boasts a massive photography collection, including

work by Ansel Adams, Ilse Bing, Alfred Stieglitz, Walker Evans and Dorothea Lange. As one of the country's largest modern art museums, SFMOMA frequently hosts blockbuster touring exhibitions as well. Past exhibits have featured Olafur Eliasson, Matthew Barney, Diane Arbus and Gerhard Richter. A rooftop garden opened in spring 2009 to commemorate the museum's 75th anniversary in 2010.

Admission: adults $12.50, seniors $8, students $7, children under 12 free. Half-price Thursday 6-9 p.m. Monday-Tuesday, Friday-Sunday 11 a.m.-5:45 p.m., Thursday 11 a.m.-8:45 p.m. Closed Wednesday.

SAN FRANCISCO MUSEUM OF MODERN ART ARTISTS GALLERY

Fort Mason Center, San Francisco, 415-441-4777; www.sfmoma.com

The SFMOMA's (San Francisco Museum of Modern Art) little sister showcases work by emerging and internationally known Northern California artists in its light-filled, two-story space. For more than 30 years, the gallery has reflected the contemporary art scene's diverse spectrum—from painting and photography to more experimental mixed media. The friendly staff of art experts, along with the casual atmosphere, may lead to a loosening of the wallet. It may not fit easily in your suitcase, but a souvenir of fine art beats a key chain any day. With items starting as low as $100, the annual spring Artists' Warehouse Sale is a great opportunity to score fine pieces at steep discounts.

SAN FRANCISCO OPERA

War Memorial Opera House, 301 Van Ness Ave., San Francisco, 415-861-4008; www.sfopera.com

The Beaux Arts architecture of the War Memorial Opera House belies the innovative spirit of the San Francisco Opera. Second only to New York's Metropolitan Opera in North America, this internationally recognized company is known for its inventive takes on classics (Puccini's La Bohème and Verdi's La Traviata) as well as for championing new work (Doctor Atomic by John Adams and The Bonesetter's Daughter, adapted from Bay Area author Amy Tan's best-selling novel). Thanks to its commitment to pulling the art form into the 21st century, there's no need to bring your opera glasses here. Its high-definition video projections allow even the folks in the balcony seats to see the divas sweat.

SAN FRANCISCO SYMPHONY

Louise M. Davies Symphony Hall, 201 Van Ness Ave., Civic Center, 415-864-6000; www.sfsymphony.org

Under the direction of Classical Music Hall of Famer Michael Tilson Thomas, the symphony has been honored for its pioneering programming and its celebration of American composers. The nearly-100-year-old orchestra's tradition of excellence has attracted a who's-who list of conductors and composers, including Leopold Stokowski, Leonard Bernstein, Igor Stravinsky, Sergei Prokofiev, Maurice Ravel, Aaron Copland and John Adams. The symphony also boasts its own chorus, whose vocal prowess has been featured on the soundtracks for *Amadeus*, *The Unbearable Lightness of Being* and

AMONG THE REDWOODS

Rise early to make the most of this route dominated by the tallest living things on earth—especially if you're planning a one-day tour.

From San Francisco, follow Highway 101 north to the town of Cloverdale. Take Route 128 northwest toward Mendocino, meandering by Anderson Valley wineries and Hendy Woods State Park. At the coast, meet up with Highway 1 and follow it north to the resort town of Mendocino, which resembles a New England fishing village perched on cliff tops. If you can spare a day, spend the night and poke around in antique and art shops or visit one of several nearby state parks. Or head back to San Francisco via Highway 20 east from the town of Fort Bragg (six miles north of Mendocino), a scenic route that leads to Highway 101, which then heads south to San Francisco, completing the 350-mile round-trip. Otherwise, continue north the next day on Highway 1 through Fort Bragg up to Leggett, where drivers can roll through a redwood tree. At Leggett, take Highway 101 north to Humboldt Redwoods State Park, home of the world's greatest redwood forest. The 30-mile-long Avenue of the Giants features the tallest of the tall, the 370-foot Champion Coast Redwood in Rockefeller Forest

After completing the Avenue of the Giants, turn around and follow Highway 101 south to San Francisco. Approximately 500 miles.

Godfather III. Hear the 11-time Grammy Award-winning symphony live in the sparkling Louise M. Davies Symphony Hall, home to the Ruffatti organ, the largest concert-hall organ in North America.

SAN FRANCISCO ZOO

1 Zoo Road, San Francisco, 415-753-7061; www.sfzoo.org

The San Francisco Zoo is home to exotic and rescued animals from all over the world, and it welcomes more than a million visitors a year to its 100-acre ocean-side spread. Followers of Animal Planet's hit "drama" Meerkat Manor will adore the zoo's outdoor meerkat exhibit. With only a low glass barrier separating human from meerkat, even the littlest fans can get an intimate look at the tight-knit family in its simulated savanna abode, replete with red soil and termite mounds. More than 900 mammals, birds, reptiles and insects call the zoo home. Kids flock to the historic "Little Puffer" miniature steam-train ride (built in 1904)—which chugs past the bear grottos and offers views of Eagle Island and the Latin American exhibit "Puente Al Sur"—and the hand-carved wooden Dentzel Carousel (built in 1921).

Admission: non-resident, adults $15, seniors $12, children ages 4-14 $9, children 3 and under free; resident, adults $12, seniors $7.50, kids 4-14 $5.50, children 3 and under free. Free first Wednesday of every month for residents. Monday-Sunday 10 a.m.-5 p.m.

SURFING

San Francisco Bay, San Francisco

Known for big waves and big sharks, Northern California surfing isn't for amateurs. If the threat of sharks isn't enough to give you goose bumps, there's always the icy-cold water to chill you to the bone. But for those ready to zip into a wetsuit and brave the fierce rip currents, the winter wave payoff can be big. Most surfing in San Francisco happens at Ocean Beach between Kelly's Cove (north end, by the Cliff House) and Sloat Boulevard at the south end (in the Sunset District, near Richmond). It picks up mighty swells and has plenty of space for a city's worth of surfers to spread out. When the waves are big, paddling out can be a rougher workout than you expect. Experienced surfers also hit San Francisco's north side at Dead Man's Break (around the corner from China Beach) and Fort Point under the Golden Gate Bridge (off the Presidio) to hang 10.

TELEGRAPH HILL
Between Powell Street and Columbus Avenue and Sansome, Francisco and Vallejo streets, San Francisco

This quaint neighborhood offers some of the best views and most verdant gardens in the city. The mostly residential district gained its moniker in the mid-1800s, when the hilltop was home to an early semaphore and optical telegraph station, which communicated with ships entering the Golden Gate. The hill no longer keeps watch over a bawdy Barbary Coast, but tourists, and some wild parrots, flock here for the beautiful vista from the 210-foot Coit Tower at its peak. In a city known for its winding stairways, it's easy to see why Telegraph Hill's Filbert Steps is one of the most famous. Surrounded by adorable cottages, Art Deco buildings, shady trees and blooming flowers, the stairway seems worlds away from the nearby buzzing of North Beach.

UNION SQUARE
Geary and Powell streets, san francisco; www.unionsquareshop.com

Union Square is one of the major tourist destinations in San Francisco, mainly because of the shopping opportunities, but also because of the plethora of hotels, theaters and bars in the area. The plaza itself, which was built in 1847 and named for the Union Army rallies that took place here, has been renovated many times, including when the world's first underground parking garage was added. But the real attractions are of course the upscale boutiques, among them Louis Vuitton, Gucci, Chanel, Prada and Marc Jacobs.

WASHINGTON SQUARE
Columbus and Union streets, North Beach, San Francisco

Situated near many different neighborhoods, Washington Square epitomizes the variety of San Francisco life. Elderly folks amble down from Chinatown for their morning tai chi exercises. American and European tourists sprawl on the grass, exhausted from gorging at nearby restaurants and shops. Craggy Italian gentlemen pause from bocce games and to reminisce about Joe DiMaggio (who was first married at Saints Peter and Paul Roman Catholic Church, which sits along the north side of the square). Local barhoppers stretch out in the sun, recovering from the debauchery of the night before. In this small, tree-lined square, people-watching is both vibrant and relaxed, much like North Beach itself.

WHALE-WATCHING
The Oceanic Society, San Francisco Marina Yacht Harbor, San Francisco, 415-441-1106, 800-326-7491; www.oceanic-society.org

Whale watching is an imprecise science. Sometimes you get lucky; other times youdon't. However, with several migration patterns taking whales right past the San Francisco coastline, you have a decent chance of seeing some kind of oceanic life when you go out on the Bay. Blue whales—the largest animals in the world—tend to migrate from June through November, as do the ever-graceful humpbacks. If you visit between December and May, you're more likely to see gray whales, which travel from their Arctic feeding grounds to Baja to breed and give birth. Even if you don't see a whale during your trip, you're likely to spy puffins, various seals and sea lions—cute alternatives if you can't catch a humpback.

Admission: $105. Saturday-Sunday 8 a.m.-4 p.m.

WINDSURFING

Crissy Field, Marine Drive, Presidio, San Francisco; www.parkconservancy.org

On any given day, brightly colored sails dot the Bay's beautiful blue waters. But don't be fooled by the pretty picture. These choppy waves aren't for beginners. Powerful tides and currents can suck novice windsurfers out to sea. Then there are the strong and variable winds to contend with and the dense fog that can reduce your vision to zero. Not to mention the hypothermia-inducing water temperatures. That said, Crissy Field is the most popular spot for those who know what they're doing and others who like to watch from the safety of the shoreline. Windy weekends draw hundreds of windsurfers into the water. Conditions are best from mid-March through September here. Beginners may want to head for tamer waters across the Bay at the Berkeley Marina or Alameda's Crown Beach.

YERBA BUENA CENTER FOR THE ARTS

701 Mission St., San Francisco, 415-978-2787; www.ybca.org

Situated alongside the picnic-ready Yerba Buena Gardens, the YBCA's two galleries form the cultural cornerstone of the surrounding entertainment complex. Unlike the relatively staid SFMOMA across the street, the YBCA doesn't have a permanent collection. The center focuses on work that explores the intersection of pop culture and fine art, such as its retrospective of underground comic artist R. Crumb and the popular Beautiful Losers exhibit, which included painting, sculpture and photography along with graffiti and clothing design born out of punk and hip-hop subcultures (and now a documentary with the same name). The center has been pushing the boundaries of art and performance ever since opening its doors in 1993. As part of its commitment to community and cutting-edge work, the center holds a triennial exhibit of emerging Bay Area artists.

Admission: when all galleries are open, adults $7, seniors, students and teachers $5; when galleries are partially open, adults $5, seniors, students and teachers $3. Free first Tuesday of every month. Tuesday-Wednesday, Friday-Sunday noon-5 p.m., Thursday noon-8 p.m.

ZEUM

221 Fourth St., San Francisco, 415-820-3320; www.zeum.org

If you take your kid to Zeum, you may realize there isn't a place this cool for adults. Open since 1998 inside the Yerba Buena Garden complex, Zeum has several exhibits where children learn how to make animated cartoons, film music videos, craft musical soundtracks and produce their own movie, talk show or television broadcast. Zeum offers workshops with visiting artists who teach wacky things like how to make blinking electronic insects. Kids

125

can also learn about and ride the historic 1906 Charles Looff Carousel. Admission: adults $10, students and seniors $8, children 3-18, children under 3 free. September-May, Wednesday-Friday 1-5 p.m., Saturday-Sunday 11 a.m.-5 p.m.; June-August, Tuesday-Sunday 11 a.m.-5 p.m. Zeum Carousel: Daily 11 a.m.-6 p.m.

SPECIAL EVENTS
BAY TO BREAKERS
The Embarcadero to Ocean Beach, San Francisco, 415-359-2800;
www.ingbaytobreakers.com

Bay to Breakers isn't your ordinary footrace. Started in 1912 and getting wackier ever since, the 7.46-mile jaunt is a mobile party, a gazillion-legged bacchanalia, Halloween in short shorts. Although technically there's no alcohol or nudity allowed during the race, Bay to Breakers features plenty of both, along with costumes galore. Folks dressed up as presidential candidates, Britney Spears through the years and the entire cast of Dukes of Hazzard have hit the ground running, or at least stumbled along. There's also a special prize for the best "centipede" teams, a.k.a. 13-member squads that remain literally and thematically linked throughout the run. More than 100,000 people come out to watch this event and more than 65,000 participate. Third Sunday in May.

CASTRO STREET FAIR
Castro and Market streets, San Francisco, 415- 841-1824; www.castrostreetfair.org

Founded by Harvey Milk in 1974, this street festival in the Castro District— the heart of the city's gay community—has drawn crowds on the first Sunday in October for more than 30 years. While many come to eat, drink beer, bargain shop and generally carouse, most turn out to watch, or take part in, the nonstop dancing in the outdoor pavilions. First Sunday in October.

CHINESE NEW YEAR FESTIVAL & PARADE
Second and Market streets, San Francisco, 415-986-1370; www.chineseparade.com

The largest and most colorful of its kind held in the country, this weeklong festival's activities include the Golden Dragon Parade—beginning at Market and Second streets—lion dancing, a carnival and cultural exhibits. February.

NORTHERN CALIFORNIA CHERRY BLOSSOM FESTIVAL
San Francisco, 415-563-2313; www.nccbf.org

For over 40 years, this festival has been taking place in Japantown to showcase the culture of the Japanese. This festival features Japanese music, dancing, flower arranging, doll and sword exhibits, a bonsai show, martial arts, calligraphy, origami, a tea ceremony, children's village, arts and crafts, films, food bazaar and a parade. April.

SAN FRANCISCO BLUES FESTIVAL
Marina Boulevard and Laguna Street, Great Meadow, Fort Mason, San
Francisco,415-979-5588; www.sfblues.com

The granddaddy of the world's blues events, since 1973 this festival has

brought together headliners and regional acts for three days of Mississippi Delta, Chicago Electric, Memphis R&B and gospel. It has been called "Nirvana at the Golden Gate," with legendary names like B.B. King, John Lee Hooker, Etta James, Taj Mahal and Stevie Ray Vaughan performing. Bring your picnics and blankets, and get ready for some blues.
Late September.

SAN FRANCISCO INTERNATIONAL FILM FESTIVAL

Sundance Kabuki Cinemas (1881 Post St., Western Addition), Castro Theatre (429 Castro St., Castro), Pacific Film Archive Theater (2575 Bancroft Way, Berkeley), Landmark's Clay Theatre (2261 Fillmore St., Western Addition); www.sffs.org

Film is the world's medium, and no fête showcases that better than this festival, which runs for two weeks. Ever since its launch in 1957, the festival has exhibited fascinating fiction, documentaries and short movies from all over the globe. Since 2007, SFIFF has even had a home worthy of its illustrious status, as Robert Redford's Sundance Institute bought and retrofitted the Kabuki Theater, adding swanky lounges and a mezzanine where you can eat and drink while you watch.
Late April through early May.

STERN GROVE FESTIVAL

Sigmund Stern Grove, 19th Avenue and Sloat Boulevard, Sunset District; www.sterngrove.org

Directly in line with San Francisco's iconoclastic tradition, the Stern Grove Festival provides free summertime concerts—with a catch. Since 1932, the non-profit association has hosted its Sunday afternoon shows in a 33-acre eucalyptus grove that is both stunningly beautiful and prone to be as chilly as an ice floe. Factor in some difficult parking, and your Stern Grove experience can go from grand to god-awful in a hurry. But for music fans, the chance to witness titans of classical, Latin, soul, jazz and opera—from Os Mutantes to Allen Toussaint—in a lush outdoor setting makes the difficulties worth braving.
Mid-June through mid-August.

WHERE TO STAY

★★★ARGONAUT HOTEL

495 Jefferson St., San Francisco, 415-563-0800, 866-415-0704; www.argonauthotel.com

Everything's in ship-shape at the Wharf's newest boutique hotel. Housed in what was once a warehouse of the largest fruit and vegetable cannery in the world, this nautical-themed hotel features plank floors in the lobby, crisp navy and yellow fabrics and white-washed furnishings, as well as amazing panoramas of the waterfront, Alcatraz and even the sea lions that live on Pier 39. The generous amenities include flat-screen TVs, Sony Stereos and CD/DVD players, in-room spa services, and the Yoga channel on every TV with complimentary yoga accessories to use during your stay. Next door, the Blue Mermaid Chowder House & Bar delivers seafood to landlubbers.
265 rooms. Restaurant, bar. Fitness center. Pets accepted. $251-350

★★BEST WESTERN AMERICANIA HOTEL

121 Seventh St., San Francisco, 415-626-0200, 800-444-5816;
www.americaniahotelsf.com

Newly renovated, Americania Hotel is retro-styled with nods to America's pastimes and notable pop-culture. Rooms are simple with mod décor with black, white and red as the basic colors; and plenty of amenities, including a flat-screen TV and an iPod docking station. There's a jukebox in the lobby, an outdoor heated pool and Custom Burger and Lounge where you get a burger with your own customized toppings.

143 rooms. Fitness room. Pool. Pets accepted. $61-150

★★BEST WESTERN TUSCAN INN AT FISHERMAN'S WHARF

425 N. Point St., San Francisco, 415-561-1100, 800-648-4626; www.tuscaninn.com

This cheery hotel aims to deliver Italian style, with a space filled with bright colors and mixed patterns that delight the eye. Amenities are what you'd expect from Best Western—a mini-bar, free local calls—along with extra perks such as nightly happy hours and a pet-friendly policy. Café Pescatore serves competent Italian food with—you guessed it—a Tuscan influence.

221 rooms. Restaurant, bar. Complimentary breakfast. Pets accepted. $151-250

★★★CAMPTON PLACE

340 Stockton St., San Francisco, 415-781-5555, 800-235-4300;
www.camptonplace.com

Campton Place is a haven of serenity right on San Francisco's frenetic Union Square. The hotel is steps from Nob Hill's shops and restaurants, which makes the sophisticated vibe and thoughtful service at this boutique hotel all the more welcome. The rooms and suites have a modern, fresh look, with pear-wood paneling, unique photography and cushy but minimal furnishings. Most rooms have window seats with a view of the city—perfect for daydreaming or curling up with a book—and the hotel's rooftop fitness center boasts terrific skyline vistas. The onsite dining room, Campton Place Restaurant, serves great contemporary American fare.

110 rooms. Restaurant, bar. Fitness center. Pets accepted. $351 and up

★★★CLIFT HOTEL

495 Geary St., San Francisco, 415-775-4700, 800-697-1791; www.clifthotel.com

You don't have to be a fashionista to stay here, but it doesn't hurt. Philippe Starck's brilliantly eclectic design vision for this boutique hotel balances a Dalí-inspired lobby with bright, calming guest rooms tricked out with floor-to-ceiling mirrors and ivory-and-lavender color schemes. Located just two blocks off Union Square, it's near all the area's tourist draws without being dominated by the noise and crowds. A young clientele dines on Latin-Asian cuisine in the Asia de Cuba restaurant, but for a little history, grab a cocktail at the Redwood Room, a landmark lounge that has been restored to its Art Deco glory.

363 rooms. Restaurant, bar. Fitness center. Business center. Spa. Pets accepted. $251-350

★★★THE DONATELLO

501 Post St., San Francisco, 415-441-7100, 800-227-3184; www.thedonatellosf.com
This European-style hotel, named for the 15th-century Italian sculptor, has some of the largest guest rooms in the city (425 square feet), each with a king size bed, flat-screen television, Internet access, CD/stereo system, wet bar and a kitchenette equipped with a microwave, toaster and refrigerator. For such an expensive city, the Donatello is a good value. The hotel, one block from Union Square, also has a private rooftop garden. Live jazz bands perform five nights a week at Zingari Ristorante, the hotel's restaurant which serves up delicious Northern Italian cuisine.
94 rooms. Complimentary breakfast. Restaurant, bar. Business center. Fitness center. $151-250

★★EXECUTIVE HOTEL VINTAGE COURT

650 Bush St., San Francisco, 415-392-4666, 888-388-3032; www.executivehotels.net
If you can't make it to Napa during your trip, stay at this vino-inspired hotel for a little taste of wine country. Nightly wine tastings and a continental breakfast will fuel your adventures, while the décor's varying shades of green evoke visions of vineyards. It's just two blocks to Union Square and Chinatown, but once you spy the French offerings at the elegant (and excellent) Masa's Restaurant, you may want to stay put.
106 rooms. Restaurant, bar. Complimentary breakfast. $151-250

★★★THE FAIRMONT SAN FRANCISCO

950 Mason St., San Francisco, 415-772-5000, 800-257-7544; www.fairmont.com
Sitting at the peak of Nob Hill, near Fisherman's Wharf and the Financial District, this century-old lavish hotel aims to dazzle you from the moment you step into its palatial lobby. Its Old World ambience extends to the rooms, where marble baths and chaise lounges invite lazy lingering. Things are livelier, but not as swanky, at the Tonga Room, a tiki restaurant with decorative indoor rain showers. The Laurel Court offers a more refined atmosphere to take in fresh seafood dishes. Higher tower rooms have good views, but the view in the lobby isn't too shabby, either—it's recently been through a beautiful restoration that makes it one of the city's most opulent.
591 rooms. Restaurant, bar. Fitness center. spa. Pets accepted. $251-350

★THE FITZGERALD HOTEL

620 Post St., Nob Hill, 415-775-8100, 800-334-6835; www.fitzgeraldhotel.com
Low rates and a stellar location make this a frequent choice for budget-conscious travelers. The room décor ranges from masculine brocades to Old World antiques, and a working gated elevator adds to the charm. Rooms are on the small side, even by city standards, but the Hidden Vine wine bar provides a place to stretch out with a full-bodied cab.
42 rooms. $61-150

★★★★★FOUR SEASONS HOTEL SAN FRANCISCO

757 Market St., San Francisco, 415-633-3000, 800-819-5053; www.fourseasons.com
San Francisco does not experience four distinct seasons—it's pretty mild no matter when you visit. Likewise, the Four Seasons provides posh lodgings

all year long. The glassy exterior of the tower looks sleek and modern, but the décor inside is more traditional, with wood-paneled walls, plush rugs and gold-accented furniture lending a classic feel to the spacious rooms. (Request a corner room to see more of the city through floor-to-ceiling windows.) The restaurant, Seasons, focuses on surf-and-turf classics with a wine list that draws liberally from vineyards in nearby Sonoma and Napa counties. To burn off those calories, head to the 127,000-squarefoot Sports Club/LA that overlooks Market Street. It takes a comprehensive approach to fitness with state-of-the-art equipment and cutting-edge classes. The Spa at Sports Club/LA is a favorite among hotel guests and locals. Before visiting the nearby San Francisco Museum of Modern Art, art aficionados should download the podcast guide to the hotel's impressive collection, which includes works by Matisse and Klee.

277 rooms. Restaurant, bar. Business center. Fitness center. Pool. spa. Pets accepted. $351 and up

★★★GRAND HYATT SAN FRANCISCO

345 Stockton St., San Francisco, 415-398-1234, 800-233-1234;
www.grandsanfrancisco.hyatt.com

Popular with tourists and business travelers alike, this 36-story hotel boasts a fantastic Union Square location and floor-to-ceiling windows. Grandviews, a restaurant on the top floor, supplies sweeping vistas of Alcatraz and the Golden Gate Bridge, along with its French-accented American cuisine. A large 24-hour fitness center provides workout options, while the rooms themselves are spacious, with plush pillows, a down blanket and a pillow-top mattress. If you're here on business, this hotel has great business packages, which often include Internet access, a morning newspaper and a complimentary shirt press. Our advice: Request a room away from Stockton Street, as the doormen's cab whistles blare on late into the night.

685 rooms. Restaurant, bar. $61-150

★★HARBOR COURT HOTEL

165 Steuart St., San Francisco, 415-882-1300, 866-792-6283;
www.harborcourthotel.com

Tucked away from the melee of Market Street, but close enough to the action of downtown, this boutique hotel serves up beautiful views of the Bay Bridge. Standard rooms, decorated in warm tones and colorful stripes, aren't enormous, but they're well-designed to offer as much space as possible. Although there is no onsite fitness center, you can work it out at the next-door YMCA.

131 rooms. Restaurant, bar. Fitness center. $61-150

★★★HILTON SAN FRANCISCO FISHERMAN'S WHARF

2620 Jones St., San Francisco, 415-885-4700, 800-228-8408; www.hilton.com

Located at a busy intersection in Fisherman's Wharf, this Hilton is a short walk to North Beach, Ghirardelli Square and the Embarcadero, making it a convenient choice for leisure travelers. Spacious guest rooms are nicely maintained and complimentary water and robes, a safe and a varied selection of bath amenities are also provided. Vintner's Grill features California cuisine at both breakfast and dinner. The breakfast buffet is not to be missed, with 85 different selections. And for a cocktail and small plates, head to Vintner's Bar, the hotel's more casual dining option.

234 rooms. Restaurant, bar. $251-350

★★HOLIDAY INN GOLDEN GATEWAY HOTEL

1500 Van Ness Ave., San Francisco, 415-441-4000; www.goldengatewayhotel.com

Take the cable car to the end of the line, and you'll find this 26-story tower with comfortable guest rooms. It's popular among people who want to escape the noise of downtown, but because it's not far from the Tenderloin, know where you're going before you head out. Top floors offer gorgeous views of the Marin headlands; floating in the outdoor heated pool is a rare treat in pool-deprived San Francisco.

499 rooms. Restaurant, bar. Business center. Fitness center. Pool. Pets accepted. $151-250

★★HOLIDAY INN SAN FRANCISCO FISHERMAN'S WHARF

1300 Columbus Ave., Fisherman's Wharf, 415-771-9000; www.hifishermanswharf.com

The best part of this hotel? It's right where tourists want to be. That and the kid-friendly atmosphere make this a popular choice for families. Rooms are large by city standards, and the long hallways seem to stretch on forever. Denny's and the Bristol Bar and Grill both serve quick, convenient meals—but opt for the nearby Alioto's or Boudin for seafood and sourdough instead.

591 rooms. Restaurant, bar. Business center. Fitness center. Pool. Spa. Pets accepted. $151-250

★★★HOTEL ADAGIO

550 Geary St., San Francisco, 415-775 5000, 800-228-8830; www.thehoteladagio.com

After a 2003 facelift, the Adagio has become a stylish option for travelers seeking a bit of contemporary design. The hotel's style mixes a dash of Spanish Colonial (Moorish archways) with clean, contemporary touches (sleek couches and whimsical light fixtures). The hotel's restaurant, Cortez, draws a hip crowd seeking Mediterranean small plates. You'll appreciate the close-to-it-all location and soothing earth tones of the modern rooms, which feature plush beds and Egyptian linens. If you need to travel a little farther than nearby Union Square, the hotel offers complimentary car service each morning for business travelers.

171 rooms. Restaurant, bar. Business center. Fitness center. $151-250

★HOTEL BOHÈME

444 Columbus Ave., San Francisco, 415-433-9111; www.hotelboheme.com

Bohemian indeed, this tiny 15-room hotel is a wonderful mixed bag of Beat-era inspiration and nostalgia as cast-iron beds, yellowing newspaper clippings and antique furniture fill the space. Although the rooms are small, and the bathrooms may require some fancy footwork to fit two people at once, the accommodations are charming. Staying here is like stepping into a writer's nook—and in fact, if you luck into room 204, you'll rest where Allen Ginsberg composed some of his poetry long ago.

15 rooms. $151-250

★★HOTEL CARLTON

1075 Sutter St., San Francisco, 415-673-0242, 800-922-7586; www.hotelcarltonsf.com

In one of the greenest cities in the country, it only makes sense to stay at an eco-friendly hotel. This one is partially powered by solar panels, cleaned with less-toxic detergents and certified green by the city. The eclectic room décor blends Lucite lamps with Moroccan furniture, pulled together with a palette of persimmon, baby blue and teal. The onsite restaurant, Saha, dishes up vegetarian-friendly Yemeni cuisine in a spicy, sexy setting.

161 rooms. Restaurant. Business center. Pets accepted. $151-250

★★★HOTEL DRISCO

2901 Pacific Ave., San Francisco, 415-346-2880, 800-634-7277; www.hoteldrisco.com

Live like a local for the night at this century-old hotel. Tucked among multi-million dollar homes in the posh Pacific Heights neighborhood, this hostelry provides a glimpse into a lively residential area. Mahogany wood encases the front desk area, while traditionally decorated guest rooms feature overstuffed sofas, marble sinks in the bathrooms, crown molding and a creamy color palette. Amenities are top-notch: A gourmet buffet breakfast served daily, a lounge with tea and coffee, evening aperitif service, a bath-goods bar in your room and evening wine service make this a very gracious stay.

48 rooms. Complimentary breakfast. $151-250

★★HOTEL GRIFFON

155 Steuart St., San Francisco, 415-495-2100, 800-321-2201; www.hotelgriffon.com

Although the city is surrounded on three sides by water, few hotels provide the chance to stay near the waterfront. Not so at Hotel Griffon, located a stone's throw from the Bay Bridge. Decked out with exposed brick walls, Berber carpeting and quilted duvets, the recently remodeled rooms are comfortable and swanky. Although there isn't an onsite restaurant, some of the best dining in town can be found nearby.

62 rooms. Complimentary breakfast. Restaurant, bar. Business center. Fitness center. $151-250

★★★HOTEL KABUKI

1625 Post St., San Francisco, 415-922-3200, 800-533-4567; www.jdvhotels.com

Honoring its Japantown location, the Hotel Kabuki brings a little east to the Western lodging experience. The recently remodeled property features a clean, modern lobby, comfortable guestrooms and a nod to Japanese culture. You're greeted with a complimentary tea service in your room, similar to the traditional Japanese tradition. A complimentary one-day pass to the communal bath (a couple blocks away) will let you experience a popular Japanese tradition. In addition to those extras, rooms have flat-screen televisions, iPod docking stations, bathrobes, desks, ergonomic chairs and Asian tea kettles. Stop by the O Izakaya Lounge where you can sip sake and enjoy small plates of inventive Asian fare.

218 rooms. Restaurant, bar. Business center. Fitness center. Spa. Pets accepted. $151-250

★★★HOTEL MAJESTIC
1500 Sutter St., San Francisco, 415-441-1100, 800-869-8966;
www.thehotelmajestic.com

Escape tourist-clogged downtown at this beautiful turn-of-the-century building, which holds the honor of being the city's oldest continuously operating hotel. Decorated with green granite, silk brocades and Victorian furniture, its large rooms have a from-the-past charm; their panel drapery, antiques, and four-poster beds make for a romantic environment. Many rooms also have fireplaces. Try to snag a reservation at Café Majestic, which turns out superb dishes from one of the city's rising chefs, Louis Maldonado. If you're interested in the supernatural, request a room on the fourth floor—it's said to be haunted by a friendly ghost.
58 rooms. Restaurant, bar. Business center. $151-250

★★★HOTEL MONACO
601 Geary St., San Francisco, 415 292-0100, 866-622-5284; www.monaco-sf.com

This Theater District boutique hotel is all about whimsy, from the lobby tarot-card readings to the rent-a-goldfish service. There's even a Grace Slick suite filled with Jefferson Airplane memorabilia and Slick's own original paintings. But just because the hotel offers hippie-dippy perks doesn't mean it skimps on posh amenities. A roomy spa offers massages and pedicures, while the Grand Café brasserie turns out regional French cuisine in a former ballroom. Frette robes, canopy beds and fleur-de-lis textiles give a nod to the South-of-France inspiration, drawing guests who crave a little fun with their luxury experience.
201 rooms. Restaurant, bar. Business center. Fitness center. Spa. Pets accepted. $251-350

★★★HOTEL NIKKO
222 Mason St., San Francisco, 415-394-1111, 800-248-3308; www.hotelnikkosf.com

Say "konnichiwa" to the San Francisco outpost of this Asian hotel chain, which has a Japanese feel without being too literal about it. The décor is traditional—lots of beige-on-beige warm tones and a few bold splashes of red—and the views of Union Square are lovely. Although the hotel caters to conventioneers and business travelers, the amenities are better than what many hotels in its class have to offer: ANZU, an Asian fusion restaurant, attracts locals for its sushi, wild mushroom risotto and sake martinis, and the sky-lit indoor pool will please fitness fans.
533 rooms. Restaurant, bar. Business center. Fitness center. Pool. Spa. $251-350

★★★HOTEL PALOMAR
12 Fourth St., San Francisco, 415-348-1111, 866-373-4941; www.hotelpalomar-sf.com

Easily identifiable by its mint-green tiled exterior, the Palomar aims to draw an artsy crowd with its Escher-esque patterned floors and René Magritte suite, where guests sleep under a ceiling of blue sky and white clouds, surrounded by prints of this modern master's work. But there's nothing surreal about the attention to detail; staffers are known to leave notes offering their assistance and the bathrooms are generously stocked with L'Occitane products. Alligator-print carpeting and persimmon wood furniture give a decidedly international flair, and the Fifth Floor restaurant is heralded for its take on Southern French cooking. All in all, it's an ideal place to get in touch with your inner artiste.

195 rooms. Restaurant, bar. Business center. Fitness center. Pets accepted. $151-250

★★★HOTEL REX

562 Sutter St., San Francisco, 415-433-4434, 800-433-4434; www.thehotelrex.com

A bibliophile's dream, this upscale boutique hotel has the rich ambience of a literary salon of the 1920s and 1930s. The lobby has a traditional bar and lounge, where you'll find soft jazz music and the occasional literary event. Walls of books, leather chairs and original portraits make you feel like you're part of the intelligentsia, while the cozy but bright rooms feature cheerful yellow walls balanced by dark wood furniture. Downstairs, Café Andrée serves breakfast, a weekend brunch and dinner, and offers ethnic dishes and homemade pasta in a dining room that looks more like a library than a hotel eatery.

94 rooms. Restaurant, bar. Business center. $151-250

★★★HOTEL VITALE

8 Mission St., South Beach, 415-278-3700, 888-890-8688; www.hotelvitale.com

Opened in 2005, this minimalist hotel has an unbeatable location across from the Ferry Building. Its rooms are modern but warm, with soothing powder-blue accents and Fresh toiletries to add to the comfort. A series of patios makes it easy to soak up views of the Bay, while a spa and yoga studio (with complimentary classes) provide opportunities to chill out. Although they don't have a pool, they do hand out passes to the YMCA lap pool. The off-lobby restaurant, Americano, draws a crowd of professional singles, giving the Vitale the feel of a cool local hangout rather than an isolated hotel.

199 rooms. Restaurant, bar. Business center. Fitness center. Spa. Pets accepted. $351 and up

★★★THE HUNTINGTON HOTEL

1075 California St., San Francisco, 415-474-5400, 800-227-4683;
www.huntingtonhotel.com

Even on a foggy night, this historic hotel's rooftop sign lights up the top of Nob Hill. Built in 1922, it retains its old-fashioned character through rich velvets, silks and damasks in the lobby and guest rooms. The hotel was originally crafted as an apartment building, so you'll appreciate the larger-than-average layouts—as well as homey touches like complimentary tea or sherry service upon your arrival. The Nob Hill spa is larger and more luxurious than the average hotel spa, and the Big 4 restaurant serves rich American cuisine in a classic wood-paneled room. Guests have included the likes of Pablo Picasso and Lauren Bacall, so you know this stately mansion has a history of gracious service.

136 rooms. Restaurant, bar. Business center. Fitness center. Pool. Spa. $351 and up

★★★HYATT AT FISHERMAN'S WHARF

555 N. Point St., San Francisco, 415-563-1234, 800-233-1234;
www.fishermanswharf.hyatt.com

Just a two-minute walk from Pier 39, this low-rise building is popular due to its location. It's a few blocks from Ghirardelli Square and the Hyde Street cable car line, which chugs past the crooked part of Lombard Street. But this touristy hotel offers another standout quality: great design. A recent refurbishing has given the lobby a bright, sophisticated look that extends to the chocolate-and-white room décor. Rooms include fluffy white duvets, chaise lounges or armchairs and large working desks with flat-screen TVs above. An outdoor heated pool, a rarity in San Francisco, adds to the appeal of the 24-hour health club.

313 rooms. Restaurant, bar. Business center. Fitness center. Pool. $151-250

★★★HYATT REGENCY SAN FRANCISCO

5 Embarcadero Center, San Francisco, 415-788-1234, 800-233-1234; www.hyatt.com

A breathtaking, 17-story atrium is the centerpiece of this angular hotel, which sits across the street from the San Francisco Bay. After zooming up a few flights in a glass elevator, you'll be able to spread out in the understated, spacious rooms; perks like Portico bath products and granite bathrooms make your stay even more luxurious. Rooms offer vistas of the water or of the city; ask to be placed on a higher floor to escape some of the street noise below. The Eclipse Café offers standard salad-and-sandwich fare, but 13 Views lounge amps up the sophistication along with providing views of the Embarcadero.

802 rooms. Restaurant, bar. Business center. Fitness center. $251-350

★★★INN AT THE OPERA

333 Fulton St., San Francisco, 415-863-8400, 800-325-2708;
www.shellhospitality.com/hotels/inn_at_the_opera

Culture vultures will appreciate the classic European-style feel of this intimate and upscale boutique hotel. While some of the rooms are a bit crowded, all of them are polished and romantic; think dark woods, brocade duvets and white tile bathrooms. They also have queen-size beds, wet bars with refrigerators and armoires with televisions. A restaurant, Ovation at the Opera, features seafood and French classics, and its sofas invite post-dinner lingering. True to its name, the hotel is near the opera house and Civic Center, beautiful areas that can be dodgy at night, so ask the concierge for directions before heading out for the evening.

48 rooms. Restaurant, bar. Complimentary breakfast. Business center. $61-150

★★★THE INN AT UNION SQUARE

440 Post St., San Francisco, 415-397-3510, 800-288-4346; www.unionsquare.com

Centrally located and wonderfully cozy, this small inn on the northwest corner of Union Square offers traditional pleasures. Standard rooms are on the petite side, so if you aren't traveling light, consider upgrading to a Penthouse suite to enjoy an in-room fireplace and whirlpool tub. Either way, you'll revel in cozy red-and-gold rooms with classy touches such as damask duvets and Georgian-style chairs. A friendly staff aims to delight, taking care of little

pleasures, from leaving fresh flowers on the desk to including chocolates with nightly turndown service. Each floor has a small sitting area where guests can enjoy complimentary continental breakfast and morning newspaper, which is provided by the inn.
30 rooms. Complimentary breakfast. Business center. Fitness center. Pool. $151-250

★★★INTERCONTINENTAL MARK HOPKINS SAN FRANCISCO

1 Nob Hill, San Francisco, 415-392-3434, 800-662-4455; www.markhopkins.net
Cable cars clatter by this San Francisco icon, which resembles a French château, and inside, the scene is as classic and old-money as ever. Rooms are traditionally styled in warm tan and brown shades and sleigh beds feature California King mattresses for extra sleeping space. The light-filled Nob Hill restaurant has seasonally changing New American cuisine, but a visit is incomplete without a stop at Top of the Mark. The lounge's legendary vistas may provide the city's best place to catch a sunset, and the bar's 100 Martinis menu is absolutely classic.
380 rooms. Restaurant, bar. Business center. Fitness center. $251-350

★★★INTERCONTINENTAL SAN FRANCISCO

888 Howard St., San Francisco, 415-616-6622, 888-811-4273;
www.intercontinentalsanfrancisco.com
On the outside, this just-opened, 32-story hotel is a bold testament to steel and blue glass. Within its walls, the modern décor warms up to include floor-to-ceiling windows and iPod docking stations in each room. Plasma TVs, a spacious 24-hour fitness center and a full-service spa featuring Murad products offer plenty of ways to energize or recharge. Luce restaurant has well-done Italian fare in a beautiful, contemporary, high-ceilinged space off the lobby. The location, near the Moscone Center, is bound to draw convention-goers, but this spot offers just as much in the way of pleasure as it does for business.
550 rooms. Restaurant, bar. Business center. Fitness center. Pool. Spa. $251-350

★★★JW MARRIOTT HOTEL

500 Post St., Nob Hill, 415-771-8600; www.jwmarriottunionsquare.com
Formerly the Pan Pacific hotel, this location just completed a top-to-bottom refurbishing. The effort has paid off and made this a stylish upscale business hotel. The sizable rooms feel fresh and modern, and thoughtful amenities include a one-touch button that summons a butler for all of your needs, 42-inch flat-screen TVs, and an ergonomically-designed workdesk and Herman Miller Aeron chair. The restaurant, Level III, is brightly appointed in rich red and orange tones; head there to sample fancy takes on comfort food, such as macaroni and cheese with black truffle oil and Kobe beef sliders.
329 rooms. Restaurant, bar. Business center. Fitness center. Pets accepted. $251-350

★★★LE MÉRIDIEN

333 Battery St., Financial District, 415-296-2900; www.starwoodhotels.com

The cavernous Financial District isn't exactly the height of chic, but Le Méridien tries to add a dash of style to this big business neighborhood. The former Park Hyatt has received a continental facelift, including streamlined rooms with chic contemporary furniture and décor in shades of taupe, red and brown. (Many rooms have balconies that offer views of the city or the Bay, so make your requests accordingly.) The Park Grill features classic décor and serves delicious American cuisine; dine alfresco on the plant-filled terrace and take in some sun and views of the city.

360 rooms. Restaurant, bar. Fitness center. Business center. $251-350

★★★★MANDARIN ORIENTAL SAN FRANCISCO

222 Sansome St., San Francisco, 415-276-9600, 800-622-0404;
www.mandarinoriental.com

Located on the upper floors of one of the city's tallest buildings, this luxury hotel offers sky-high views of the city — from the Golden Gate Bridge to the Transamerica Pyramid to the Bay Bridge. (Binoculars are placed in every room.) Power lunches take place at the hotel restaurant, Silks, which incorporates California produce into Asian fusion cuisine; MO bar is more casual, offering great cocktails and small plates from the kitchen. The hotel's fitness center provides state-of-the-art facilities with treadmills with their own TV's and headsets. While the rooms can feel almost austere—the gold and red accents work hard to perk up the subdued, contemporary furnishings, beige carpet and walls—the staff's warmth more than makes up for it. Asian influenced hospitality extends from feng shui room design to complimentary jasmine tea service, making this Eastern-influenced location one of the most memorable stays in the West.

158 rooms. Restaurant, bar. Business center. Fitness center. Pets accepted. $351 and up

★★★MARRIOTT FISHERMAN'S WHARF

1250 Columbus Ave., San Francisco, 415-775-7555, 800-228-9290; www.marriott.com

Other hotels may exude more character, but what this mid-range spot lacks in dazzle, it makes up for with tidy rooms, dependable service and a tourist friendly location. Rooms are comfortable with down comforters, luxurious linens and feather pillows. Spada restaurant offers a chance to chow down on fresh-from-the-ocean seafood, but we recommend heading to one of the neighborhood's many eateries for a better taste of San Francisco. For some pampering, head to the hotel's spa, the Golden Green Spa which features a variety of treatments such as body scrubs, facials, massages and foot baths.

285 rooms. Restaurant, bar. Business center. Fitness center. Spa. Pets accepted. $151-250

★★★OMNI SAN FRANCISCO HOTEL

500 California St., San Francisco, 415-677-9494, 800-788-6664;
www.omnisanfrancisco.com

Built in 1926 and remodeled in 2000, the former Financial Center Building retains all of the richness of its past splendor. Sparkling chandeliers, polished brass and delicate ironwork dress up the lobby and the rooms are just as elegant. Though the furnishings are purely traditional, with colonial-style beds and armoires, and plenty of subdued fabrics, they've been updated with modern amenities such as Italian linens and iPod alarm clocks. There's even a children's suite with games, toys and kiddie-sized furniture. Don't be fooled by the casual name of Bob's Steak and Chop House—the atmosphere is upscale and the steaks are top-notch.

362 rooms. Restaurant, bar. Fitness center. Business center. Pets accepted. $151-250

★★★PALACE HOTEL
2 New Montgomery St., San Francisco, 415-512-1111, 888-627-7196; www.sfpalace.com

Designed to rival Europe's best hotels, this San Francisco landmark in the Financial District first opened in 1875. After a devastating fire, this grand hotel was rebuilt and restored to its Victorian grandeur, from crystal chandeliers to a sky-lit indoor pool. The rooms aren't the largest in town, but mahogany furniture and 14-foot-high ceilings make up for what they lack in space. Be sure to enjoy afternoon tea at the Garden Court restaurant, a historic landmark, which has a beautiful domed stained-glass ceiling; or for an upscale Japanese dinner, make a reservation at Kyo-ya, where ambiance is more modern, but service is equally refined.

553 rooms. Restaurant, bar. Business center. Fitness center. Pool. Spa. $251-350

★★★PARC 55 HOTEL
55 Cyril Magnin St., San Francisco, 415-392-8000, 800-595-0507; www.parc55hotel.com

Only a half block from Market Street, this enormous 32-story tower attracts families and tour groups who love the hotel's proximity to major shopping areas and public transportation. The rooms are decorated in dark woods and deep earth tones, and though standard rooms can be small, they're laid out well; and they have bay window views. Dining options abound, including inexpensive curries at Siam Thai and surf-and-turf choices at the Cityhouse Restaurant and local microbrews at Cityhouse Bar. While varied guest services are offered here, the focus is on meeting the needs of business travelers (like one-hour pressing service).

1,010 rooms. Restaurant, bar. Business center. Fitness center. $151-250

★★★THE PRESCOTT
545 Post St., San Francisco, 415-563-0303, 888-271-3632; www.prescotthotel.com

Need proof that the Prescott is dripping with class? Cinema legends such as Robert Redford and Elizabeth Taylor have stayed here. You'll be impressed by the Italian linens and cherry furniture that give this eco-friendly boutique hotel a European flair. Although not all of the rooms have benefited from a recent renovation effort, beds throughout are comfortable and the Italian linens are crisp. Complimentary Internet access if provided, along with in-room spa services and a Yoga channel on every television, along with yoga accessories. Room service is a delight; dishes are delivered from Wolfgang Puck's New American restaurant, Postrio.

164 rooms. Restaurant, bar. Fitness center. Pets accepted. $151-250

★★★★★THE RITZ-CARLTON, SAN FRANCISCO

600 Stockton St., San Francisco, 415-296-7465, 800-241-3333; www.ritzcarlton.com

Even the most blasé traveler would have to be impressed by this stately mansion atop Nob Hill. Built in 1909 as the headquarters of the Metropolitan Life Insurance Company, the hotel recently underwent a $12.5 million renovation that has restored its palatial polish, giving the opulent Old Europe design theme a little more gilt and sparkle. Club level suites feature options such as 1,000-thread-count sheets and a 1,200-square-foot private balcony. But if you can't stay in the Presidential Suite, don't worry—the smaller rooms are only slightly less lavish, featuring a palette of butter cream and taupe, with walnut and mahogany furniture that adds warmth. You'll have excellent options for food, too: The Dining Room is frequently booked due to its excellent Asian fusion cuisine, and on sunny days, catch the alfresco jazz brunch (complete with a caviar station) at The Terrace. Throughout the hotel, the legendary service is gracious whether you arrive by Jaguar or by hopping off the cable car outside.

336 rooms. Restaurant, bar. Business center. Fitness center. Spa. Pool. Pets accepted. $351 and up

★★★SAN FRANCISCO MARRIOTT UNION SQUARE

480 Sutter St., San Francisco, 415-398-8900, 800-912-0973; www.marriott.com

What was previously the Hotel 480, is now a $40 million renovated Marriott. This large, high-rise hotel provides a full range of guest services and amenities, including a large work desk, CD player, Internet access, and coffeemaker. Rooms are colorful with bright yellow walls and red accents colors in the bedding, which includes a pillow-top mattress, feather pillows and a down blanket. Bar480 and Lounge offer an eclectic spot for dinner and cocktails. Union Square is just one block away, and the Powell Street cable car conveniently stops at the hotel's corner.

400 rooms. Restaurant, bar. Fitness center. Business center. Pets accepted. $251-350

★★★SERRANO HOTEL

405 Taylor St., San Francisco, 415-885-2500, 866-289-6561; www.serranohotel.com

Although the Serrano nudges up next to the sketchy Tenderloin district, it nonetheless delivers a great stay. The Spanish-inspired lobby is the setting for complimentary wine each night (and tarot card reading), and the guest rooms, though some fall on the small side, are clean and filled with light. The Ponzu restaurant serves Asian fusion fare and is surprisingly quiet on the weekends; it's better for a quick drink than a full meal. In-room amenities include umbrellas, robes, pre-arrival turndown, high-speed Internet access and cordless phones. The hotel's attentive service—including a morning limousine ride to the Financial District—makes up for any dodgy dealings a few blocks away.

236 rooms. Restaurant, bar. Business center. Fitness center. Pets accepted. $151-250

★★★SHERATON FISHERMAN'S WHARF HOTEL

2500 Mason St., San Francisco, 415-362-5500, 800-325-3535;
www.sheratonatthewharf.com

Looking for a family-friendly, sunny spot? A $33 million renovation freshened the décor and amplified the amenities at this hotel. Pale woods, slanted windows and cheerful colors make for a vaguely nautical environment; a heated outdoor pool and close proximity to Pier 39 and Ghirardelli Square make this spot popular among visitors who eschew fusty, fussy hotels. Sol, a breakfast restaurant, will fuel you for a busy day; an outdoor seating area with fire pits will help you unwind at night. Other notables include a large fitness center and a manned business center.

531 rooms. Restaurant, bar. Business center. Fitness center. Pool. $151-250

★★★★★ST. REGIS HOTEL, SAN FRANCISCO

125 Third St., San Francisco, 415-284-4000; www.starwoodhotels.com/stregis

Since opening in 2005, this hotel has been refining the concept of luxury, retaining the detail-oriented service focus, but removing any hints of stodginess. It's located in a historic building in the vibrant SOMA neighborhood close to the San Francisco Museum of Modern Art. Rooms feature stylish contemporary décor in creams and dark woods, with standard features such as flat-screen TVs, crisp Pratesi linens and plush robes. Bathrooms are clad in marble and feature rainfall showerheads, deep bathtubs (that may inspire you to order from the hotel's Signature Bath menu), petite LCD televisions for catching up on the morning news and Remède amenities. The in-house Rèmede Spa is the pinnacle of extravagant pampering, while the ground-floor restaurant, Ame, offers Japanese-influenced fare conceived by Hiro Sone and Lissa Doumani of St. Helena's Terra Restaurant. When you go out, the staff will be happy to shuttle you to your destination—in a Bentley, of course.

260 rooms. Restaurant, bar. Business center. Fitness center. Pool. Spa. Pets accepted. $351 and up

★★★THE STANFORD COURT, A RENAISSANCE HOTEL

905 California St., San Francisco, 415-989-3500, 800-227-4736; www.marriott.com

This hotel stands at the former spot of railroad magnate Leland Stanford's mansion, but you're the one who will feel at home. The décor is 20th century through and through, from the lobby's Tiffany dome to Baccarat crystal chandeliers brought over from the Grand Hotel in Paris. With a $35 million revamp in 2008, all rooms are new with luxurious bedding, large baths, plush bathrobes and in deluxe view rooms, vistas of the bay and city. After spending a day downtown, enjoy a glass of wine at Aurea, the hotel's restaurant/bar, which serves seasonal Californian cuisine (or stop by during the day when it operates as a café).

367 rooms. Restaurant, bar. Business center. Fitness room. Pets accepted. $151-250

★★THE UNION STREET INN

2229 Union St., San Francisco, 415-346-0424; www.unionstreetinn.com

Set in an Edwardian home filled with antiques, this bed and breakfast features six distinctively decorated rooms. All are elegant without being stuffy, and some offer perks such as a private deck or Jacuzzi. Within the main house, you'll enjoy lighting a fireplace in the maroon-walled New Yorker room. A beautiful garden patio shows off roses and lavender, and when the fog rolls in, you can head to the sitting room and feast on the always-available cookies and tea.

6 rooms. Complimentary breakfast. $151-250

★★★W SAN FRANCISCO

181 Third St., San Francisco, 415-777-5300; www.whotels.com

Urban cool permeates this lively, stylish spot adjacent to the Museum of Modern Art in the SOMA district. The hotel restaurant, XYZ, is almost always filled with a fashionable crowd enjoying the latest in California cuisine, and Bliss spa adds a dash of fun to your pampering experience. The bright white rooms are hypermodern, with light wood contrasting with the pops of colorful textiles. Beds have their signature pillow-top beds and goose-down covers. The black-clad staff aims to please, from the chauffeur service to the "pillow menu" that lets you choose exactly how to lay your head.

404 rooms. Restaurant, bar. Business center. Fitness center. Pool. Spa. Pets accepted. $251-350

★★WASHINGTON SQUARE INN

1660 Stockton St., San Francisco, 415-981-4220; www.wsisf.com

Tucked among the Italian restaurants of North Beach and across the street from the Saints Peter and Paul church, is this well-maintained, 16-room bed and breakfast. Best for solo travelers and couples, it's a quiet, homey place whose simple but elegant rooms have a continental influence. Afternoon tea and evening wine and cheese encourage guests to mingle.

16 rooms. Complimentary breakfast. No children under 12. $151-250

★★★THE WESTIN SAN FRANCISCO MARKET STREET

50 Third St., San Francisco, 415-974-6400, 888-627-8561; www.westinsf.com

There's no big mystery behind this business-traveler mainstay, just a contemporary hotel with a great downtown location near Yerba Buena Gardens and San Francisco Museum of Modern Art. Sometimes that's all you need, especially when the rooms are spacious and comfortable. Westin's legendary beds live up to their reputation for plush softness, and floor-to-ceiling windows let tons of light stream in while providing a chance to watch the bustling downtown traffic. Although the earth toned décor isn't the most groundbreaking, it's quite the opposite at Ducca, where you can eat Venetian cuisine and kick back with a Peroni on the well-designed patio.

676 rooms. Restaurant, bar. Business center. Fitness center. Pets accepted. $251-350

★★★THE WESTIN ST. FRANCIS

335 Powell St., San Francisco, 415-397-7000, 866-500-0338; www.westinstfrancis.com

Opened in 1904, this historic hotel's design reflects its origins—an opulent, columned lobby with large crystal chandeliers -dangling from high ceilings, and the famous 10-foot-high Magneta Grandfather clock. Blocks from Union Square, this hotel offers two wings with distinctly different experiences, both of which were recently renovated. The Historic Building is classic and sophisticated, offering Empire-style rooms painted in creams and powder blues. The Tower Building's glass elevators show their 1970s origins, but the contemporary rooms are wholly modern. Chef Michael Mina's eponymous restaurant draws an epicurean crowd with its New American tasting menu, while Clock Bar offers smaller bites in a more casual environment. There's also a full-service spa and a large health club.

1,195 rooms. Restaurant, bar. Business center. Fitness center. Spa. Pets accepted. $151-250

WHERE TO EAT

★★A16
2355 Chestnut St., San Francisco, 415-771-2216; www.a16sf.com

A16's popular pizza is made in an oven that is the centerpiece of the kitchen. But, nearly everything's outstanding at this small, noisy, casual, always-hopping spot. From the chef's certification as a pizzaiolo focusing on the Neapolitan-style pizzas to the intense wines grown in the rich soil of Pompeii, this place aims to be rustic and authentic—and, judging by the crowd, is also very hip.

Italian. Lunch, dinner. Reservations recommended. Outdoor seating. Bar. $36-85

★ACE WASABI'S ROCK AND ROLL SUSHI
3339 Steiner St., San Francisco, 415-567-4903

An open kitchen and sushi bar separate the front and rear dining rooms at this hot spot located in the trendy Marina District. The front room's décor is modern, with the high chairs and counter of the bar in gray stone. The rear room features walls of exposed brick and red tabletops. Rock and roll music and friendly young servers make this an appealing place for young sushi lovers.

Japanese. Dinner. Bar. $16-35

★★★ACQUERELLO
1722 Sacramento St., San Francisco, 415-567-5432; www.acquerello.com

Other Italian restaurants may see their names in food blogs and their chefs on TV, but Acquerello doesn't need all that razzmatazz, and probably doesn't want it. The restaurant's stately, white-linen ambience and its graciously formal service make all that attention seem a little vulgar. Here, you'll get a top-notch tasting menu complete with an amuse bouche and cheese cart; à la carte offerings done up Italian-style from antipasti (such as warm pancetta-wrapped figs with balsamic vinegar) to primi (risotto with apples and braised pork belly) to secondi (seared sea bass with piquillo peppers, capers and olive relish). Don't miss the Italian wine pairings; if you really like something, you'll get a free refill. But be sure to save room for desserts, especially the housemade biscotti.

Italian. Dinner. Closed Sunday-Monday. Reservations recommended. $36-85

★★★AME

The St. Regis San Francisco, 689 Mission St., San Francisco, 415-284-4040;
www.amerestaurant.com

A wall of flame between bar and dining room. A huge red center table. A dramatic open kitchen. All of this means you're entering a high-style zone. The menu at this contemporary spot is equally flawless, with food so sophisticated it's hard to describe. Think New American, with a strong Japanese influence and touches of French and Italian. Chef Hiro Sone is in charge of dinner, which slinks elegantly from raw (pristinely cut sashimi, tartare or barely smoked fish) to cooked (anything from sake marinated cod to lamb two ways). His wife, Lissa Doumani, takes on pastry chef duties, showcasing perfect seasonal fruit in tarts, pastries and ice creams. Order from an edited version of the menu, paired with deliciously intricate cocktails, in the also-stylish bar.

Contemporary American. Dinner. Reservations recommended. Bar. $36-85

★★ANNABELLE'S BAR & BISTRO

68 Fourth St., San Francisco, 415-777-1200; www.annabelles.net

A block south of Market Street, this bistro's interior is divided into three rooms, with the mahogany bar at the entry and two dining rooms beyond. Décor reflects the early 20th century, with octagonal tile flooring, wood wainscoting and chairs, and several stained-glass accent windows. Originally opened in 1913, the restaurant serves up American cuisine.

American. Lunch, dinner, late-night. Reservations recommended. Bar. $16-35

★ANTICA TRATTORIA

2400 Polk St., San Francisco, 415-928-5797; www.anticasf.com

Creamy tomato bisque colored walls and rubbed wood floors provide a comfortable setting for a dinner of Italian comfort food at Antica Trattoria, a storefront restaurant located at the corner of Polk and Union streets in the Russian Hill district. A small wine bar is located at the rear of the dining room, and the kitchen is partially open.

Italian. Dinner. Closed Monday. Reservations recommended. $16-35

★★★ANZU

Hotel Nikko, 222 Mason St., San Francisco, 415-394-1100, 800-248-3308;
www.restaurantanzu.com

An elegant addition to the Hotel Nikko, Anzu draws locals and international travelers with its blend of Eastern and Western cuisine. The house specialties include prime cuts of beef, and there's a Tokyo-trained master chef steering the full-service sushi bar. The restaurant perches on a balcony overlooking the hotel's unusual lobby and it showcases works by local artists. Visitors can sample an array of sake cocktails in a lounge with bar seating. Enjoy a Sunday brunch with jazz musicians, great food and plenty of champagne.

International, Japanese. Breakfast, lunch, dinner, Sunday brunch. Reservations recommended. Bar. $36-85

★★★★AQUA

252 California St., San Francisco, 415-956-9662; www.aqua-sf.com

The go-to spot for business lunches and networking dinners, Aqua must mind its p's and q's lest a deal be lost over lackluster lobster. The Financial District restaurant goes the distance—service is famously elegant (some might even say showy) and the atmosphere is serene and contemporary. The menu emphasizes seafood and zeroes in on small portions featuring clean flavors accented by bold spices. Dungeness crab salad might be punctuated by a piquant curry-poppy-seed vinaigrette, while Kumamoto oysters pair with celery agnolotti and pomegranate. High-end classics like caviar service, truffles and foie gras dapple the menu. If you're still talking business after the main course, order some delicious wine or dessert to seal the deal.

French, Seafood. Lunch (Monday-Friday), dinner. Reservations recommended. Bar. $36-85

★★★AZIE

826 Folsom St., San Francisco, 415-538-0918; www.restaurantlulu.com

This renovated warehouse, a sister restaurant to nearby Lulu, serves its trademark French-Asian fusion fare in a dramatic, intimate interior—some booths have their own curtains. There's an eight-seat chef's counter that overlooks the busy exhibition kitchen where you can see the food being prepared. The food, served on unusual, colorful glass plates, ranges from an extensive selection of appetizers, including iron skillet spicy prawns and moules frites, to entrées like miso monkfish, slow roasted pork belly and tandoori steak. The bar is a great place to enjoy a cocktail before or after a meal.

French, Asian. Dinner. Reservations recommended. Bar. $36-85

★★★AZIZA

5800 Geary Blvd., San Francisco, 415-752-2222; www.aziza-sf.com

Aziza's swirling Moroccan patterns, graceful arches and rich jewel tones contrast with the foggy Richmond District's architecture. The food is equally dramatic: fresh, organic local ingredients with a deft, light Moroccan treatment. Basteeya, traditionally a pigeon pie, lightens up in a version pairing chicken and almonds with phyllo dough and confectioner's sugar. Fluffy couscous is topped with chicken, prawn, lambs or fresh veggies; exotically scented spices like cardamom and ras el hanout work their way in everywhere from spectacular produce-based cocktails to can't-miss desserts such as watermelon granita with rose parfait.

Moroccan. Dinner. Closed Tuesday. $16-35

★★★BACAR

448 Brannan St., San Francisco, 415-904-4100; www.bacarsf.com

Wine rules at Bacar. The first thing you see when you walk in is a wine wall stocked with bottles that span the restaurant's three floors. (The rest of the place is equally dramatic: Lots of arching windows and skylights balance the metal, rough wood and brick former-warehouse décor.) The unfussy seasonal dishes were designed to be extremely wine-friendly (not too spicy, with sweet and savory in balance), and served either à la carte or with snappy pairings. The downstairs lounge, Bacar Below, calls itself a wine salon but is also a cocktail and bar snacks hot spot. Bacar is often full of youngish groups celebrating. Uncork a bottle from the wine wall to jump-start the festivities. California menu. Dinner, late-night (Friday-Saturday). Closed Sunday. Reservations recommended. Bar. $36-85

★BAKER STREET BISTRO

2953 Baker St., San Francisco, 415-931-1475; www.bakerstbistro.com
Located in Cow Hollow, this tiny but popular neighborhood French bistro draws customers from all over the city. With only about 15 tables and basic furnishings and décor, the restaurant relies on its excellent "bang-for-the-buck" factor. The menu, which changes daily, is comprised of a handful of appetizers, entrées and a solid wine list. A collection of local artwork is available for sale.
French. Lunch (Tuesday-Friday), dinner, Saturday-Sunday brunch. Closed Monday. Reservations recommended. Outdoor seating. $16-35

★★BAR CRUDO

655 Divisadero St., San Francisco, 415-409-0679; www.barcrudo.com
This newly relocated restaurant features a larger space than its previous location on Bush Street (which had only eight tables), with high ceilings and a clean, contemporary feel. The menu still consists of cooked, chilled or raw fresh seafood. The Belgian-focused beer list is almost as impressive as the world-spanning whites on the wine list.
Seafood. Dinner. $16-35

★★BASIL

1175 Folsom St., San Francisco, 415-552-8999; www.basilthai.com
Located in a commercial part of SoMa, this small Thai restaurant is off the beaten path and serves authentic cuisine that changes seasonally. The menu is made up of curries, noodles and wok-prepared dishes. The narrow dining room has contemporary décor and furnishings with Asian touches: hardwood floors, bamboo plants, framed cartoon art, a small Asian fountain, and pale yellow walls.
Thai. Lunch (Monday-Friday), dinner. Bar. $16-35

★★BETELNUT PEJIU WU

2030 Union St., San Francisco, 415-929-8855; www.betelnutrestaurant.com
Food trends come and go, and in San Francisco, pan-Asian screams mid-'90s—but Betelnut is still proudly continent-skipping. The menu references India, Hawaii, Mongolia, Hunan, Shanghai, Szechwan, Korea, Taiwan, Indonesia, Japan, Thailand, Vietnam and even Sri Lanka. The food isn't completely authentic, but it's consistent and flavorful. Spicy Szechwan green beans, minced chicken with lettuce cups, and "little dragon" dumplings of pork and shrimp with ginger vinegar are especially tasty, and the small plates go nicely with strong tropical cocktails and beer (pejiu wu translates to "beer house," so you'll have to order the house specialty).
Pan-Asian. Lunch, dinner. Reservations recommended. Outdoor seating. Bar. $16-35

★★★BIG 4

The Huntington Hotel, 1075 California St., San Francisco, 415-771-1140; www.big4restaurant.com

Dark wood, deep-green booths, lead-glass mirrors and lots of greenery give Big 4 a clubby feel. The restaurant is named for the old-boys' club of 19th-century railroad magnates C.P. Huntington, Charles Crocker, Leland Stanford and Mark Hopkins. Today, a modern-day old-boys' crowd packs in for lunch and happy hour, boosting the members-only atmosphere. A glowing fireplace and live piano music make this wonderfully old-school dinner date spot. Even the menu is timeless: Filet mignon, petrale sole, wild game (sometimes caribou, sometimes alligator!) and crab cakes are all well executed with touches like truffles, beautiful produce and a superior wine list. American. Breakfast, lunch, dinner. Reservations recommended. Bar. $36-85

★BISCUITS AND BLUES

401 Mason St., San Francisco, 415-292-2583; www.biscuitsandblues.com

This lively blues club in downtown San Francisco serves food in its quarters below street level. Nightly live blues entertainment takes place in a dark, unadorned room. The music complements the Southern cuisine—gumbo, catfish, fried chicken, fried yams, and jambalaya. Sip a New Orleans iced tea or a Southern punch and let the music take you on a journey below the Mason-Dixon line.
Southern. Dinner. Closed Sunday-Monday. Reservations recommended. Bar. $16-35

★★BISTRO AIX

3340 Steiner St., San Francisco, 415-202-0100; www.bistroaix.com

Surrounded by slick wine bars and overpriced small-plates spots, Bistro Aix is unpretentious and comfortably well-worn—at least by the standards of the yuppie Marina District. The mostly French fare ranges from quite good to excellent, especially the very Gallic salads and bistro classics like steak frites. The reasonably priced wine list has some good bottles from Southern France.
American, French. Dinner. Closed Monday-Tuesday. Reservations recommended. Outdoor seating. Bar. $16-35

★★★BIX

56 Gold St., San Francisco, 415-433-6300; www.bixrestaurant.com

You don't come to Bix for the food. That's not to say the food at this Jackson Square restaurant is not good—it is, and sometimes it's even great. It's just that this supper club emphasizes the "club" part of its concept, and you may remember the high-ceilinged Art Deco décor, live jazz, speakeasy alley location, snazzily dressed crowd, tableside service and top-notch cocktails more than the eats. The downstairs bar is often hopping; upstairs tables are quieter. No matter where you sit, you should try a cocktail from the ever-changing menu, with each expertly mixed using organic ingredients (though the place has such a jazz club vibe that a classic martini goes down easy, too). Traditional dishes are your best bet: mini lamb burgers, steak tartare, truffled french fries. The warm chocolate brioche bread pudding, bananas foster and fig and almond brown butter cake will remind you that clubby Bix also has a "supper" portion as well.

American. Lunch (Friday), dinner. $36-85

★★BOCADILLOS
710 Montgomery St., San Francisco, 415-982-2622; www.bocasf.com

Suits line up in the morning for hard-boiled eggs and toast, Greek yogurt with honey or eggs with Catalan sausage; lunchers go for tiny (three-bite), flavorful sandwiches such as chorizo with walnuts and BLTs. In the evenings, the minuscule spot loosens its tie and morphs into a mellow tapas joint. Even with the warm woods and brick wall there's a lunch-counter feel, but the food is exceptional. After a glass of sherry and a few hearty tapas (think housemade chorizo or braised tripe "basquaise"), you'll realize the worth of this dream child of Piperade chef Gerald Hirigoyen.

Tapas. Breakfast (Monday-Friday), lunch (Monday-Friday), dinner. Closed Sunday. $16-35

★★★BOULEVARD
1 Mission St., San Francisco, 415-543-6084; www.boulevardrestaurant.com

Boulevard is the grande dame of San Francisco dining: still sexy, not quite avant-garde, but gracious. She certainly impresses upon first sight with her delicate, pre-1906 carthquake, belle époque building, with an open kitchen (sit at the counter to watch the cooks in action), swirling peacock mosaic, art nouveau light fixtures and spectacular Bay views. And she's still up for a party: Business lunchers, couples, tourists and locals mingle here, whether dressed to the nines or sporting San Francisco casual (jeans are fine). The French-kissed American food is satisfying though a bit inconsistent. Your best bet is to order an appetizer or two (such as the dayboat sea scallops with pork belly, butternut squash and roasted chestnuts, topped with a picked squash relish) and then go for one of the grilled meats (the roasted rack of lamb with garlic and thyme is simplistic perfection). The superb wine list proves that like Boulevard, things often get better with age.

Contemporary American. Lunch (Monday-Friday), dinner. $36-85

★★★CAFÉ MAJESTIC
1500 Sutter St., San Francisco, 415-441-1280; www.cafemajesticsf.com

Despite its recent renovation, one step into this café feels like going back 100 years in time. The café opened in 1902 as a fine-dining establishment serving continental favorites like broiled lobster, crab Louie and grilled lamb chops. Today, the menu offers an oven-roasted rack of lamb and Dungeness crab salad (no lobster sadly) and a century's experience in fine-dining. The walls of the Art Deco-influenced room are adorned with drawings by Henri Matisse. Next door, the walls of The Butterfly Bar are lined with—you guessed it—a framed collection of rare butterflies. Pop in for a Majestic Martini (Belvedere, Chambord, pineapple juice and champagne) and have a gander.

American. Breakfast, dinner (Tuesday-Saturday). Bar. $36-85

★★CAFÉ TIRAMISU
28 Belden Place, San Francisco, 415-421-7044; www.cafetiramisu.com

On pedestrian-only Belden Place in the Financial District, this café has a

Tuscany-like taupe façade and numerous outdoor European-style tables that are always filled in good weather. Whether you're eating in the main dining room, the cozy downstairs space, or on the attractive alley, the place is always bustling, pleasing customers with northern Italian pastas, meat dishes, and seafood options.

Italian. Lunch (Monday-Friday), dinner. Closed Sunday. Reservations recommended. Outdoor seating. $16-35

★★★★CAMPTON PLACE RESTAURANT

340 Stockton St., San Francisco, 415-955-5564, 866-332-1670; www.camptonplace.com

Campton Place likes to find new talent (just google "Laurent Manrique," "Bradley Ogden," "Daniel Humm" or "Todd Humphries"). These rising-star chefs tend to move on quickly, but not much changes within the sedate dining room. Oversized banquettes and gleaming silver define Campton as upscale, with menu and service to match. Adroit waitstaff present dishes, from amuse bouche to petits fours, with a flourish. The food zooms in on high-end, locally sourced ingredients (even the foie gras is labeled "artisan") with trendy touches like foams dabbed here and there. Semi-celeb pastry chef Boris Portnoy trained his team well before he departed. Desserts are surprising, well-balanced little gems: English cucumber soup with pistachio, mint and yogurt sorbet sounds bizarre but tastes divine. Hotel guests rave about breakfast (malted walnut waffles; tiger prawn frittata).

American, Mediterranean. Breakfast, lunch (Monday- Saturday), dinner, Sunday brunch. $36-85

★★CANTEEN

817 Sutter St., San Francisco, 415-928-8870; www.sfcanteen.com

You might be perplexed by Canteen. This tiny space with eclectic diner décor offers a brief menu and only a few seatings per night. But go just once and you'll understand: It may be cramped, but the food defies the surroundings. Chef Dennis Leary (not the actor) used to helm upscale Rubicon; here, he can't be bothered with trappings like space, décor and service. Leary's too busy reinventing flavor combinations on the daily-changing menu, including duck breast with a ragout of butter beans, pork and thyme. Brunch might include blueberry French toast topped with coffee. It's like a fine dining experience, without obsequious service, but certainly without any fuss. Tip: You have to request dessert up front when you order dinner (another one of Leary's quirks), but it's worth it, especially for the wonderfully fragrant vanilla soufflé.

American. Lunch (Wednesday-Friday), dinner (Tuesday-Saturday; prix fixe dinner Tuesday), Saturday-Sunday brunch. Closed Monday. $36-85

★★★CARNELIAN ROOM

555 California St., San Francisco, 415-433-7500; www.carnelianroom.com

No matter what they serve here (and it happens to be contemporary American fare and expensive cocktails), it would be secondary to the view of the bay, the bridges and the city. Located on the 52nd floor of downtown's Bank of America building amid a lot of wood, antiques and old-world artwork, the Carnelian Room draws crowds for its compelling vistas. Entrées include duck breast with soft polenta, rainbow chard, baby turnips and sour bing cherry reduction, and braised beef short rib with horseradish, corn potato, roasted cherry tomatoes and Maui onion salad.

American. Dinner. Reservations recommended. Bar. $36-85

★★★CHAYA BRASSERIE

132 the Embarcadero, San Francisco, 415-777-8688; www.thechaya.com

Chaya offers an interesting twist on two very popular cuisines—French and Japanese. Menu options include sliced roasted venison with black pepper-corn sauce and purple potato purée and roasted rack of lamb with vegetable pot-au-feu and black olive tapenade. A combination of industrial and elegant décor make for sleek, sophisticated dining rooms. Orange steel beams resembling the Golden Gate Bridge and massive rectangular chandeliers add to the setting. Located on the Embarcadero, the restaurant features floor-to-ceiling windows and outdoor tables that provide spectacular views of the bay.

Japanese, French. Lunch (Monday-Friday), dinner. Reservations recommended. Outdoor seating. Bar. $36-85

★★CHOW

215 Church St., San Francisco, 415-552-2469; www.chowfoodbar.com

Serving casual, reasonably priced California fare on the edge of the Castro District, Chow swarms with impatient diners eager to sample the kitchen's dishes made with fresh, seasonal ingredients. A long bar/counter at the front of the restaurant adds to the hustle and bustle, as does the click-clack on wood floors and tables. A shady rear patio extends the seating options in fair weather.

American. Breakfast, lunch, dinner, Saturday-Sunday brunch. Children's menu. Outdoor seating. $16-35

★★COCO500

500 Brannan St., San Francisco, 415-543-2222; www.coco500.com

The fried green beans chef-owner Loretta Keller perfected when this spot was a French bistro called Bizou are still on the menu, and they pair dazzlingly with the drinks now that the space has been reimagined as a moody after-work hangout. Some might remember the quieter bistro with nostalgia, but times (and neighborhoods) change. Keller has the trendy-cocktail thing down with small-batch spirits, organic drink ingredients and a lovely teak bar. The American food skews French (duck liver terrine, salt-cod brandade), but the local produce is called "California dirt" on the menu. The well-crafted nonalcoholic "sober cocktails" (including a "no-jito") are great options for lunch, when the place is less noisy.

American, Mediterranean. Lunch (Monday-Friday), dinner. Closed Sunday. Reservations recommended. $36-85

★★★COI

373 Broadway, San Francisco, 415-393-9000; www.coirestaurant.com

Walking from the strip-club-heavy street into Coi's serene, earth-toned, windowless dining room is a tumble down an expensive rabbit hole. You know you're far from home when the waiter presents a tiny concoction of grapefruit, ginger, tarragon and black pepper, neighbored by a dot of essential

oils of the four ingredients, telling you to inhale before taking a bite: The aromas make the flavors explode. The journey continues through 11 tiny, intricate and surprising courses—one could be a griddled porcini mushroom with coconut tapioca, another might be a slow-cooked egg with morels and green garlic. The lounge serves tasty, but less interesting, à la carte dishes like udon noodles and suckling pig terrine. Nearly everything is housemade (butter, bread, some of the cheese) and locally-sourced (the left side of the menu serves as a bibliography to nearby farms, ranches and foragers). When not guiding you through the very good wine list, the sommelier brings out plates and advises on the menu along with the rest of the staff.
Modern California men. Dinner. Closed Sunday-Monday. $$$$

★DAVID'S
474 Geary St., San Francisco, 415-276-5950; www.davidsdelicatessen.com
A longtime San Francisco institution just a few blocks from Union Square, this Jewish deli has been in its current location, and under the same ownership, for more than 50 years. Counter seating and unadorned tables also haven't changed much. The restaurant offers New York-style Jewish deli fare like knishes, kugel, and piled-high sandwiches on rye.
Deli. Breakfast, lunch, dinner. $16-35

★★DELFINA
3621 18th St., San Francisco, 415-552-4055; www.delfinasf.com
Spilling out onto the sidewalks of the Mission with its hipster servers, loud music, slick beams-and-mirrors décor and trendy Neapolitan pizzas, Delfina defines San Francisco Cal-Italian. And it seems the city can't get enough: Ten years after it ushered in a huge trend with its organic and house-made ingredients (pasta, sausage, gelato), Delfina still requires reservations well in advance. Maybe it's Craig Stoll's 2008 James Beard Award win, or maybe it's the primo location. Most likely, it's the food.
American, Italian. Dinner. Outdoor Dining. $36-85

★★★★★THE DINING ROOM
The Ritz Carlton, 600 Stockton St., San Francisco, 415-296-7465;
www.ritzcarltondiningroom.com
Dinner at the Ritz is a formal occasion, suitable for deal brokering, marriage proposals and all matters that require impressive surroundings. The city's only Five Star restaurant is known for service with a quiet flourish amid lavish trimmings like shining silver carts carrying champagne, desserts or cheese. Every dish created by chef Ron Siegel is a shining, unique little jewel. He's known for haute French cuisine with Japanese touches—most evident in pairing subtle flavors like shiso and yuzu, and his delicate way with seafood. In the beautifully crafted nine-course tasting menu, a different meal is served to every other person at the table. An innovative recent menu played with the concept of "salt and pepper," using flavored salts (vanilla, ginger) and peppers (alepepo, Szechuan pepper) to set off abalone, foie gras and sorbet, among other ingredients. Spring for the wine pairing; the 12,000-bottle cellar is nothing short of astonishing.
French, Japanese. Dinner. Closed Sunday-Monday. Reservations recommended. Bar. $86 and up

★★★E & O TRADING CO.

314 Sutter St., San Francisco, 415-693-0303; www.eotrading.com

On the edge of the Financial District, located next to the large Stockton-Sutter parking garage, this sleek fusion restaurant is decorated with lanterns and specializes in Southeast Asian cuisine. The menu features traditional street foods found sold by street vendors in Asia including dishes like Indonesian corn fritters, Vietnamese shaking beef and garlic prawn satay. The bar provides microbrew beer in addition to bottled beers from India, Vietnam and Indonesia and an extensive list of wine and cocktails. Happy Hour features specially priced cocktails and small plates during the week.

Asian. Lunch (Monday-Saturday), dinner. Reservations recommended. Bar. $16-35

★★EMPRESS OF CHINA

838 Grant Ave., San Francisco, 415-434-1345; www.empressofchinasf.com

Presiding over Grant Avenue in Chinatown for almost 40 years, this landmark has played host to a parade of politicians and celebrities. The restaurant, on the sixth floor of the China Trade Center, treats visitors to 180 degree views of the city that include Coit Tower and the Bay Bridge. Alas, the ambience surpasses the food.

Chinese. Lunch, dinner. Bar. $36-85

★★EOS

901 Cole St., San Francisco, 415-566-3063; www.eossf.com

This popular Asian/fusion restaurant is located in Cole Valley. The facade is green with large windows, and the interior features a modern decor with cement flooring, black granite tables, and dark wood chairs. Track and pendant lighting highlight the tables and artwork. The best seats in the house are at the open kitchen counter, where diners can watch executive chef Daniel Guerrini and staff in action.

International, Asian. Dinner. Bar. $16-35

★★★FARALLON

450 Post St., San Francisco, 415-956-6969; www.farallonrestaurant.com

At this downtown restaurant, an over-the-top, under-the-sea theme dominates the atmosphere and the menu. Pat Kuleto designed the unique space, with its porthole windows, nautical scenes, mosaic mural ceiling, shell-patterned chairs and jellyfish chandeliers. Chef Mark Franz's fare changes daily but could include options like house-made caviar, pan-roasted king salmon, Maryland striped bass and oysters on the half shell. Grilled fillet of beef and a few other non-seafood items are also available. The tasty dessert menu features artisan cheeses including one from the Cowgirl Creamery, strawberry rhubarb pie, whole wheat carrot cake and chocolate blackout cream cake.

Seafood. Dinner. Reservations recommended. Bar. $36-85

★FATTOUSH

1361 Church St., San Francisco, 415-641-0678; www.fattoush.com

This Palestinian-owned neighborhood-style restaurant in a 1903 building cooks up Middle Eastern fare in a Noe Valley locale. Dine on dishes such as sabanech (lamb shank with spinach and black-eyed beans) and mashwi

(skewers of prawns and halibut) at the colorful wood tables, which are enhanced by cushions and other Arabic touches. The ivy-covered patio is open when the weather permits.
Middle Eastern. Lunch (Wednesday-Friday), dinner, Saturday-Sunday brunch. Outdoor seating. $16-35

★★★FIFTH FLOOR
Hotel Palomar, 12 Fourth St., San Francisco, 415-348-1555; www.fifthfloorrestaurant.com
Now under the direction of chef Jennie Lorenzo, this Fifth Floor's spare, chic, recently redesigned dining room is a comfortable space to sample creative, seasonal new American cuisine. Dig into dishes such as stuffed quail with asparagus and pea succotash, or roasted lamb sirloin with green beans and black olive tapenade. Master Sommelier Emily Wines—yep, that's really her name—knows her stuff, and has worked out a tasting menu with Lorenzo that pairs the hearty, satisfying menu with anything from sparkling to handcrafted beers. It's a sure bet that any high-end restaurant renovation these days will include a casual lounge for bar-food nibblers and downturn diners. Fifth Floor doesn't disappoint, with croquettes and cocktails, beer and burgers, and a nice selection of wines by the glass.
French. Dinner. Closed Sunday. Reservations recommended. Bar. $36-85

★★FIGARO RISTORANTE
414 Columbus Ave., San Francisco, 415-398-1300; www.figaroristorante.com
Feel as if you stepped into a ristorante in Italy when dining at Figaro, located on the main artery in North Beach. An elaborate ceiling mural, a small espresso bar and Italian music enhance the scene. A traditional Italian menu is constant throughout the year. The self-proclaimed "house of gnocchi" also whips up a tasty tiramisu.
Italian. Lunch, dinner..Reservations recommended. Outdoor seating. Children's menu. Bar. $16-35

★FIREFLY RESTAURANT
4288 24th St., San Francisco, 415-821-7652; www.fireflyrestaurant.com
Low amber lights and mismatched décor screams flash-in-the-pan quirky neighborhood spot, but Firefly has been going strong since 1993 thanks to its dependable food. The seasonal, expertly cooked California fare is worth seeking out, even if you're nowhere near this sleepy corner of Noe Valley.
American. Dinner. $16-35

★★★FLEUR DE LYS
777 Sutter St., San Francisco, 415-673-7779; www.fleurdelyssf.com
The tented ceiling in the main dining room of this upscale eatery provides a little drama, setting off the posh flowers and gleaming tableware to deliver a grand first impression. The food arrives in small, appealing portions, with witty nods to hearty French tradition: Alsatian Choucroute (sauerkraut) is trioed as soup, in strudel, and in fondant with caviar; boneless quail with roasted parsnips, leeks and foie gras. The wine list is thoughtful, offering pairing options with à la carte meals and with the omnivore or vegetarian tasting menus. Service, a Fleur de Lys hallmark,

is classic and professional, and the bar makes a cozy stop for pre- or post-dinner drinks.

French. Dinner. Closed Sunday-Monday. Reservations recommended. Bar. $86 and up

★★FOREIGN CINEMA
2534 Mission St., San Francisco, 415-648-7600; www.foreigncinema.com
The walk down the long hall to Foreign Cinema's impressive indoor-outdoor space leads you far away from the Mission's hustle and bustle. In the covered, heated patio, the restaurant screens moody foreign movies (anything from Fellini classics to *The Diving Bell and the Butterfly*) against a concrete wall. Inside, a huge fireplace makes the dining room as cozy as 20-foot ceilings and salvage-chic décor gets. Focus instead on the consistently rewarding food, by Zuni Café vets (and spouses) Gayle Pirie and John Clark. Try fried eggs deglazed with balsamic vinegar for brunch, or beef carpaccio so thoroughly spattered with horseradish sauce, fried herbs, capers and waffle chips that it appears to move on the plate (and that's a good thing). Wine and cocktails are both solid, and there are even kids' and between-meals menus. .
French, Mediterranean. Dinner, Saturday-Sunday brunch. $16-35

★★FRINGALE
570 Fourth St., San Francisco, 415-543-0573; www.fringalesf.com
When Gerald Hirigoyen and J.B. Lorda opened Fringale in 1991, its Basque-accented French bistro fare was new and terribly exciting. Flash forward to today: Hirigoyen is gone, Lorda is retired, Basque food is everywhere (partly due to Hirigoyen's Piperade and Bocadillos) and the towering, ring-molded presentation recalls the '90s. It's surprising, then, that Fringale is still so tasty. Substainal French classics like the salad of frisée, bacon and poached egg and duck confit with little Puy lentils are still a treat. Bonus: The whole menu is available for takeout.
French. Lunch (Tuesday-Friday), dinner. $36-85

★★GLOBE
290 Pacific Ave., San Francisco, 415-391-4132; www.globerestaurant.com
An energetic Financial District destination serving American-Italian fare, Globe stays open late, thus earning it a reputation as a favorite stop for chefs after they close their own restaurants. Two skylights add a bright, sunny glow to the restaurant's industrial décor: a zinc-topped bar and counter and exposed-brick walls with frequently changing artwork.
American, Italian. Lunch, dinner, late-night.. Outdoor seating. Bar $16-35

★★★GRAND CAFE
Hotel Monaco, 501 Geary St., San Francisco, 415-292-0101; www.grandcafe-sf.com
Grand in both scale and style, this Parisian brasserie in the Theater District's Hotel Monaco indulges frequent patrons' love of all things theatrical with its high ceilings, ornate moldings, and tall bronze sculptures. The seasonal French bistro menu may include fresh oysters, oven-roasted half chicken and bouillabaisse. They also have a caviar menu and a large weekend brunch menu. Sit in the main dining hall or receive equivalent choice and service in the spacious bar area, which is open late so you can have some cocktails

after a performance.
American, French. Breakfast (Monday-Friday), lunch (Monday-Friday), dinner, late-night, Saturday-Sunday brunch. Reservations recommended. Children's menu. Bar. $36-85

★★GREENS

Fort Mason, Building A, San Francisco, 415-771-6222; www.greensrestaurant.com
Greens' prime location in historic Fort Mason has glorious Bay views—the former waterfront military base is a cool combination of piers, parks and little museums. Annie Somerville has dished out upscale vegetarian fare since 1979 and matches it to local wines, specialty teas and organic coffees. Some dishes are available vegan; you can also buy many of them from the takeout counter and make use of the prime location.
Vegetarian. Lunch (Tuesday-Saturday), dinner, Sunday brunch. $36-85

★★★HARRIS'

2100 Van Ness Ave., San Francisco, 415-673-1888; www.harrisrestaurant.com
If it weren't for the cityscape and bucolic California murals on the wall, you might not even remember Harris' is in San Francisco. In Pacific Heights, you'll find this steakhouse with the feel of a men's club. The huge leather banquettes, traditional, dry martinis and classic dishes like steak Diane, Kobe rib eye and prime rib (accompanied by sides like béarnaise sauce, baked potatoes and creamed spinach) make for tried-and-true steakhouse success, no matter where you are. The proudly touted "corn-fed Midwestern beef" is hardly California cuisine, but other local touches include a wine list that's enormous, California-heavy and very, very good.
American. Dinner. $36-85

★★HELMAND PALACE

2424 Van Ness Ave., San Francisco, 415-362-0641
Try Helmand Palace's most famous entrée, kaddo bourani—candied pumpkin with ground beef sauce and garlic yogurt. It may sound odd, but it's a delicious sweet-savory balance. Order it with the mantwo—beef-filled pasta, misrepresented on the menu as "pastry," with addictive split pea sauce. Everything's interesting at this quiet, low-lit Afghani spot, including the many vegetarian options. Whatever you order will be preceded by pillowy, warm flatbread and a trio of cilantro, pepper and yogurt sauces.
Afghani. Dinner. $16-35

★★HOG ISLAND OYSTER COMPANY

Ferry Building Marketplace (Market Street and the Embarcadero), San Francisco, 415-391-7117; www.hogislandoysters.com
The few tables at Hog Island Oyster Company are always crowded on nice days (especially during Monday and Thursday happy hours, when the oysters are $1 and pints are $3.50). They're less packed and more fun in the fog, when the Bay view is so very San Francisco and you can try a grilled cheese with three melted cheeses from nearby Cowgirl Creamery paired with a light, smoky Sweetwater oyster stew. This restaurant serves the fruits of the renowned Hog Island oyster farm in Tomales Bay to the north. The oysters are treasured by local and not-so-local chefs, and are definitely worth the

perpetually long wait in the Ferry Building halls.

Seafood. Lunch, dinner (closes at 6 p.m. Saturday- Sunday); happy hour (Monday & Thursday 5-7 p.m.) $36-85

★★IDEALE RESTAURANT

1315 Grant Ave., North Beach, 415-391-4129; www.idealerestaurant.com

It may not be the city's best Italian, but Ideale Restaurant is hands down the best Italian in North Beach. Here, the welcome is as warm as the brightly painted walls and as pleasing as the mostly Roman food and moderate prices. Standouts include raw zucchini with truffle oil and shaved Parmigiano-Reggiano and the thin-crust pizza is crispier than the very hip Naples-style versions elsewhere, but it's authentic to Rome.

Italian. Dinner. Closed Monday. $16-35

★★★INCANTO

1550 Church St., San Francisco, 415-641-4500; www.incanto.biz

Chef-owner Chris Cosentino is known for his love of offal, or those "nasty bits" of meat like kidneys, brains and trotters. If that isn't immediately appealing, consider that Cosentino has competed on Iron Chef America and The Next Iron Chef on the strength of that love. But if offal sounds awful, there are a lot of other delicacies on Incanto's menu, particularly handmade pasta and house-cured pork salami. The rustic Italian stone arches throughout the dining room make for an ideal setting, and the nearly all-Italian wine list contains an impressive number of flights, half liters, and wines by the glass, so you can taste for yourself what best pairs with beef tongue ravioli.

Italian. Dinner. Closed Tuesday. Reservations recommended. Bar. $36-85

★★JAI YUN

680 Clay St., San Francisco, 415-981-7438; www.menuscan.com/jaiyun

This place does authentic Chinese in Chinatown—we're talking a chef (albeit a local-celebrity one) who doesn't speak English, doesn't serve from a menu, and uses ingredients like pork knuckle and chicken knees. Jai Yun is an adventure, and a worthwhile one: Every dish is impeccably prepared, with contrast in texture as important as the flavor. When you make your reservation, you'll be asked how much you want to spend, and you'll be treated to some 10 courses depending on the night and party size.

Chinese. Dinner. Closed Thursday. $36-85

★★★JARDINIÈRE

300 Grove St., San Francisco, 415-861-5555; www.jardiniere.com

The food at this extravagantly designed, pre-theater powerhouse by Traci Des Jardins (Food Network fans may remember her from *Iron Chef* and *The Next Iron Chef*) and Paul Kuleto skews California cuisine with American, Asian and French influences. All of it is nicely portioned and elegantly presented, with indulgent touches like foie gras and caviar. Couples looking to get cozy will appreciate the two-tiered, exposed-brick dining room with swervy metal balcony railings and a glowing fiber optic Lucite dome. Casual diners veer to the front of the space, where the J Lounge offers everything from small plates to full caviar service offered alongside cocktails crafted from high-end spirits such as Neisson Rhum Agricole and St. George absinthe.

American, French. Dinner. Reservations recommended. Bar. $36-85

★★KISS SEAFOOD
1700 Laguna St., Western Addition, 415-474-2866

With just three tables and a bar, dining at Kiss feels more like you're visiting someone's home. Just as you would at a dinner party, let your host make the choices, with one of two omakase (chef's choice) meals. One offering is $42 and the other is $60, and you'll get five or six bang-up plates for your buck from chef Naka San. The sushi at this Japantown joint is consistently pristine, but the poetic soups made of cherry blossoms or delicate clams swimming in miso go way beyond dinner-party fare.

Japanese. Dinner. Closed Monday, first Sunday of the month. $36-85

★★★KOKKARI ESTIATORIO
200 Jackson St., San Francisco, 415-981-0983; www.kokkari.com

This huge, two-story taverna with an open rotisserie, wood-burning fireplaces and rough-hewn wood is equally popular with groups and couples. The food goes well beyond the Greek-American trinity of gyros, spanakotiropita and moussaka (though you can order delicious versions of the last two). Even better are crispy, batter-fried smelts; whole grilled fish; tomato oven-baked beans; and the Kokkari Salad with arugula, cherry tomatoes and myzithra cheese. The kitchen's not afraid to keep it simple: The two best desserts are fresh fruit with mint and thick yogurt drizzled with honey and studded with walnuts. The wine list includes many interesting Greek bottles, and classic cocktails go down easy.

Greek. Lunch (Monday-Friday), dinner (Monday-Saturday). Closed Sunday. $36-85

★★★KYO-YA
Palace Hotel 2 New Montgomery St., San Francisco, 415-546-5090; www.kyo-ya-restaurant.com

Kyo-Ya is one of the Bay area's best Kaiseki restaurants. An elaborate cuisine originating with tea ceremonies in 16th-century Kyoto, kaisekis are known for dainty presentation and delicate flavors delivered over many courses, moving from appetizers, soup, glowing sashimi and variously prepared savories to ages-old ochazuke (green tea over rice). If you can't commit to the time involved in such a lengthy meal, you can also order many of these dishes à la carte, or try master sushi chef Akifusa Tonai's beautiful sushi and sashimi. The hushed, minimalist décor is appealing; at lunch (when you can order a delicious bento box), you'll likely sit alongside businessmen on expense accounts.

Japanese. Lunch, dinner (Monday-Friday). Closed Saturday-Sunday. $36-85

★★★★LA FOLIE
2316 Polk St., San Francisco, 415-776-5577; www.lafolie.com

La folie means "madness," and you shouldn't visit unless you're ready to lose your head a little. The luxe French menu, gigantic portions, heady wine list and lushly draperied décor will leave you giddy, if only from the spillover of excitement from the newly engaged couple at the next table. The richest dishes are best (standouts include a terrine of pigs' feet, lobster and sweetbreads; butter-poached lobster; cheese soufflé; and lots of black truffle). The vegetarian tasting menu is consistently flavorful, while desserts (preceded by a sparkling selection of complimentary petit fours and confections) lean to silky creations made out of chocolate. Service is some of the most affable and attentive in the city, down to congratulatory chocolates for the recently betrothed lovebirds.

French. Dinner. Closed Sunday. Reservations recommended. Bar. $86 and up

★LA TAQUERIA
2889 Mission St., San Francisco, 415-285-7117
You can easily find cheaper, bigger meals elsewhere, but here, what a burrito lacks in size it makes up for in flavor and quality. Juicy, salty carnitas (pork confit) or carne asada (steak) share tortilla space with well-seasoned pinto beans and hot-as-Hades salsa—that's it. You're allowed to add jack cheese or chunky fresh avocado, if you wish, but diehards will argue that that's not a real burrito. The breezy tiled patio is the perfect place to cool down with a watermelon aqua fresca or a Mexican beer.

Mexican. Lunch, dinner. $15 and under.

★★LAÏOLA
2031 Chestnut St., San Francisco, 415-346-5641; www.laiola.com
Vibrant and a touch chaotic, with a young crowd overflowing to sidewalk tables, Laïola could be a trendy tapas tavern in Barcelona. The Iberian wine (or sangria, house-made citrus limoncellos or cocktails) flows freely. But this isn't just a party spot: Seasonal tapas are crafted from top-notch ingredients, from acorn-fed, Iowa-raised La Quércia Rossa ham (which closely resembles impossible-to-get Spanish jamón ibérico) to the sweet, fresh peas in a dish of tender Napa Valley lamb.

Spanish. Dinner. $16-35

★★LE CHARM FRENCH BISTRO
315 Fifth St., San Francisco, 415-546-6128; www.lecharm.com
This small French-style bistro in SOMA offers an indoor dining room and an informal, seasonal courtyard. Terra-cotta walls, chocolate and black carpeting, a very high ceiling, and chocolate velvet drapes beside the windows and patio door decorate this cozy restaurant. The gourmet menu is moderately priced and features prix fixe options; basically, it's a fantastic spot for quality, classic French cuisine at bargain prices.

French. Lunch, dinner. Closed Monday. Outdoor seating. $36-85

★★★LUCE
888 Howard St., San Francisco, 415-616-6566; www.lucewinerestaurant.com
Luce is what you get when rustic farm-to-table cooking sensibilities collide with elegant but restrained culinary craftsmanship. Chef Dominique Crenn took her experience growing up on a farm to the rising San Francisco restaurant, focusing on organic, local ingredients and highlighting their superior taste and freshness. Northern Italy is a notable influence in Crenn's cuisine,

much of which has a Tuscan flair. To truly take advantage of Luce's love affair with local ingredients, snag a table during the restaurant's weekly Sunday Supper, a four-course meal appropriately titled "Farm to Table" that features produce and meat from neighboring farms in San Francisco.
American. Breakfast (Monday-Friday), lunch (Monday-Friday), dinner. Saturday-Sunday brunch. $86 and up

★★★★MASA'S
Hotel Vintage Court, 648 Bush St., San Francisco, 415-989-7154;
www.masasrestaurant.com
San Francisco's most elegant dining room can be found at Masa's: White linen-swathed tables and toile d'Juoycovered chairs contrast with rich chocolate walls, behemoth red lampshades suspended from the ceiling, an abundance of flowers and a dramatic bronze sculpture in the room's center. The 900-plus-bottle wine list and a variety of tasting menus aim for a night of lush comfort—and the French dishes, though not the most creative in town, don't disappoint. On the contrary, they are packed with flavor and often incorporate ingredients like caviar, crab or bone marrow. Dessert also comes in waves, with sorbet clearing the way for delights like chocolate soufflé and petits fours. Perfect service, great wine, a romantic atmosphere and rich, spot-on flavors: Everything at Masa's is well executed.
French. Dinner. Closed Sunday-Monday. $86 and up

★★★MAYA
303 Second St., San Francisco, 415-543-2928; www.mayasf.com
This lively upscale Mexican restaurant in SoMa is located on the ground floor of a large office complex and set back from Second Street. At the long bar, sip a potent margarita, mojito or sangria while waiting for your table in one of two stylish dining areas. You'll soon be savoring the mole s, gazpacho with crabmeat and chayote relleno. There is patio dining at the front entrance.
Mexican. Lunch, dinner. Reservations recommended. Bar. $16-35

★★★★MICHAEL MINA
The Westin St. Francis, 335 Powell St., San Francisco, 415-397-9222;
www.michaelmina.net
Three is the magic number at Michael Mina: Choose one of three menus (prix fixe, tasting or vegetarian tasting). If you go for prix fixe, you'll get three courses, with an emphasis on playful trios. A dish titled "American classics: crustacean trio" will arrive as a "shrimp cocktail" of sweet sushi-grade prawns with horseradish panna cotta and tomato-water gelée; a tiny Maine lobster roll; and a wee Dungeness crab po' boy. Dessert could be a simple cheese trio or a flight of exquisite Mexican-influenced sweets: mole pudding, tres leches cake and flan. If you find this all too fussy (or pretentious), you're welcome to order a one-plate dish for each course, including the addictive tuna tartare and heady lobster pot pie that made Mina famous when he was at Aqua. But where's the fun in that?
Contemporary American. Dinner. Reservations recommended. Bar. $86 and up

★★★MORTON'S, THE STEAKHOUSE
400 Post St., San Francisco, 415-986-5830; www.mortons.com

This steakhouse chain, which originated in Chicago in 1978, grabs the serious meat lover with its selection of belt-busting carnivorous delights—the house specialty is a 24-ounce porterhouse—as well as fresh fish, lobster and chicken entrées. The beef is shipped directly from Chicago to all the Morton's locations. The wine list features more than 200 and there are specialty cocktails, "Mortinis," to indulge in—like the Heavenly Cosmopolitan or Heavenly Palm Beacher.

Steaks. Dinner. Reservations recommended. Bar. $36-85

★MO'S GRILL
1322 Grant Ave., San Francisco, 415-788-3779; www.mosgrill.com

North Beach takes a break from Italian fare at this hamburger joint, which beckons with its neon signage. Mo's is still willing to serve a "bloody," high-quality burger (if you want it that way), along with thick fries and milkshakes. Angus beef is ground fresh Daily in house, and 7-ounce patties are cooked over volcanic rocks.

American. Breakfast, lunch, dinner. $15 and under

★★★MYTH
470 Pacific Ave., San Francisco, 415-677-8986; www.mythsf.com

This quintessential San Francisco restaurant, located in the historic Jackson Square area, combines excellent food, amiable service and a sophisticated setting. Chef Sean O'Brien, who trained for years with Chef Gary Danko, has put together a menu replete with French, Japanese and California influences. The wine list is world class. The dining room's banquettes create privacy and cozy tables have a view of the kitchen. There is also an eight-person kitchen table available.

California, French, Japanese menu. Dinner. Closed Sunday-Monday. Bar. Reservations recommended. $16-35

★★★NOPA
560 Divisadero St., San Francisco, 415-864-8643; www.nopasf.com

It isn't really "north of the Panhandle"—it's northeast. But the abbreviation is hip, and so is this restaurant. A cavernous, bi-level former bank, NoPa usually hums (loudly) with a scenery crowd who are there for the hipster art and cocktails as much as the food. You can always hang out at the bar, chance the no-reservations communal table or show up late—the kitchen's open until 1 a.m. Many of the hefty dishes (calamari with chorizo, chickpeas and endive; chicken with Romano beans) are roasted in the wood oven, and most ingredients are local and organic.

American. Dinner. Bar. $36-85

★★★NORTH BEACH
1512 Stockton St., San Francisco, 415-392-1700, 866-860-0013;
www.northbeachrestaurant.com

This Tuscan restaurant has thrived in the city's Italian district for more than 30 years and feels authentic, with tiled floors, vaulted ceilings (made by Italian craftsmen) and original artwork. Waiters in tuxes serve fresh fish, veal and pasta. House specialties include spaghetti with vodka sauce, sand dabs and pasta with bay shrimp and cream sauce. Slide up to the granite bar and peruse the sizable wine selection of nearly 600 vintages. The list also includes 75 types of grappa. If the weather's nice, take a seat on the sidewalk seating area.

Italian. Lunch, dinner. Reservations recommended. Outdoor seating. Bar. $36-85

★★★ONE MARKET
1 Market St., San Francisco, 415-777-5577; www.onemarket.com

When he opened One Market in 1993, Bradley Ogden was a rising star with a quirky, pioneering take on farm-fresh New American food, as exemplified by a huge, witty à la carte menu. Over the years, said menu didn't change much, and so One Market settled into a reliably upscale destination for Financial District power diners. Enter Ogden's latest executive chef, Mark Dommen, who has updated the basic-and-fresh style with modern twists (think foie gras emulsions and smoked sea salt). He also added full plates, with sides specially made to go with the entrées. The enormous, efficient dining room isn't romantic, but the very good desserts are—especially the homemade ice cream and Ogden's signature butterscotch pudding.

American. Lunch (Monday-Friday), dinner (Monday-Saturday). Closed Sunday. Reservations recommended. Bar. $36-85

★O'REILLY'S
622 Green St., San Francisco, 415-989-6222; www.oreillysirish.com

This raucous watering hole and eatery serves Guinness and Irish fare on the outskirts of North Beach. Dine on dishes like the Irishman's quesadilla (with shredded corned beef), fish and chips, or chicken pot pie while perusing Irish memorabilia, bric-a-brac, photos, and murals. Eat outside on the sidewalk if the sun is shining.

Irish. Breakfast, lunch, dinner. Outdoor seating. Children's menu. Bar. $16-35

★★PALIO D'ASTI
640 Sacramento St., San Francisco, 415-395-9800; www.paliodasti.com

Named for the Palio, a medieval bareback horse race in the Italian town of Asti, this spacious Financial District restaurant features a large mural depicting the event, which was reborn more than 35 years ago. Menus change seasonally and reflect different regions: northern Italy in the winter, southern Italy in the summer, and Rome in the spring. Fresh white truffles (when in season) and house-made pastas are specialties.

Italian. Lunch, dinner. Closed Saturday-Sunday. Reservations recommended. Children's menu. Bar. $36-85

★★PARAGON
701 Second St., San Francisco, 415-537-9020; www.paragonrestaurant.com

Just a half block away from the ballpark that's the home of the San Francisco Giants, this brick-fronted brasserie with glass awning serves American fare to casual business folks and an after-work drinking crowd, as well as baseball fans looking for a pre- or post-game meal. The large, contemporary space has a long bar (which serves more than 80 vodkas from all over the globe) backed by an enormous mirror.

American. Lunch (Monday-Friday), dinner. Closed Sunday. Reservations recommended. Outdoor seating. Bar. $16-35

★PERRY'S
1944 Union St., San Francisco, 415-922-9022; www.perryssf.com

For more than 30 years, Perry's has been a popular standby for its weekend brunch and tasty burgers, salads, and chowder. Sidewalk tables on trendy Union Street offer prime people-watching. Front and rear dining rooms, along with the atrium, feature historic one-inch octagonal tile floors, bentwood chairs, and blue and white gingham cloth-covered tables. High chalkboards with daily menus and a huge eclectic collection of memorabilia cover the walls.

American. Breakfast, lunch, dinner, late-night, Saturday-Sunday brunch. Outdoor seating. Children's menu. Bar. $16-35

★★PIPERADE
1015 Battery St., San Francisco, 415-391-2555; www.piperade.com

Piperade, with its amber lighting and cozy dining room, isn't particularly trendy but is somehow still sexy, the kind of place filled with happy regulars. The food, by Basque chef Gerald Hirigoyen, is hearty and a little unusual—very salty, very piquant, very satisfying. Start with small plates like house-cured salt cod set off by oyster tartare and lemon crème fraîche. Entrées include lamb chops with manchego potato gratin, as well as pipérade itself—fried peppers and Serrano ham with a poached egg served in a skillet. Desserts (turron mousse cake with roasted almonds) are so luscious they'll have you pondering a trip to Hirigoyen's homeland to see if they can be as good as Piperade's.

French. Lunch (Monday-Friday), dinner. Closed Sunday. $36-85

★★★PLUMPJACK CAFÉ
3127 Fillmore St., San Francisco, 415-563-4755; www.plumpjack.com

A few blocks off Union Street, Plumpjack Café draws a sophisticated crowd with its pleasing California fare. Fresh, locally sourced ingredients dominate the frequently changing menu. Local politician Gavin Newsom is a part owner of this Cow Hollow spot, which is part of an empire that includes the Matrix Fillmore bar (located across the street) and a Lake Tahoe branch. Since the restaurant is slightly cramped, it makes sense that after 14 years, they're finally remodeling. And to do so, the restaurant is closed until early 2010 (so call ahead before heading there) when they have their grand reopening to show off their fresh makeover.

American. Lunch, dinner. Reservations recommended. $36-85

★★★RANGE
842 Valencia St., San Francisco, 415-282-8283; www.rangesf.com

The cocktail list at this chic eatery is as long as the dinner menu, though there's hardly room for a bar crowd in the tiny, hip (think mid-century modern crossed with industrial) space. But the drinks are lovingly prepared, as is the New American food. An ever-changing menu comes studded with intriguing ingredients like morels or wild nettles, and desserts (strawberry ice cream puffs, chocolate and armagnac soufflé) are heavenly. Range is bar-like in its lack of elbowroom and noise problem, so it won't set the mood for romance. But it definitely sees its share of urbanites sipping classic cocktails or smooth Belgian beers.

Contemporary American. Dinner. $36-85

★★★★RESTAURANT GARY DANKO

800 North Point St., San Francisco, 415-749-2060; www.garydanko.com

Restaurant Gary Danko boasts the most tableside dazzle in town, including tea service, caviar service, cheese cart and flambéed desserts. The décor is theatrical, too, with large paintings, dim lighting, and a bathroom so large and luxurious it's practically a spa. But it's not all looks and no substance: The tea is rare and steeped to perfection; and the cheeses are a kaleidoscope of different styles, animals and continents. The wine list may read like a dictionary, but your smart and friendly server will happily guide you through it. The food is a blend of California, French and Mediterranean with dishes such as lobster risotto and quail stuffed with mushrooms, quinoa and foie gras; you can order three, four or five courses or go for the tasting menu. Everything's available at the bar, making Danko a smart stop for a swanky last-minute meal.

Contemporary American. Dinner. Reservations recommended. Bar. $86 and up

★★★RUTH'S CHRIS STEAK HOUSE

1601 Van Ness Ave., San Francisco, 415-673-0557; www.ruthschris.com

For over 40 years, this popular nationwide chain has dished out an array of tasty steaks. Come for generous portions of corn-fed Midwestern beef in all its incarnations: rib eye, T-bone, fillet and so on. The steaks are brought to your table still sizzling with butter. Of course, there are lamb chops, stuffed chicken breast, grilled portobello mushrooms and more on the menu in case beef isn't your thing. Comfort-food side dishes also appear on the menu, including creamed spinach and potatoes au gratin.

Steak. Dinner. Reservations recommended. Bar. $36-85

★SCHROEDER'S

240 Front St., San Francisco, 415-421-4778; www.schroederssf.com

Opened in 1893, Schroeder's is an old-world German beer hall and restaurant located in the Financial District. The spacious, wood-paneled dining room features large murals of traditional German beer hall scenes above the bar, along with a collection of beer steins on display.

German. Lunch, dinner. Closed Sunday. Reservations recommended. Bar. $16-35

★★SCOMA'S

Pier 47 on Al Scoma Way, San Francisco, 415-771-4383; www.scomas.com

Located in touristy Fisherman's Wharf, San Francisco's longtime seafood restaurant is almost an institution. The white-and-blue color scheme enhances the aquatic theme, and the dining room faces the fishing boat moorings. There is a large bar and adjacent lounge at the entry, with three smallish,

separate dining areas to the rear of the restaurant.
Seafood. Lunch, dinner. Bar. $36-85

★SEARS FINE FOOD
439 Powell St., San Francisco, 415-986-0700; www.searsfinefood.com
Diners flock to this San Francisco institution established in 1938 for the Swedish pancakes. A half block from Union Square, the main dining room here is divided into two sections: one at the front window overlooking Powell Street and another with a long dining counter and bar. Old family photos and Norman Rockwell prints enliven the walls.
American. Breakfast, lunch, dinner. Reservations recommended. Bar. $16-35

★★SEBO
517 Hayes St., San Francisco, 415 864 2122; www.sebosf.com
If you're fishing for super-high-quality seafood, stop by this small, skylit, no-reservations restaurant with a laidback minimalistic atmosphere. It attracts restaurateurs and other off-duty sushi chefs, as well as locals wanting to experience the exclusivity of the tiny 20-seated joint. The American chef-owners fly the fish in Daily: It's usually wild, typically from Japan and always unexpected.
Japanese. Dinner. Closed Monday. $36-85

★★★★SILKS
Mandarin Oriental, San Francisco, 222 Sansome St., San Francisco, 415-276-9888; www.mandarinoriental.com/sanfrancisco
The antique kimono fabric displayed under glass on the walls at Silks says a lot about the ambience: classic and elegant. This is a spot for ladies who lunch, power brokers and guests of the luxe Mandarin Oriental hotel in which the restaurant is hidden. Gleaming silver, heavy linen, attentive service and a hushed atmosphere lay claim to tradition. But the Asian-inflected food dreamed up by chef de cuisine Orlando Pagan is innovative: pan-seared scallops share a plate with pine nut tabouli, cherry tomatoes and bacon emulsion; grilled pork chops are served with cannelloni beans and bell peppers. After dinner, slink into the nearby MO bar for a nightcap or linger at the table over coffee and petite fours.
American. Breakfast, lunch (Monday-Friday), dinner (Wednesday-Saturday). $36-85

★★THE SLANTED DOOR
1 Ferry Building, San Francisco, 415-861-8032; www.slanteddoor.com
A mix of tourists, foodies and executives converge behind the Slanted Door—some attracted by mesmerizing views of the Bay and bridge, others by cocktails, but most by owner Charles Phan, who has a reputation as the city's best Vietnamese chef. Snake past the revelers who jam-pack the long bar and low-slung cocktail couches. Food includes crispy imperial rolls, caramelized catfish claypot and tender shaking beef—nothing you couldn't get elsewhere for much less money, until you factor in a wine list heavy on German and Austrian riesling and unparalleled tea service.
Vietnamese. Lunch, dinner. Reservations recommended. Bar. $16-35

★★SLOW CLUB

2501 Mariposa St., San Francisco, 415-241-9390; www.slowclub.com

The Slow Club's moniker is a misnomer because your wait is rarely long, and besides, time flies at the glowing, backlit bar, where delicious cocktails are mixed from intriguing ingredients like blackberry brandy. Once seated, service is efficient to the point of abrupt. If you're hungry, you'll appreciate the efficiency, and the large portions and American flavors kill pangs quickly. American. Breakfast (Monday-Friday), lunch (Monday-Friday), dinner (Monday-Saturday), Saturday-Sunday brunch. $16-35

★★★★SPRUCE

3640 Sacramento St., San Francisco, 415-931-5100; www.sprucesf.com

A revamped auto barn with black décor, overstuffed leather seats, an imposing backlit bar and a glowing wine cabinet, Spruce feels like an updated steakhouse. The dry martini has been replaced by fancier quaffs, and the American menu boasts far more than beef—but the self-satisfied, no-surprises vibe is the same. The food is downright delicious (buttered Maine lobster with golden potato gnocchi; duck-fat-fried potatoes), and the kitchen and service are polished and confident. Come for the scene and the staggering wine list, which is so amazing that there's a page for each vinification of a single grape from a single country (for example, riesling and Germany). Spruce is great for lunch, if you're willing to travel to the sleepy neighborhood, shell out $14 for a tasty burger, and avoid a third glass of wine, should you have things to do later in the day. American. Lunch (Monday-Friday), dinner. $$$

★SWAN OYSTER DEPOT

1517 Polk St., San Francisco, 415-673-1101

Swan doesn't take reservations, it doesn't accept credit cards, the line always spills out the door, and the servers can be gruff. It's all part of the semi-rowdy, old-time San Francisco atmosphere (which is much more authentic than the versions found at Fisherman's Wharf). Cool off on a hot day with cold, cracked Dungeness crab, or warm up on a foggy night with satisfyingly creamy clam chowder. Seafood. Lunch. $15 and under

★★TADICH GRILL

240 California St., Financial District, 415-391-1849

Tadich is a last bastion of old-school San Francisco, from white-coated waiters to sourdough on the tables. Tadich doesn't take reservations, but pre-dinner martinis and people-watching at the bar are part of the fun. Service is hurried but jovial, and the more local and simply prepared the dish, the better. Best bets are cioppino, calf's liver steak with onions, broiled petrale sole filet, oysters Rockefeller and Dungeness crab Louie. Seafood. Lunch, dinner. Closed Sunday. $16-35

★★★TOMMY TOY'S

655 Montgomery St., San Francisco, 415-397-4888; www.tommytoys.com

Since 1985 this downtown eatery has combined the taste and technique of China with French-influenced presentation (no chopsticks) and flair. Ask about the Daily special at lunch and dinner; you can also opt for the six-course signature dinner, which may include oven-baked seafood bisque topped with a French puff pastry and Peking duck with lotus buns.

Chinese, French. Lunch, dinner. Reservations recommended. Bar. $36-85

★★★TOWN HALL

342 Howard St., San Francisco, 415-908-3900; www.townhallsf.com

When they helmed the staid but classy Postrio, the Rosenthal brothers must have been jonesing to mix things up. Town Hall's two-story building is a former ship engine manufacturing plant reconceived with New England school-house elements; lots of brick and large windowpanes are juxtaposed with a huge mirror and chandeliers, and there's a nice heated patio outside. The seasonal menu is a zingy take on Contemporary American (read: Southern with a few regional specialties). Tempura squash blossoms with four-cheese stuffing and pesto are so succulent you won't want to share; gumbo is a favorite when it shows up on the menu. The ballpark-adjacent spot swells to capacity at lunch, pre-weekend and during home games, but quiets down on weeknights.

Contemporary American. Lunch (Monday-Friday), dinner. $36-85

★★★TWO

22 Hawthorne St., San Francisco, 415-777-9779; www.two-sf.com

The Google-defying name refers to many things: A double-two street address and two types of service (to-go and table). It's also chef David Gingrass's second go-round in this location. The first incarnation was the more formal Hawthorne Lane; these days, the large, multi-roomed restaurant is so informal there are food magazines to peruse at the bar. The casual approach draws an after-work crowd, and the spaciousness makes it a good option for large groups. The food is sometimes uneven, but it's interesting (a foie gras PB&J with peach chutney on fig bread is unforgettable: piquant, sweet, unctuous, impossibly rich and homey all at once), and the burger at lunch wins kudos among locals. The TWO-Go Box lunches are some of the best noontime takeout in town, and the monthly, bubbly-fueled cooking classes are a rockin' good time.

American. Lunch, dinner. Closed Sunday. $36-85

★★★XYZ

W Hotel, 181 Third St., San Francisco, 415-817-7836; www.xyz-sf.com

This eatery in the W Hotel serves self-described urban continental fare with a French influence (that's California cuisine to laymen). They use local, organic and sustainable ingredients and therefore, focus on changing seasonal menus. For spring you'll find choices such as the ravioli with white bean, ricotta and arugula; filet mignon with braised cippolini onions, savoy spinach and fingerling potatoes; and tuna carpaccio with oro blanco grapefruit, olive tapanade and purple asparagus. The adjacent three-story bar is a popular place to mingle over cocktails with the stylish SOMA crowd.

American. Breakfast, lunch, dinner, late-night, Saturday-Sunday brunch. Reservations recommended. Bar. $36-85

★★YANK SING

49 Stevenson St., San Francisco, 415-541-4949; 101 Spear St. (inside Rincon Center), San Francisco, 415-957-9300; www.yanksing.com

If you're a dim sum purist, know this: Yank Sing's signature Shanghaiese xiao long bao (soup-filled dumplings) may be untraditional, but they're delicious—as is everything that arrives on the cart at San Francisco's most upscale dim sum palace. Dumplings are a highlight, especially sweet and savory shrimp-based har gau and shiu mai. Fried soft-shell crabs, flaky curry chicken puffs, and sticky rice packets are also delicious.

Chinese. Lunch, Saturday-Sunday brunch. Bar. $35-86

★★ZUNI CAFÉ

1658 Market St., San Francisco, 415-552-2522; www.zunicafe.com

The liquor bottles stacked against the floor-to-ceiling bar window face out to busy Market Street and add to Zuni's dazzle, along with exposed brick walls, the open kitchen and a copper bar. Though it had a snooty heyday, the scene now is less see-and-be-seen than see-and-devour-the-chicken—Zuni's roasted bird for two is justly famous for its crisp-skinned juiciness (plus it's organic, as is all of the meat here).

French, Provençal. Lunch, dinner. Closed Monday. $36-85

SPAS

★★★NOB HILL SPA

The Huntington Hotel 1075 California St., San Francisco, 415-345-2888, 800-227-4683; www.huntingtonhotel.com

Trudge uphill to one of the city's classic hotels, and you'll be rewarded with a posh spot for top-notch pampering. The bi-level space offers 10 treatment rooms, an indoor pool, saunas and steam rooms, and a workout area—all of which are overseen by friendly, but unobtrusive staffers. Indulge in a High Skin Refiner Facial ($205), which helps smooth out wrinkles and lines, or the Ultimate Massage ($295)—a 110-minute customized blissfest in which you're kneaded with aromatherapeutic oils and hot stones that'll leave you so relaxed you may need a ride home. Or take some time to compose yourself first by ordering a light lunch (Nob Hill is one of the rare spas to offer more than cucumbers and water on its spa menu) while taking in the city views from the balcony patio.

★★★★REMÈDE SPA

The St. Regis San Francisco, 125 Third St., San Francisco, 415-284-4000; www.stregis.com

If heaven has a spa, it must look like this: pristine ivory walls with dark wood accents, a glassy 50-foot indoor lap pool, plush velour sofas and a staff that plies you with truffles and champagne. Since it's in the posh St. Regis hotel, the service is as refined and gracious as you'd expect—and the services are as luxurious as they are effective. You can't go wrong with the Remède Customized Facial ($95–$255), which tops off thorough pore cleansing and a customized face mask with a decadent essential-oil scalp massage and skin-softening mud-and-paraffin wraps for hands and feet. It's an experience that's so lavish and pampering it's almost sinful.

SAN JOSE

See also Gilroy, Los Gatos, Santa Clara, Santa Cruz

Once a small farm town, San Jose has always had grand ambitions. The state capital before California even became a state, it is now the nerve center of the computer and high-tech industries. Several area universities—San José State University, Santa Clara University and Stanford University—graduate thousands of engineers and computer scientists every year. Now known as the capital of Silicon Valley, San Jose was founded as Pueblo de San Jose de Guadalupe in the name of Charles III of Spain. It became part of the United States in 1846.

WHAT TO SEE
ALUM ROCK PARK

16240 Alum Rock Ave., San Jose, 408-277-2757

These 720 acres are known as "Little Yosemite" and are named for a giant rock boulder once thought to be aluminum. You can go hiking, bicycling and riding on the many bridle trails. There are picnic grounds and a playground. Daily.

CHILDREN'S DISCOVERY MUSEUM

180 Woz Way, San Jose, 408-298-5437; www.cdm.org

This museum's hands-on exhibits explore the relationships between the natural and created worlds and the people who live in them. Exhibits include "Streets," a 5/8-scale replica of an actual city, with street lights, parking meters and fire hydrants, and "Waterworks," in which pumps and valves move water through a reservoir system.
Tuesday-Saturday 10 a.m.-5 p.m., Sunday noon-5 p.m.

HAPPY HOLLOW PARK & ZOO

1300 Senter Road, San Jose, 408-277-3000; www.happyhollowparkandzoo.org

Since 1961, this park within Kelley Park has been keeping kids and parents busy and happy. The park and zoo are closed for a major million-dollar renovation until March 2010. Plan on visiting in the spring when you'll find the new education center, animal care facility, retail shop, animal barn, new rides and exhibits, public art and a greener design.
Monday-Friday 10 a.m.-5 p.m., Saturday-Sunday 10 a.m.-6 p.m.; no admittance during last hour open.

JAPANTOWN SAN JOSE

Jackson and Sixth streets, San Jose, 408-298-4303; www.japantownsanjose.org

One of the few remaining urban districts of its kind to survive the Japanese internment during World War II, this district has a rich history that dates back to the first Japanese immigrants who settled here in1900. Centered on the intersection of Sixth and Jackson streets, modern Japantown is home to a mix of businesses and merchants. The area includes an abundance of Asian groceries and eateries, art galleries, martial arts studios and gift shops, a number of which were first established in the early 1900s. On Sunday mornings, there is a farmers' market with an Asian bent on Jackson between Sixth and Seventh streets.

J. LOHR WINERY TASTING ROOM

1000 Lenzen Ave., San Jose, 408-288-5057; www.jlohr.com

Visit the home of J. Lohr wines, known for their chardonnay, cabernet sauvignon, syrah, white riesling, valdiguié and merlot. J. Lohr is committed to keeping their vineyards sustainable and organic. Stop by for a free tasting. Tasting room: Daily 10 a.m.-5 p.m.

MUNICIPAL ROSE GARDEN

Naglee and Dana avenues, San Jose, www.sjparks.org

More than 4,000 rose plants take up these six acres, showing off their beautiful colors. The best time to visit the garden is in May when they're at full bloom. To see them in bloom, visit from April to November. There are picnic areas and walking paths.
Daily. 8 a.m.-sunset.

OVERFELT GARDENS PARK

368 Educational Park Drive, San Jose, 408-251-3323; www.sjparks.org

This 33-acre botanical preserve includes extensive natural areas and wildflowers, a formal botanic garden and a wildlife sanctuary. Migratory waterfowl and other wildlife inhabit three lakes. The Chinese Cultural Garden has a bronze and marble statue of Confucius overlooking a reflecting pond, an ornate Chinese gate and three Chinese pavilions—all gifts from the Chinese community.
Daily.

RAGING WATERS SAN JOSE

2333 S. White Road, San Jose, 408-238-9900; www.rwsplash.com

This water-themed amusement park has 23 acres of slides and attractions. There's a 350,000-gallon wave pool and an activity pool.
Admission: adults $30.99, seniors and children under 48 inches $22.99. Adult prices may be lower online; visit the Web site for more information. Mid-June-late August, Daily; mid-May-mid-June, late August-September, Saturday-Sunday.

ROSICRUCIAN EGYPTIAN MUSEUM & PLANETARIUM

1664 Park Ave., San Jose, 408-947-3636; www.egyptianmuseum.org

This museum holds one of the largest collections of Egyptian antiques west of the Mississippi, including human and animal mummies, an exhibit on the Egyptian afterlife and a full-scale replica of a nobleman's tomb with images of daily life in the Nile Valley.
Admission: adults $9, students and seniors $7, children 5-10 $5 and children under 5 free. Monday-Friday 9 a.m.-5 p.m., Saturday-Sunday 11 a.m.-6 p.m.

SAN JOSE FARMERS' MARKET

San Pedro Square, San Pedro St., San Jose, 408-279-1775; www.sjdowntown.com

From late May to December, head to San Pedro Square in downtown San Jose on Fridays to shop for local produce, fresh flowers and gourmet foods, and enjoy cooking demonstrations and musical performances. Among the

special events is the twice monthly Chef at the Market event, where a popular local chef prepares a dish for all to sample.
May-December, Friday 10 a.m.-2 p.m.

SAN JOSE FLEA MARKET

1590 Berryessa Road, San Jose, 408-453-1110; www.sjfm.com
Flying in the face of Silicon Valley's high-tech reputation, the San Jose Flea Market is a decidedly low-tech spectacle. The largest open-air market in the nation, it encompasses 120 acres and 8 miles of retail-laden pathways. Founded in 1960 by a landfill operator who saw too may good items going to waste, the market now attracts more than 4 million visitors a year to its shops, carts, restaurants and other attractions. The quarter-mile long Produce Row overflows with fresh fruits and vegetables of all descriptions; there's also a carousel, arcade, two playgrounds and street musicians.
Wednesday-Sunday, sunrise-sunset.

SAN JOSE MUSEUM OF ART

110 S. Market St., San Jose, 408-271-6840; www.sjmusart.org
The top museum in Silicon Valley, this downtown facility is best known for its permanent collection of contemporary works from the 20th and 21st centuries, with a focus on those by West Coast artists. Often edgy and abstract, these pieces run the gamut from oil paintings to room-sized installations and together comprise one of the top collections of modern art in the area, rivaling that of San Francisco's better-known MOMA. On a seasonal basis, high-quality showcases for regional contemporary artists and high-concept, themed exhibitions dominate the calendar.
Admission: adults $8, students and seniors $5, children under 6 free.
Tuesday-Sunday 11 a.m.-5 p.m.

SANTANA ROW

3055 Olin Ave., San Jose, 408-551-4611; www.santanarow.com
Visit this upscale shopping center adjacent to the Hotel Valencia to take advantage of brand stores including Diesel and Gucci, as well as mall staples like Crate & Barrel and Borders Books and Music. There's also a fitness center, day spas, a movie theater, restaurants and an open-air café that regularly draw in the residents of Santana Row's lofts and townhomes.

THE TECH MUSEUM OF INNOVATION

201 S. Market St., San Jose, 408-294-8324; www.thetech.org
See how a microchip is made, design a roller coaster or make a movie in the Digital Studio at this 132,000-square-foot facility with 240 interactive exhibits. The Hackworth IMAX Theater, which has a dome that has become a landmark in the San Jose skyline, screens films in a larger-than-life setting with groundbreaking computer graphics and technology.
Admission: $8. Daily 10 a.m.-5 p.m.

WEST SAN CARLOS STREET ANTIQUE ROW

West San Carlos Street and Bascom Avenue, San Jose, 408-947-8711;
www.sancarlosstreet.com

This 15-block stretch of West San Carlos Street has one of the highest concentrations of antique shops on the Pacific Coast. The selection runs the gamut from European crystal to African art to Western Americana. There are multidealer collectives among the shops, including Laurelwood Antiques (1824 W. San Carlos), Briarwood Antiques & Collectibles (1885 W. San Carlos) and Antiques Colony (1915 W. San Carlos). A number of resale shops are packed with vintage and almost new clothing and décor, and there are also a few standard thrift stores.

WINCHESTER MYSTERY HOUSE

525 S. Winchester Blvd., San Jose, 408-247-2101; www.winchestermysteryhouse.com

Construction began on this architectural oddity in 1884 at the command of eccentric widow Sarah Winchester (of the Winchester Rifle family). Without the guidance of any overall blueprint, it went on until Winchester died in 1922. By then her home had grown to 160 rooms—with 47 fireplaces, 17 chimneys, 950 doors, staircases that go nowhere and cabinets that are the sole entry to entire wings. Also here are two museums, including one dedicated to the Winchester Rifle, and extensive gardens. Check Web site for hours and prices.

YOUTH SCIENCE INSTITUTE

16260 Penitencia Creek Road, San Jose, 408-258-4322; www.ysi-ca.org

This Science center offers natural science classes, exhibits and nature trips. Located within historic Alum Rock Park, YSI's Alum Rock Science and Nature Center has been open to the public since 1953. The lush Penitencia Creek, which bisects the site, flows year-round. Once home to the Ohlone Indians, Alum Rock Park features rugged ridges with spectacular views of the Santa Clara Valley, geologic formations including mineral springs and evidence of seismic events, and a variety of native flora and fauna.
Tuesday-Sunday noon-4:30 p.m.

SPECIAL EVENTS
METRO FOUNTAIN BLUES FESTIVAL

San Jose State University, San Carlos Plaza, San Jose, 408-924-6262; www.as.sjsu.edu

Silicon Valley's preeminent annual musical event held in early May at San Carlos Plaza on the San Jose University campus. This free concert showcases a lineup of about 10 local and national blues talents every year, from Mississippi Delta and Chicago legends to up-and-coming guitar prodigies.
Early May.

SAN JOSE FESTIVAL FOR INDEPENDENCE

Woz Way at W. San Carlos Street, San Jose, 408-294-2100; www.ehclifebuilders.org

This celebration of cultural diversity in San Jose features food booths, arts and crafts, rides, games, entertainment and fireworks. It raises funds to support an agency's building of housing for the homeless.
July 4.

SANTA CLARA COUNTY FAIR

Santa Clara County Fairgrounds, 344 Tully Road, San Jose, 408-494-3247;
www.thefair.org

This county fair has children's stage acts, livestock shows, a demolition derby, concerts and fireworks. There is a youth fair talent and performing arts competition, children can display their artwork to win prizes and more.
Early August.

TAPESTRY ARTS FESTIVAL

Downtown San Jose, www.tapestryarts.org

More than 350 visual artists and craftspeople display works ranging from ceramics and paintings to jewelry, clothing and woodwork at this three-day festival celebrating the arts that began in 1976. There are rock, blues, jazz and classical music performances, as well as dance and theater on three stages; more than 40 food booths; and hands-on art activities for children.
Labor Day weekend.

WHERE TO STAY

★★★CROWNE PLAZA HOTEL

282 Almaden Blvd., San Jose, 408-998-0400, 800-972-3165; www.crowneplaza.com

Palm trees line the street in front of this downtown San Jose hotel situated across from the Center for the Performing Arts, the San Jose McEnery Convention Center, and the Tech Museum of Innovation. Attractive and modernly decorated guest rooms feature tones of crimson, beige, and mahogany, and include flat-screen TVs, CD players, and beds with a number of fluffy pillows. The hotel is easily accessible to major freeways and approximately 3 miles from the airport.
239 rooms. Restaurant, bar. Business center. Fitness center. Pets accepted.
$151-250

★★DOUBLETREE HOTEL

2050 Gateway Place, San Jose, 408-453-4000, 800-222-8733; www.doubletree.com
505 rooms. Restaurant, bar. Business center. Fitness center. Pool. Pets accepted. $151-250

★★★THE FAIRMONT SAN JOSE

170 S. Market St., San Jose, 408-998-1900, 800-441-1414; www.fairmont.com

This 20-story twin-tower complex has spacious accommodations, a well-equipped business center and an in-house spa. The four onsite restaurants offer something for every palate, from the Grill on the Alley's steaks and seafood and to the Chinese dishes of Pagoda. The hotel's spa, Tova Day Spa, offers a variety of different treatments from massages to facials. There's an outdoor heated pool and a full 24-hour fitness center.
808 rooms. Restaurant, bar. Business center. Fitness center. Pool. Spa. Pets accepted. $151-250

★★★HILTON SAN JOSE

300 Almaden Blvd., San Jose, 408-287-2100, 800-774-1500; www.sanjose.hilton.com
This hotel, which is connected to the McEnery Convention Center in down-

town San Jose, rises 18 stories above the Silicon Valley. It is located minutes from the San Jose International Airport and multiple Fortune 500 companies. Rooms feature the pillow-top mattresses, Internet access, a refrigerator, two-line speaker phones, coffee maker, a smart desk and auto wake-up call service. The City Bar and Grill serves reliable American cuisine.
354 rooms. Restaurant, bar. Business center. Fitness center. Pool. Pets accepted. $61-150

★★★HOTEL DE ANZA
233 W. Santa Clara St., San Jose, 408-286-1000, 800-843-3700;
www.hoteldeanza.com
This beautifully restored 1931 Art Deco hotel, listed on the National Register of Historic Places, has quirky, colorful rooms with amenities that include two TVs, CD and DVD players and large work desks. Fruit, cookies, coffee and bottled water are offered throughout the day. Restaurant options include the Hedley Club, a popular spot for cocktails and wine. La Pastaia Restaurant offers rustic Italian cuisine, suitable for a more romantic occasion.
Restaurant, bar. $251-350

★★★HOTEL VALENCIA SANTANA ROW
355 Santana Row, San Jose, 408-551-0010, 866-842-0100; www.hotelvalencia.com
From the faux mink bed cover to the toiletries provided by California apothecary Lather, this hotel is made for those seeking high-tech luxury on the Row. Wireless Internet is accessible anywhere on the property and high-speed hook-ups are available at the room desks, bedside and through large flat-screen TVs. Carnivores head for the hotel's Citrus steakhouse, while the Vbar and Cielo Wine Terrace & Bar are among the most popular night spots in town.
212 rooms. Restaurant, bar. Complimentary breakfast. Business center. Fitness center. Pool. Spa. $151-250

★★★THE SAINTE CLAIRE
302 S. Market St., San Jose, 408-295-2000; www.thesainteclaire.com
This National Historic Landmark in downtown San Jose has been restored to its 1926 elegance. The lobby features high ceilings; chandeliers; and intricate, decorative woodwork, while spacious guest rooms offer many contemporary amenities. Flat-screen TVs, CD and DVD players, refrigerators and cordless phones are found in each room, as are beds with multiple down pillows and plump duvets. Il Fornaio restaurant offers authentic Italian cuisine and serves freshly baked Italian artisan breads from their bakery, Panetteria.
170 rooms. Restaurant, bar. Business center. Fitness center. $151-250

★★★SAN JOSE MARRIOTT
301 S. Market St., San Jose, 408-280-1300, 800-314-0928; www.sanjosemarriott.com
Business travelers and vacationers will appreciate the Marriott San Jose's convenient downtown location in the heart of Silicon Valley. It is connected to the San Jose McEnery Convention Center, three miles from the San Jose International Airport, and in close proximity to area attractions. Vibrantly decorated guest rooms feature flat-screen TVs, work desks, and beds with

luxurious pillow-top mattresses and triple sheeting. Dine at chef Michael Mina's Arcadia, where you'll enjoy innovative American cuisine and top-notch wine. There's a heated outdoor pool and whirlpool as well as a full fitness center.

506 rooms. Restaurant, bar. Business center. Fitness room. Pool. $251-350

★★★SHERATON SAN JOSE HOTEL

1801 Barber Lane, Milpitas, 408-943-0600, 800-325-3535; www.starwoodhotels.com

Recently renovated, this hotel is a good choice for business travelers. This conveniently located hotel is situated just four miles from the San Jose International Airport in Milpitas. Request a room overlooking the pool's tropical courtyard, featuring gardens, waterfalls and palm trees. Mountain-view rooms and rooms with balconies are also offered. Whichever view you choose, rooms are outfitted with Internet access, the Sheraton Sweet Sleeper Bed, bathrobes, and flat-screen TVs.

229 rooms. Restaurant, bar. Business center. Fitness center. Pool. $61-150

WHERE TO EAT

★★★EMILE'S

545 S. Second St., San Jose, 408-289-1960; www.emilesrestaurant.com

Since 1973, Emile's has served European-influenced Californian cuisine. Hand-sculpted brass work and fresh flowers on every table complement the cuisine at this French San Jose restaurant. Choose a dish from the a la carte menu, the tasting menu or a three-course prix fixe menu. You'll enjoy items such as sautéed veal medallions with morel mushroom sauce; scallops, lobster and prawns in a lobster sauce served in a puff pastry shell along with fresh vegetables. Desserts include rhubarb soufflé, warm apple tart with caramel sauce and pistachio ice cream, and house-made sorbets.

French. Dinner. Closed Sunday-Monday. Bar. $16-35

★★★LA PASTAIA

Hotel De Anza, 233 W. Santa Clara St., San Jose, 408-286-8686; www.lapastaia.com

Located within the downtown Hotel De Anza, La Pastaia serves contemporary, rustic Italian dishes. The charming dining room features a fireplace, some tiled walls and some red walls with Italian posters and artwork and colorful tiled floors. Appetizers include salumi, grilled portobella mushrooms and calamari. The dinner menu features dishes such as chicken breast sautéed with chestnuts, dried figs, Sangiovese with soft polenta. The lunch menu also includes tasty paninis.

Lunch, dinner. Outdoor seating. $16-35

★O'FLAHERTY'S IRISH PUB

25 N. San Pedro St., San Jose, 408-947-8007; www.oflahertyspub.com

If you're looking for a traditional Irish pub experience, head to this spot near downtown San Jose. Fish and chips, chowder, sandwiches, and salads grace the menu, and traditional, live Irish music provides entertainment on Tuesdays and Saturdays. Enjoy your meal with a refreshing Guinness, Smithwick's, Bass or Harp.

Irish. Lunch (Monday-Friday), dinner, late-night. Outdoor seating. Bar. $15 and under

SANTA CLARA

See also Mountain View, Palo Alto, San Jose, Santa Cruz

Nicknamed the "Mission City," Santa Clara may sound placid, but it's located in the heart of Silicon Valley and is home to Great America, an amusement park that packs enough thrills to make you appreciate some tranquility.

WHAT TO SEE
GREAT AMERICA

4701 Great American Parkway, Santa Clara, 408-988-1776; www.cagreatamerica.com

This 100-acre park offers theme park thrills in an array of rides, live stage shows and entertainment for children of all ages. Some of the most thrilling rides include the FireFall, where you're raised up to 60 feet and then taken on a 360 degree journey of twists, turns and spins through fire and water effects. There are also family rides, a Nickelodeon-themed playland with rides and more.

Admission: adult $54.99, children and seniors $35.99. April-October, days and times vary; call or visit Web site for schedule.

INTEL MUSEUM

2200 Mission College Blvd., Santa Clara, 408-765-8080; www.intel.com/museum

Have you ever wondered how computer chips are made? Or how microprocessors work? If so, consider visiting this 10,000-square-foot museum, located in the main lobby of Intel's corporate headquarters. Surf the Internet or play computer games in the Application Lab, where a huge microprocessor simulates the brain of a computer.

Admission: Free. Monday-Friday 9 a.m.-6 p.m., Saturday 10 a.m.-5 p.m.

SANTA CLARA UNIVERSITY

500 El Camino Real, Santa Clara, 408-554-4000; www.scu.edu

This university is the oldest institution of higher learning in California. Self-guided tours of the Mission Gardens are available, including the Adobe Lodge and a wall from the original 1820s mission. Olive trees and grinding stones in the gardens also date to the early mission period. Visit the Mission Santa Clara de Asis, which is a replica of the 1777 mission. This one was dedicated in 1928 and contains 12,000 cover tiles salvaged from earlier missions. It's surrounded by beautiful gardens.

SPECIAL EVENTS
SANTA CLARA ART & WINE FESTIVAL

Central Park, 909 Kiely Blvd., Santa Clara, 408-615-3140;
www.santaclaraartandwine.com

Local and regional artists display their work at this annual free festival. There are almost 175 different booths to explore and plenty of international food, wine, beer and live entertainment on three stages.
September.

WHERE TO STAY
★★★HYATT REGENCY SANTA CLARA
5101 Great America Parkway, Santa Clara, 408-200-1234; www.santaclara.hyatt.com

This contemporary, sprawling hotel underwent a recent renovation that produced stylish rooms with Mid-Century modern furnishings, wireless Internet, flat-screen TVs and iPod docks. The resort-like outdoor pool and fitness center are just some of the onsite activities. Tresca, the hotel's main restaurant, features innovative American cuisine.

501 rooms. Restaurant, bar. Fitness center. Pool. $61-150

★★★SANTA CLARA MARRIOTT
2700 Mission College Blvd., Santa Clara, 408-988-1500, 800-228-9290;
www.marriott.com

This recently renovated hotel has rooms with wireless Internet access, luxury bedding and flat-screen TVs. Parcel 104, the onsite restaurant that is under the direction of chefs Bradley Ogden and Robert Sapirman, is a local favorite for fresh, seasonally-inspired California cuisine. The large patio and fire-pit make for comfortable outdoor dining in warm weather. The hotel's fitness center is stocked with cutting-edge equipment, and the grounds include a palm-tree lined outdoor pool.

748 rooms. Restaurant, bar. Fitness center. $151-250

SANTA CRUZ
See also Los Gatos, San Jose, Santa Clara

Santa Cruz is a trip—and lots of people don't mean that literally. It's a lefty/counter-culture/free-thinker haven whose tree-lined streets are shared by hippies sporting tie-dyed ensembles, activists fighting for everything from veganism to medical marijuana, beach bums and surfers, University of California Santa Cruz students and nature types enjoying the great outdoors and tourists taking it all in. They're all drawn to the hushed redwoods and dramatic beaches, migrating whales and butterflies, historic attractions and Victorian houses and, most of all, the laidback vibe. This is a town where stores proudly sell T-shirts and stickers reading "Keep Santa Cruz Weird." Most of the action is on Pacific Avenue, where street musicians, students, panhandlers, tourists and locals mingle amid a mix of quirky restaurants, indie shops and chain stores. There are 29 miles of public beaches and a boardwalk that retains its early 20th-century charms.

WHAT TO SEE
AÑO NUEVO STATE RESERVE
New Year's Creek Road, Highway 1, Pescadero, 650-879-0227; www.parks.ca.gov

This wild, windswept coastal reserve is where thousands of massive elephant seals come to mate and give birth each winter. You can experience this and the undeveloped area by making reservations for a guided walk (which is the only way to see this reserve). Mid-December-March,
Daily 8 a.m.-sunset.

BARGETTO WINERY

3535 N. Main St., Soquel, 831-475-2258; www.bargetto.com
Located in the Santa Cruz Mountains, Bargetto Winery has been producing wines at this family vineyard since 1933. For $5, you can taste five wines and enjoy the scenic courtyard. Tours are also available by appointment only. Daily noon-5 p.m.

BIG BASIN REDWOODS STATE PARK

Santa Cruz Mountains, 831-338-8860 www.bigbasin.org
Hikers and horseback riders congregate at one of the state's most popular parks—and its first redwood preserve—for 80 miles of trails over the 18,000 acres. Established in 1902, this state park is one of California's oldest and a great place to see wildlife in their natural habitat, from mountain lions to coyotes to quail and woodpeckers. There are also waterfalls and canyons. Waddell Creek, located within Big Basin, has a beach and is well-known as one of the best spots for windsurfing; however, due to the strong winds and often heavy surf, it's not recommended for the novice wind surfer. Daily 6 a.m.-10 p.m.

MYSTERY SPOT

465 Mystery Spot Road, Santa Cruz, 831-423-8897; www.mysteryspot.com
Discovered in 1939, this 150-foot-long area defies conventional laws of gravity and perspective—it's where balls roll uphill and trees grow sideways. You have to see this mystery to believe it.
Admission: $5, children 3 and under free. Guided tours. Memorial Day-Labor Day, Daily 9 a.m.-7 p.m.; Labor Day-Memorial Day, Daily 10 a.m.-5 p.m.

NATURAL BRIDGES STATE BEACH

2531 W. Cliff Drive, Santa Cruz, 831-423-4609; www.parks.ca.gov
This state beach is well known for its Monarch Grove, where more than 100,000 monarch butterflies migrate to each winter. The beach has a natural bridge (an ocean-formed sandstone arch) from where you can view sealife below including starfish, crabs, migrating whales, seals and otters. There are areas for fishing, picnicking and nature trails.
Daily 8 a.m.-sunset.

SANTA CRUZ BEACH BOARDWALK

400 Beach St., Santa Cruz, 831-423-5590; www.beachboardwalk.com
The town's emblem and the best and oldest remaining California beachside amusement park, it stars the 1920s-era Giant Dipper, a still-thrilling wooden rollercoaster, and a preserved carousel from 1911. Once you've maxed out on rides, air hockey and guilty-pleasure fair food like fried artichoke hearts (from nearby artichoke capital Castroville), kick back on the beach and watch the kites loop through the air. There is also a bowling alley, arcades, numerous restaurants and souvenir shops and a concert venue, Cocoanut Grove, that has been a cornerstone of the park since it opened. Annual events held here include a clam chowder cook-off in February and free Friday concerts during the summer. Memorial Day-Labor Day.

SANTA CRUZ MISSION STATE HISTORICAL PARK

144 School St., Santa Cruz, 831-425-5849; www.parks.ca.gov

Constructed from 1822 and 1824, Casa Adobe (Neary-Rodriguez Adobe) is the only remaining building of the old Santa Cruz Mission. Located in downtown Santa Cruz, it's hard to miss. Thursday-Sunday 10 a.m.-4 p.m.

SANTA CRUZ SURFING MUSEUM

Mark Abbott Memorial Lighthouse, 701 W. Cliff Drive, Santa Cruz, 831-420-6289;
www.santacruzsurfingmuseum.org

Located in an old lighthouse, this surfing museum features more than 100 years of natural and cultural history of the northern Monterey Bay region. There are surf boards from the when they originated to newer designs and photographs from the 1930s showing surfing as its changed over the years. A gift shop features unique T-shirts, hats, sweatshirts, books and other gifts. Admission: Free. July 4 Labor Day, Wednesday-Monday 10 a.m.-5; Labor Day-July 4: Thursday-Monday noon-4 p.m.

SANTA CRUZ WHARF

Pacific Avenue and Beach Street, Santa Cruz, 831-420-5270;
www.santacruzparksandrec.com

One of few piers of this type to permit auto traffic, the Santa Cruz pier has plenty of restaurants, shops, fish markets and boat rentals. Santa Cruz Wharf is a huddle spot for honking sea lions. From April to November, keep an eye out for the flashing flippers of a humpback. Beach Street turns into the two-mile West Cliff Drive, with cliffs on one side and stately Victorian mansions (many now bed and breakfasts) on the other.

SEACLIFF STATE BEACH

Highway 1, Santa Cruz, 831-685-6442; www.parks.ca.gov

This fishing pier leads to "The Cement Ship," (it's real name is the Palo Alto) which was purposely sunk here in 1929 to serve as an amusement center. This is a popular swimming beach, with seasonal lifeguards. You can fish off the pier but because the ship is unsafe, it's closed to the public. There are picnicking areas and campsites.
Daily 8 a.m.-sunset.

UNIVERSITY OF CALIFORNIA, SANTA CRUZ

1156 High St., Santa Cruz, 831-459-0111; www.ucsc.edu

Made up of 10 colleges, University of California, Santa Cruz is set on a 2,000-acre campus overlooking Monterey Bay. The Institute of Marine Sciences offers guided tours of the Long Marine Laboratory (this campus has the largest amount of marine research programs in the country). There are art galleries, astronomical exhibits, an agroecology farm and arboretum to explore.

SPECIAL EVENTS
MONTEREY BAY STRAWBERRY FESTIVAL

Ramsay Park, Watsonville, 831-566-1230; www.mbsf.com

More than 12,000 acres of lush California land in the Pajaro Valley produce

ALONG THE RUSSIAN RIVER

Named for the Russian trappers who plied its redwood-thick banks in the early 1800s, the river and its surroundings retain a tranquil, old-world appeal. Make this drive in one day or turn it into a leisurely two-day excursion.

Follow Highway 101 to Petaluma in Sonoma County. Head west on Bodega Avenue and later Valley Ford Road, which cross through rolling farmlands and old ranchos to Highway 1 at the town of Valley Ford. Highway 1 then leads west and north to Bodega Bay, a coastal fishing village. Continue up the winding coastal road, stopping at one of the turnoffs to Sonoma Coast State Beach or to the town of Jenner, overlooking the Pacific at the mouth of the Russian River. This is a scenic place to enjoy a sunlit lunch while looking out on the ocean or to spend a night.

Next, head inland (east) for about 12 miles on route 116 to Guerneville, a rustic Russian River resort town. Walk the mist-shrouded trails of the Armstrong Redwoods state reserve just to the north. On the return trip, take route 116 southeast to highway 101, which leads south to San Francisco. Approximately 175 miles.

some of the best strawberries in the country. Almost 50,000 people turn out at this festival each year to eat unusual delicacies such as strawberry tamales. Compete with fellow strawberry lovers in fruit- and pie-eating contests or enjoy the fruity aroma as you chow down on more traditional summertime fare like local pizzas and sausages while enjoying entertainment, arts and crafts.

First weekend in August.

SANTA CRUZ COUNTY FAIR

2601 E. Lake Ave., Watsonville, 831-724-5671; www.santacruzcountyfair.com

More than 50,000 people turn out for this fair, which starts on Tuesday with a barbecue and band and continues through the week and weekend with concerts, games and animal exhibitions. There are also contests and food and drink vendors.

Early September.

WHERE TO STAY

★★★CHAMINADE

1 Chaminade Lane, Santa Cruz, 831-475-5600, 800-283-6569; www.chaminade.com

This beautiful contemporary Spanish mission-style hotel sits on a mountain ridge and offers guests panoramic views of Monterey Bay. Rooms are bright and stylish with plush down duvets, microfiber bathrobes, Internet access, granite bathrooms, and luxe toiletries. Guests choosing to stay on the grounds can opt for a relaxing spa treatment or dip in the heated pool, a game of tennis, volleyball or badminton, or a workout in the fitness center. End the day with a meal at one of the two onsite restaurants; Sunset features beautiful views and buffets and a Sunday champagne brunch. Linwood's Bar and Grill serves California cuisine with a colorful dining room, fireplace and outdoor patio.

156 rooms. Restaurant, bar. Fitness center. Pool. Spa. $251-350

★★DREAM INN SANTA CRUZ

175 W. Cliff Drive, Santa Cruz, 831-426-4330, 800-716-6199;
www.dreaminnsantacruz.com

Renovated in 2008, this contemporary hotel is the only beachfront hotel along the Santa Cruz Monterey Bay coastline and overlooks the Santa Cruz Beach Boardwalk. Each room has a private balcony or patio, flat-screen TVs, iPod docking stations and bathrobes. Guests can walk to the beach or enjoy the outdoor heated pool.

165 rooms. Restaurant, bar. Business center. Pool. Beach. $151-250

WHERE TO EAT

★★BITTERSWEET BISTRO

787 Rio del Mar Blvd., Aptos, 831-662-9799; www.bittersweetbistro.com

American, Mediterranean. Dinner. Outdoor seating. Children's menu. Bar. $36-85

★★CAFE SPARROW

8042 Soquel Drive, Aptos, 831-688-6238; www.cafesparrow.com

French. Lunch (Monday-Saturday), dinner, Sunday brunch. $36-85

★★CROW'S NEST RESTAURANT

2218 E. Cliff Drive, Santa Cruz, 831-476-4560; www.crowsnest-santacruz.com

Seafood, steak. Lunch, dinner. Outdoor seating. Children's menu. Bar. $16-35

★★GABRIELLA CAFÉ

910 Cedar St., Santa Cruz, 831-457-1677; www.gabriellacafe.com

American. Lunch, dinner, Saturday-Sunday brunch. Closed Monday.

★GILBERT'S SEAFOOD GRILL

25 Municipal Wharf, Santa Cruz, 831-423-5200; www.gilbertssantacruz.com

Seafood. Lunch, dinner. Children's menu. Bar. $16-35

SANTA ROSA

See also Bodega Bay, Calistoga, Healdsburg, Sonoma, St. Helena

Minutes from more than 150 wineries, this rapidly expanding city is surrounded by vineyards and mountains. The rich soil and even climate of the Sonoma Valley lured famed horticulturist Luther Burbank here, where he lived and worked for 50 years, developing innumerable new and improved plant life. Many farm and ranch products originate from the area.

WHAT TO SEE

LUTHER BURBANK HOME & GARDENS

Santa Rosa and Sonoma avenues, Santa Rosa, 707-524-5445; www.lutherburbank.org

A Registered National, State, city and Horticultural Historic Landmark, this is where the locally famous horticulturist, Luther Burbank lived. His work is on display along with a greenhouse, gardens, a carriage house and exhibits. April-October, Tuesday-Sunday 10 a.m.-3 p.m. Gardens: Daily 8 a.m.-sunset.

REDWOOD EMPIRE ICE ARENA

1667 W. Steele Lane, Santa Rosa, 707-546-7147; www.snoopyshomeice.com

Built by Charles M. Schulz, the creator of the *Peanuts* comic strip, this ice arena, known as Snoopy's Home Ice, is a great place to cool off on a hot summer day. The rink offers skate rentals, events and has a restaurant onsite. Next door is the Charles M. Schulz Museum, known as the Snoopy Gallery which also contains a gift shop.

Hours vary; call or visit Web site. Snoopy's Gallery: Daily 10 a.m.-6 p.m.

SAFARI WEST WILDLIFE PRESERVE AND AFRICAN TENT CAMP

3115 Porter Creek Road, Santa Rosa, 707-579-2551, 800-616-2695;
www.safariwest.com

Board a safari vehicle and head into the hills in search of the more than 600 exotic mammals and birds that call this place home. Animals include cheetahs, giraffes, antelopes, zebras and more.

See Web site for schedules and pricing.

SONOMA COUNTY MUSEUM

425 Seventh St., Santa Rosa, 707-579-1500; www.sonomacountymuseum.org

This museum contains changing exhibits and permanent collections on Sonoma County and Northern California regional history. Guided tours are available by appointment and there are special events throughout the year. Admission: adults $5, students and seniors $2, children under 12 free. Tuesday-Sunday 11 a.m.-5 p.m.

SPECIAL EVENTS
LUTHER BURBANK ROSE PARADE

Downtown, Santa Rosa, www.roseparadefestival.com

This annual parade has been ongoing in Santa Rosa since 1894. Today, parade-goers will see plenty of floats with flowers, marching bands, equestrian groups and military veterans. Third Saturday in May.

SONOMA COUNTY FAIR

1350 Bennett Valley Road, Santa Rosa, 707-545-4200; www.sonomacountyfair.com

This two-week fair includes carnival rides, livestock shows, horse racing, a talent show, competitions for budding magicians, scarecrow building and bubblegum bubble blowing. A highlight of the fair each year is the Hall of Flowers exhibit, where participants create themed floral displays.

Late July-early August.

WHERE TO STAY
★★★HILTON SONOMA WINE COUNTRY

3555 Round Barn Blvd., Santa Rosa, 707-523-7555, 800-445-8667;
www.winecountryhilton.com

On top of a hill and located in the center of more than 140 world-class Sonoma County wineries and golf courses, this hotel gives guests access to surrounding towns as well as hiking, biking and sailing at nearby state parks. Recently renovated, the hotel feature spacious rooms, some with private decks. There is a large outdoor heated pool, whirlpool, a renovated fitness

center, a jogging track, in-room spa services and a business center. Nectar Restaurant and Lounge features seasonal regional ingredients.
250 rooms. Restaurant, bar. Business center. Fitness center. Pool. Spa. Pets accepted. $151-250

★★★HOTEL LA ROSE

308 Wilson St., Santa Rosa, 707-579-3200, 800-527-6738; www.hotellarose.com
Located in Santa Rosa's historic Railroad Square, this European-style boutique hotel is a short walk from downtown shops, restaurants and movie theaters and across the street from the visitor's center in the old train station. The hotel's original building dates to 1907 with a more contemporary annex on an adjacent street. Guest rooms are equipped with armoires, duvets, lots of pillows and marble bathrooms. Visit Josef's, the hotel restaurant, for continental cuisine.
47 rooms. Restaurant, bar. Complimentary breakfast. $61-150

★★★HYATT VINEYARD CREEK HOTEL & SPA–SONOMA COUNTY

170 Railroad St., Santa Rosa, 707-284-1234, 800-633-7313; www.hyatt.com
From the guest rooms and suites to the outdoor sculpture garden, an artistic flair sets this hotel apart from others. At the spa, choose from a full menu of treatments, including seven types of massage and six types of facials. Several treatments use crushed grape seeds and olive oil to soften and smooth skin. Using Sonoma county ingredients, the hotel's restaurant, Seafood Brasserie, serves dishes that taste of French country cooking.
155 rooms. Restaurant, bar. Fitness center. Pool. Spa. $151-250

★★★KENWOOD INN & SPA

10400 Sonoma Highway, Kenwood, 707-833-1293, 800-353-6966; www.kenwoodinn.com
Set among 2,000 acres of vineyards, this Mediterranean villa recalls the Tuscan countryside. The cozy and charming rooms have striped fabric headboards, iron scroll work and terra-cotta tile floors that capture the romance of Italy. Most rooms have featherbeds, private jetted tubs, fireplaces and either patios or sitting areas. Amenities include two pools, fountains, landscaped gardens, a wine bar and a full-service spa. The Restaurant features traditional Italian dishes made with local ingredients. A private wine bar located within the courtyard features rare wines and light fare.
29 rooms. No children allowed. Complimentary breakfast. Restaurant, bar. Pool. Spa. -$351 and up

★★★VINTNERS INN

4350 Barnes Road, Santa Rosa, 707-575-7350, 800-421-2584; www.vintnersinn.com
On the grounds of a 92-acre vineyard, this Southwestern-style inn surrounds an attractive central courtyard with a fountain. Spacious guest rooms have beamed ceilings, bathrobes, featherbeds, honor bars, decks or patios and whirlpool tubs. All suites and upstairs fireplace rooms have wood-burning fireplaces. You can book an in-room massage or take advantage of the vineyard trail and go for a job or walk. There's also a bocce ball court and a fitness room. A complimentary breakfast is provided along with a welcoming

bottle of wine.

44 rooms. Restaurant, bar. Complimentary breakfast. Fitness center. $251-350

WHERE TO EAT

★★CA'BIANCA RISTORANTE ITALIANO

835 Second St., Santa Rosa, 707-542-5800; www.cabianca.com

Italian. Lunch (Monday-Friday), dinner. Outdoor seating. $16-35

★★★EQUUS

Fountaingrove Inn, 101 Fountain Grove Parkway, Santa Rosa, 707-578-0149;
www.fountaingroveinn.com

The California wine country menu of this contemporary restaurant inside the Fountaingrove Inn changes seasonally and relies on local Sonoma County produce. Entrées include sun-dried tomato and mushroom ravioli with artichokes, pancetta, and tomato basil sauce; and seared sea scallops with curry sauce, coconut basmati rice and grilled pineapple relish. The restaurant also features an extensive wine list emphasizing West Coast wines.

American. Lunch, dinner. Reservations recommended. Bar. $16-35

★★GARY CHU'S

611 Fifth St., Santa Rosa, 707-526-5840; www.garychus.com

Chinese. Lunch, dinner. Closed Monday. $16-35

★★★JOHN ASH & CO.

4330 Barnes Road, Santa Rosa, 707-527-7687; www.vintnersinn.com

Located next to the Vintners Inn, a country retreat operated by winemakers Ferrari-Carano, this sophisticated dining room serves simple dishes made with fresh, local ingredients from local farmers and producers as well as the restaurant's own gardens. Entrées might include Moroccan spiced loin of California lamb with couscous or housemade chicken and sun-dried tomato sausage. The Front Room Bar and Lounge offers signature cocktails, wines and lighter fare.

American. Dinner. Reservations recommended. Outdoor seating. Bar. $36-85

★★JOSEF'S RESTAURANT & BAR

308 Wilson St., Santa Rosa, 707-571-8664; www.josefsrestaurant.com

Continental, French. Lunch (Tuesday-Friday), dinner. Bar. $16-35

★★★KENWOOD

9900 Highway 12, Kenwood, 707-833-6326; www.kenwoodrestaurant.com

This restaurant has many dining rooms to choose from with views of the Sugarloaf Mountains and the Kunde Vineyards. Enjoy a simple California menu, including grilled chicken with wild rice, curry sauce, and raisin chutney. For dessert, try the pineapple carpaccio with coconut ice cream or the dark chocolate truffle. Then retreat to the bar for a drink in front of the fire.

American. Lunch, dinner. Closed Monday-Tuesday. Reservations recommended. Outdoor seating. Bar. $16-35

★★LA GARE
208 Wilson St., Santa Rosa, 707-528-4355; www.lagarerestaurant.com
French, Continental. Dinner. Closed Monday-Tuesday. Reservations recommended. Children's menu. $16-35

SONOMA
See also Calistoga, Napa, Petaluma, Santa Rosa, St. Helena

The quieter sister to nearby Napa, Sonoma has plenty of top-notch wineries, luxurious inns and spas, and superlative dining, but without the crowds. The oldest town in the wine region, Sonoma was arranged around the eight-acre plaza like a traditional Mexican village because up until 1846, it was under Mexican rule. On June 14 of that year, a group of settlers rebelled in the so-called "Bear Flag Revolt," and for a brief 25 days, Sonoma was declared the capital of California. The U.S. government then annexed California, ending Sonoma's days as the seat of state government. Today, the history of the town is well preserved. City Hall, built in the heart of the plaza in the early 20th century, is still used and the Franciscan mission San Francisco Solano, dating back to 1823, is open to the public. In addition to the history, Sonoma's shops, restaurants and famed wineries are well worth the visit. The town's more than 9,000 residents stay for the pleasant weather and scenery, with the Pacific coastline to the west and the Mayacamas Mountains to the east.

WHAT TO SEE
BARTHOLOMEW PARK WINERY
1000 Vineyard Lane, Sonoma, 707-935-9511; www.bartpark.com

Grapes have been grown on this land since the 1830s, but Bartholomew Park has existed as a winery only since 1994. With winemaker Jim Bundschu (of the long-time Sonoma family behind nearby Gundlach Bundschu winery's Rhinefarm) at the helm, expect to find limited-production single vineyard wines that range from soft, full merlots to crisp, refreshing whites. Pick up a picnic in town and plan on a hike through the winery's trails, which on a clear day deliver views across the valley to San Francisco. Afterward, buy a cold bottle of sauvignon blanc from the tasting room and take a seat at one of the picnic tables that overlook the vineyards for an unforgettable lunch.
Daily 11 a.m.-4:30 p.m.

BUENA VISTA CARNEROS HISTORIC TASTING ROOM
18000 Old Winery Road, Sonoma, 707-938-1266, 800-926-1266;
www.buenavistacarneros.com

Founded in 1857, Buena Vista is California's oldest premium winery and a California historic landmark. The 1862 Press House stands as the estate's tasting room, and history buffs will particularly enjoy the tour, as it recounts Buena Vista's past and the life of Count Agoston Haraszthy, the man behind today's winemaking techniques. There are a number of different tasting options—from library vintages to seated food and wine pairings—so be sure to call ahead for details (reservations recommended).
Daily 10 a.m.-5 p.m.

GENERAL JOSEPH HOOKER HOUSE

414 First St. East, Sonoma, 707-938-0510; www.sonomaleague.org

This historic house was built for Civil War hero General Joseph Hooker and was originally known as the Vasquez House. In 2008, the home was renamed to honor Hooker's legacy. Find vintage exhibits and extensive photographic and historical archives on Sonoma's history in this house that dates back to 1850. It's now maintained by the local historical society, which serves homemade pastries and tea to visitors.

Wednesday, Saturday 1-4 p.m.

GLORIA FERRER CAVES & WINERY

23555 Highway 121, Sonoma, 707-993-1917; www.gloriaferrer.com

The first sparkling wine house to settle in the Sonoma Carneros region, Gloria Ferrer is an idyllic stop for a glass of Brut Rosé and a nibble on some of their delicious, addicting house-roasted spicy almonds. The daily tours include a peek at century-old winemaking equipment and a journey into the estate's cellar. Unlike other wineries in the area, Gloria Ferrer does not provide tasting samples; rather they sell their wines by the full glass or bottle. Grab a flute, head out to the sun-drenched Vista Terrace and relax as you overlook the estate vineyards. For those who prefer still wines, the winery also offers a limited-release pinot noir rosé and a variety of more robust pinot noirs. Winery Tour: $10.

Daily 10 a.m.-5 p.m.; tour reservations recommended for parties of 10 or more.

RAVENSWOOD

18701 Gehricke Road, Sonoma, 707-933-2332, 888-669-4679;
www.ravenswood-wine.com

This Sonoma winemaker's well-priced zinfandels may be ubiquitous (you can find the vintner's blends in most grocery stores across the U.S.), but they're some of the most robust, deliciously drinkable American reds around. Winemaker Joel Peterson's mantra is "no wimpy wines," and that philosophy shows in the full-bodied wines Ravenswood produces. A visit to the rustic tasting room gives you a chance to sample some of the winery's limited-production vineyard designate zinfandels, all of which are acclaimed for their rich taste (think big flavor with notes ranging from vanilla to cedar to raspberry, depending on the vineyard). Tour and tasting: $15.

Daily 10 a.m.-4:30 p.m.

SONOMA STATE HISTORIC PARK

363 Third St. W., Sonoma, 707-938-9560; www.parks.ca.gov

This state park is made up of six historical locations around Sonoma Plaza: General Vallejo's house, Mission San Francisco Solano, the Blue Wing Inn, the Sonoma Barracks, the Toscano Hotel and the remains of La Casa Grande. The barracks holds a museum and gift shop.

Daily 10 a.m.-5 p.m.

VELLA CHEESE COMPANY

315 Second St. East, Sonoma, 707-938-3232, 800-848-0505; www.vellacheese.com

Not much has changed over the past 70 years for this cheese company. Housed in a century-old stone building originally intended for a brewery, it remains a family-run operation that puts quality before all else. Whether you're in the mood for a slice of sharp raw milk cheddar or a wheel of dry monterey jack, locals and visitors will agree that little tastes better with a bottle of local wine than a serving of fresh Vella cheese. Monday-Saturday 9:30 a.m.-6 p.m.

SPECIAL EVENTS

VALLEY OF THE MOON VINTAGE FESTIVAL

Sonoma Plaza, Broadway and E. Napa Streets, 707-996-2109; www.sonomavinfest.org

Sonoma's oldest wine festival first celebrated the end of the grape-growing season and the harvest in 1896. Today, the tradition continues with a grape stomp, winemaking contest, parade, food, arts and crafts and of course, wine tasting. Late September.

WHERE TO STAY

★★EL DORADO HOTEL

405 First St. W., Sonoma, 707-996-3220, 800-289-3031; www.eldoradosonoma.com

The contemporary surroundings of the El Dorado Hotel make the perfect home base for exploring historic Sonoma. Guest rooms are filled with modern four-poster beds with down comforters, DVD and CD players, flat-screen TVs and refrigerators. French doors lead to private balconies with lovely views of the historic Sonoma Plaza. The El Dorado kitchen offers a menu of sophisticated California-influenced cuisine for every meal of the day, which can be enjoyed in the sleek dining room or the beautiful stone-floored covered patio.
27 rooms. Restaurant, bar. Pool. $151-250

★EL PUEBLO INN

896 W. Napa St., Sonoma, 707-996-3651, 800-900-8844; www.elpuebloinn.com

53 rooms. Complimentary breakfast. Fitness center. Pool. $151-250

★★★THE FAIRMONT SONOMA MISSION INN & SPA

100 Boyes Blvd., Sonoma, 707-938-9000, 800-862-4945; www.fairmont.com/sonoma

A favorite since the 1920s, this idyllic country retreat sits on Boyes Hot Springs—a sacred healing ground for Native Americans—and just beyond the valley's famous vineyards. Many of the sophisticated yet country-comfortable guest rooms have French doors that open to a private patio or balcony. Romantic suites hold fireplaces and four-poster beds. American fare has been served for more than 50 years at the Big 3 Diner, while Santé earns praise for its imaginative cuisine. Guests can relax by the pool or play a round of golf on the historic 1925 course. Inspired by the thermal mineral springs that flow underneath the inn, the spa is a destination unto itself, wowing guests with its comprehensive treatment menu.
228 rooms. Restaurant, bar. Business center. Fitness center. Pool. Spa. $351 and up

★★★THE LODGE AT SONOMA, A RENAISSANCE RESORT & SPA

1325 Broadway, Sonoma, 707-935-6600, 800-468-3571; www.thelodgeatsonoma.com

About six blocks south of the historic Sonoma Plaza, the lodge is set back from Broadway by a large circular drive with a central fountain. Tuscan-colored stucco buildings with red-tiled roofs have patios or balconies. Luxurious guest rooms hold fireplaces, loveseats and bathrooms with spa-jetted tubs, granite counters and rain showers. Feather beds, silk throws and 300-thread-count linens and duvets add to the elegance. Enjoy a lovely meal at the hotel's restaurant, Carneros Bistro and Wine Bar, where you can sample wine from the award-winning wine list.

182 rooms. Restaurant, bar. Spa. $251-350

LEDSON HOTEL

480 First St., Sonoma, 707-996-9779; www.ledsonhotel.com

In the heart of downtown Sonoma, on the town plaza, sits the historic Ledson Hotel. Located above the Harmony restaurant, the hotel is accessed through the rear of the restaurant by elevator. Guest rooms are individually decorated and feature inlaid wood floors, oriental rugs, fireplaces, and balconies. Unique chandeliers and bathrooms with gold fixtures add to the over-the-top elegance.

6 rooms. Complimentary breakfast. Bar. $251-350

★★★MACARTHUR PLACE

29 E. MacArthur St., Sonoma, 707-938-2929, 800-722-1866; www.macarthurplace.com

A country estate just a few blocks from the town plaza, this inn sits among seven acres of fragrant, blooming gardens. The Victorian-style buildings house 64 guest rooms with down comforters, plush robes, CD/DVD players with iPod connection, fireplaces and oversized bathrooms that deliver California country charm and comfort. A nightly wine and cheese reception whets the appetite, but save room for the juicy steaks and succulent seafood at Saddles, the hotel's steakhouse.

64 rooms. Restaurant. Complimentary breakfast. Fitness center. Spa. $251-350

WHERE TO EAT
★★CAFÉ LA HAYE

140 E. Napa St., Sonoma, 707-935-5994; www.cafelahaye.com

American. Dinner. Closed Sunday-Monday. Reservations recommended. Outdoor seating. $16-35

★★★CARNEROS BISTRO & WINE BAR

1325 Broadway, Sonoma, 707-931-2042; www.thelodgeatsonoma.com

This bistro is adjacent to the Lodge at Sonoma, sharing the circular drive. An extensive wine list, wine bar and wine education classes are offered along with an innovative menu of international fare. An open kitchen runs the length of the dining room. Dishes might include risotto fritters and squash soup as starters and organic game hen, pork tenderloin and cheese steak as entrees. Check for special events and live entertainment, and keep an eye out for celebrity bartenders.

International. Breakfast (Monday-Friday), lunch, dinner, Sunday brunch.

Reservations recommended. Outdoor seating. Children's menu. Bar. $36-85

★★DELLA SANTINA'S
133 E. Napa St., Sonoma, 707-935-0576; www.dellasantinas.com
Italian. Lunch, dinner. Outdoor seating. $16-35

★★DEUCE
691 Broadway, Sonoma, 707-933-3823; www.dine-at-deuce.com
American. Lunch, dinner. Reservations recommended. Outdoor seating. Bar. $16-35

★★★EL DORADO KITCHEN
405 First St. West, Sonoma, 707-996-3030; www.eldoradosonoma.com
This eatery shows off the talent of chef Justin Everett, who creates contemporary California cuisine such as free range Petaluma chicken with quinoa and squash blossom pesto. The dishes are paired with selections from local artisan vintners, and the list includes more than 20 wines by the glass. The neighboring El Dorado Kitchenette has pastries galore, as well as gourmet sandwiches, salads and house made ice cream.
American. Lunch, dinner, Sunday brunch. Reservations recommended. Outdoor seating. Bar. $36-85

★★★ESTATE
400 W. Spain St., Sonoma, 707-933-3663; www.thegeneralsdaughter.com
Inside a 19th-century Victorian farmhouse, this restaurant specializes in regional Italian fare and takes it's inspiration from artists among other things. Take a seat in the colorful grand parlors or order outdoors from the rose-covered wraparound porches. Original artwork is creative and inspired by old Italian films. The Italian menu features organic ingredients and includes salumi, cheese, wood-fired pizzas, polenta, pastas, fresh fish, chicken, pork and steak and much more.
Italian. Dinner. Outdoor seating. Bar. $36-85

★★THE GIRL & THE FIG
110 W. Spain St., Sonoma, 707-938-3634; www.thegirlandthefig.com
Prepare yourself for fresh, rustic, French-influenced cooking at this simple, rustic restaurant on Sonoma's town square. The waitstaff can range from affable to absent, but once you dig into dishes such as fig and arugula salad with fresh balsamic dressing, or skillet steak with asparagus and truffle mac 'n' cheese, you'll forget about the service. A wine list heavy with local syrahs provides the perfect complement to the California cuisine offered on the constantly changing menu. The outdoor patio is a divine spot to indulge in weekend brunch or a romantic dinner.
American, French. Lunch, dinner, Sunday brunch. Reservations recommended. Outdoor seating. Bar. $16-35

★★SADDLES
MacArthur Place Hotel, 29 E. MacArthur St., Sonoma, 707-938-2929;
www.macarthurplace.com
Steak. Lunch, dinner. Outdoor seating. Bar. $36-85

★★★SANTÉ RESTAURANT
Fairmont Sonoma Mission Inn, 100 Boyes Blvd., Sonoma, 707-938-9000;
www.fairmont.com/sonoma
Wine country cooking is the focus at this elegant, casually sophisticated restaurant inside the Fairmont Sonoma Mission Inn. Dishes are made with fresh local ingredients and focus on the natural flavors. The dining room has linen-topped tables, fireplaces and plenty of candlelight, perfect for a romantic meal. A tasting menu might include white asparagus salad with marinated heirloom beets, or sweet corn and black truffle risotto. The award-winning wine list features more than 500 local and regional wines.
American. Dinner. Reservations recommended. Outdoor seating. Bar. $36-85

ST. HELENA
See also Calistoga, Napa, Santa Rosa, Sonoma, Yountville
In a region rich with world-class dining and wine-tasting options, St. Helena reigns supreme among wine country-bound connoisseurs. An ideal base for wide-ranging exploration, the city is home to the Culinary Institute of America at Greystone and its restaurant. Notable vintners—including Beringer Wine Estates, Charles Krug Winery and V. Sattui Winery—are based here. The streets of downtown St. Helena have a small-town feel, and are lined with ice-cream shops, antique stores, upscale boutiques and spas.

WHAT TO SEE
BEAULIEU VINEYARD
1960 St. Helena Highway South, St. Helena, 707-967-5233, 800-373-5896;
www.bvwines.com
Founded more than 100 years ago by venerable winemaker Georges de Latour, this historic Vineyard contributed to the development of premium chardonnay and pinot noir, which lead to the official designation of Carneros as a separate and unique appellation. Tours cover the historic production facilities and enjoy a tasting based on your wine preference. Samples of reserve wines are available for a small fee in the reserve tasting room.
Daily 10 a.m.-5 p.m.

BERINGER VINEYARDS
2000 Main St., St. Helena, 707-967-4412; www.beringer.com
Beringer has welcomed guests since 1934, making it the oldest continuously operating winery in the Napa Valley. Sign up for one of the comprehensive tours, which include a walk through hand-dug, aging tunnels as well as informative talks about how wine is made and aged—followed, of course, by wine tasting.
May 30-October 23, 10 a.m.-6 p.m.; October 24-May 29, 10 a.m.-5 p.m.

CHARBAY WINERY & DISTILLERY

4001 Spring Mountain Road, St., Helena, 707-963-9327; www.charbay.com

Although wine is only a small percent of the focus here, the result is no less impressive. Infused flavored vodkas, from original and green tea to pomegranate and ruby red grapefruit, along with other spirits including whiskey, rum and pastis, keep this family-run property busy year-round. The worthwhile one-hour tour outlines the basics of distillation and gives you a chance to sample Charbay's prized Oakville Cabernet Sauvignon—unfortunately, the law prohibits tastings of the distilled spirits.

Daily 10 a.m.-4 p.m.

CHARLES KRUG WINERY

2800 Main St., St. Helena, 707-967-2229, 800-682-5784, www.charleskrug.com

The first winery founded in the Napa Valley, Charles Krug has been owned by the Mondavi family since 1943. As the Napa Valley made the transition from regional to international prominence, this winery led the way, building the first tasting room 50 years ago. Currently, it is undergoing a major restoration and tours may not be available during your visit, so call ahead.

Daily 10:30 a.m.-5 p.m.

THE CULINARY INSTITUTE OF AMERICA AT GREYSTONE

2555 Main St., St. Helena, 707-967-2320, 800-333-9242; www.ciachef.edu

Serious chefs and enthusiastic foodies will want to make the pilgrimage to the West Coast outpost of the famed Culinary Institute of America. Housed in a beautiful old stone building, the CIA specializes in professional development for chefs but also offers one-hour cooking demonstrations (Monday and Friday 1:30 p.m. and 3:30 p.m.; also Saturday-Sunday 10:30 a.m. and 1:30 p.m.) and several restaurants, including the Wine Spectator Greystone Restaurant.

DEAN & DELUCA

607 St. Helena Highway S., St. Helena, 707-967-9980; www.deandeluca.com

You don't have to visit New York to enjoy this gourmet grocer's quality foods, not to mention its respect for regional tastes. Along with products from around the world, the shop showcases fresh, local ingredients and area specialties, most dramatically in its prepared food section. You'll also find local produce, artisan cheeses, 1,400 kinds of California wine, an espresso bar and more.

Sunday-Thursday 7a.m.-7p.m., Friday-Saturday 7 a.m.-.-8 p.m.

FRANCISCAN OAKVILLE ESTATE

1178 Galleron Road, St. Helena, 707-963-7111, 800-529-9463; www.franciscan.com

This award-winning, 25-year-old winery aims to educate the public on all things wine in one of four tasting areas: a tasting bar, an open tasting room with fireplace, a private estate tasting room and a shady patio. Franciscan sponsors private tastings, seminars and book signings.

Daily 10 a.m.-5 p.m.

KELHAM VINEYARDS

360 Zinfandel Lane, St. Helena, 707-963-2000; www.kelhamvineyards.com

A true family affair, the Kelhams have been farming on their 60-acre vineyard for more than 35 years. Before producing its own label, the vineyard harvested its premium grapes for such esteemed vintners as Cakebread, Mondavi and Beaulieu. Unlike some of the larger estates in the area, Kelham's offers only formal wine tastings, a seated affair either in the tasting room or out on the veranda, where vineyard owner and host Susanna Kelham explains the intimate process behind each of the wines presented. Tours and tastings by appointment only.

KULETO ESTATE VINEYARD

2470 Sage Canyon Road, St. Helena, 707-963-9750; www.kuletoestate.com

Spanning 761 acres of wild hillside land on the eastern edge of Napa Valley, this family estate blends unique architecture—think Frank Lloyd Wright meets a Tuscan villa—with award-winning wines and expansive natural surroundings overlooking Lake Hennessey. Originally a designer and restaurateur, the vineyard's founder, Pat Kuleto, carried his love of food and wine directly to the soil, harvesting hillside-grown grapes for more than a decade and yielding wines full of richness and depth. The intimate tour includes four wines and complimentary food pairings.

Tours and Tastings: $35. Daily, by appointment only.

LOUIS M. MARTINI WINERY

254 St. Helena Highway South, St. Helena, 707-968-3361, 800-321-9463;
www.louismartini.com

One of the first to venture into the Carneros region now famous for its pinot noir, the Martini family helped put Napa Valley on the international wine map with its innovative grape growing and winemaking techniques. This third-generation, family-owned winery gives regular tours and tastings and includes a fine reserve tasting room along with charming gardens and picnic areas.

Daily 10 a.m.-6 p.m.

MERRYVALE VINEYARDS

1000 Main St., St. Helena, 707-963-7777; www.merryvale.com

Specializing in wine education, this winery offers a variety of programs for both the experienced connoisseur and the novice. The popular Saturday and Sunday 10:30 a.m. Wine Component Tasting seminars include a tour of the historic winery with its spectacular cask room. With 2,000-gallon oak casks on display, the cask room is regarded as one of the most enchanting places to drink wine in Napa Valley. Merryvale produces distinct chardonnays as well as bordeaux-blend red wine.

Daily 10 a.m.-6:30 p.m.

THE MODEL BAKERY

1357 Main St., St. Helena, 707-963-8192; www.themodelbakery.com

This bakery is a St. Helena institution, with an 80-plus year history. Don't miss the signature pain du vin, cheese baguettes and walnut bread. There are

also creamy soups and hearty brick-oven baked pizza. The shop is a great place to pick up a picnic lunch.
Monday-Friday 6:30 a.m.-5:30 p.m., Saturday 7 a.m.-5:30 p.m., Sunday 7 a.m.-5 p.m.

ST. CLEMENT VINEYARDS

2867 St. Helena Highway, St. Helena, 800-331-8266; www.stclement.com
Originally built in 1878 by a San Francisco manufacturer of fine mirror and glass, the Rosenbaum House is the focal point of St. Clement, offering peerless views from the front porch's café and an intimate tasting room inside. The tour elaborates upon the history of the Victorian mansion and the surrounding winery, though much of the fruit used to produce St. Clement's wine is purchased from other vineyards. Cabernet sauvignon, chardonnay, sauvignon blanc and merlot are made at this boutique winery, but the shining star is the Oroppas, a meritage-style blend.
Daily 10 a.m.–5 p.m. Reservations recommended.

V. SATTUI WINERY

1111 White Lane, St. Helena, 707-963-7774; www.vsattui.com
When you're ready to picnic, head to this family-owned, 108-year-old winery, which has one of the best gourmet food shops in the valley. While you can sample wines on the premises—the winery only sells directly to customers—it's better to stock a picnic basket from an amazing assortment of cheeses, meats, breads, spreads and sweets for a picnic on its lovely grounds.
April-October,
Daily 9 a.m.-6 p.m.; November-March, Daily 9 a.m.-5 p.m.

SPECIAL EVENTS
AUCTION NAPA VALLEY

Napa Valley Vintners, St. Helena, 707-963-3388; www.napavintners.com
The world's largest and most successful wine charity event since it began in 1981, the auction has contributed more than $85 million to the community. More than 1,800 people from around the world attend to hunt bargains and pick up rare vintages from the 214 Napa Valley participating wineries. A limited number of day passes are available to the general public, as are individual tickets to the gala dinner.
First weekend in June.

WHERE TO STAY
★★★THE INN AT SOUTHBRIDGE

1020 Main St., St. Helena, 707-967-9400, 800-520-6800; www.innatsouthbridge.com
Renowned architect William Turnbull Jr. had the small-town squares of Italy in mind when he designed this upscale, contemporary inn. Soft cream stucco buildings house spacious guest quarters with vaulted ceilings, fireplaces and French doors opening onto private balconies with views of the courtyard and beyond. The scenic property also includes Merryvale Winery, Tra Vigne restaurant and Pizzeria Tra Vigne.
21 rooms. Restaurant, bar. Complimentary breakfast. Fitness center. Spa. $$351 and up

★★★★MEADOWOOD NAPA VALLEY

900 Meadowood Lane, St. Helena, 707-963-3646, 800-458-8080; www.meadowood.com

On 250 wine-country acres, Meadowood is large, but its staff is attentive—from the esteemed resident wine tutor to the guest services manager assigned to each arriving visitor. Guests can play a game of croquet, tennis or golf, or while away the hours poolside. The suites, cottages and lodges blend classic country style with California sensibilities featuring stone fireplaces, skylights, vaulted ceilings, private decks and luxurious bathrooms—not to mention plenty of modern amenities such as flat-screen TVs, DVD/CD players, coffee and tea pots and toasters. The Grill is available for casual dining under the shade of an umbrella, and the Restaurant turns out gastronomic delights. 85 rooms. Restaurant, bar. Fitness center. Pool. Spa. $351 and up

WHERE TO EAT
★★★GO FISH

641 Main St., St. Helena, 707-963-0700; www.gofishrestaurant.net

This casual seafood restaurant with a wide-scoped menu offers a break from the regional cuisine with a little bit of everything. From the outside you may think steakhouse, from the reputation you may think sushi, but at Go Fish you can order a rib eye, Alaskan halibut, lemon thyme risotto, raw oysters or fish and chips.

Seafood. Lunch, dinner. Reservations recommended. Bar. $36-85

★★MARKET: AN AMERICAN RESTAURANT

1347 Main St., St. Helena, 707-963-3799; www.marketsthelena.com

American. Lunch, dinner. Closed Monday. Reservations recommended. Bar. $16-35

★★★MARTINI HOUSE

1245 Spring St., St. Helena, 707-963-2233; www.martinihouse.com

The cuisine at this 1923 Craftsman-style bungalow is fresh and flavorful, but for many the extensive drink list is reason enough to show up. The restaurant has a 600-bottle wine list, many specialty cocktails and a large beer selection. The earthy ingredients woven throughout the menu complement the restaurant's casual upscale appeal. The garden, surrounded by vine-covered arbors and an antique fountain, is an ideal spot for outdoor dining.

American. Lunch, dinner. Reservations recommended. Outdoor seating. Bar. $36-85

★★★PRESS

587 St. Helena Highway South, St. Helena, 707-967-0550; www.presssthelena.com

Possibly wine country's best bet for beef aficionados, Press caters to carnivores by offering a wide selection of steaks—dry-aged Kansas grass-fed prime Angus, California Kobe Waygu, and 100 percent Japanese Kobe Kuroge Waygu—and companion dishes designed to enhance their flavor. The restaurant also features a raw bar with fresh oysters, shrimp and lobster.

Steaks. Lunch (Friday-Saturday), dinner, Sunday brunch. Closed Monday-Tuesday. Reservations recommended. Outdoor seating. Bar. $86 and up

★★★★TERRA
1345 Railroad Ave., St. Helena, 707-963-8931; www.terrarestaurant.com

Chef and owner Hiro Sone has been wowing diners at Terra, his cozy, intimate Napa Valley restaurant, since 1988. Set one block off the main drag on Railroad Avenue in St. Helena, Terra is located in a charming, old stone building, rustically finished with vintage red-tiled floors, exposed stone walls and wood-beamed ceilings. The food is spectacular—a successful blend of flavors from Italy, France and Asia. Signature dishes change with the seasons and include grilled free range veal chop with forest mushrooms, grilled Hokkaido scallops, and chocolate truffle cake with espresso ice cream and fudge sauce. With gracious hospitality and warmth, the staff at Terra makes you feel like you're dining at home.

French, Italian. Dinner. Closed Tuesday. Reservations recommended. $36-85

★★★★THE RESTAURANT AT MEADOWOOD
900 Meadowood Lane, St. Helena, www.meadowood.com

Remaining true to Meadowood's natural, serene setting, The Restaurant concentrates on the purity of regional flavors, using several ingredients from the resort's onsite garden. The result is a menu replete with fresh, delectable choices, including organic strawberries and foie gras with aged Balsamic and garden arugula, and roasted turbot with artichoke, caperberry and preserved lemon. From the extensive list of 950 wines, sommelier Rom Toulon assists in pairing varietals to fully complement the essence of each dish. There are numerous prix fixe and à la carte options, but those in the know leave their evening in the hands of executive chef Christopher Kostow, whose nightly tasting menu epitomizes the casual elegance of California's wine country. A modern dining room with stone fireplaces, white wainscoting and rows of windows revealing the beautiful grounds adds to the dreamlike experience. American. Dinner. Closed Sunday. Reservations recommended. Outdoor seating. Children's menu. Bar. $86 and up

★★★TRA VIGNE
1050 Charter Oak Ave., St. Helena, 707-963-4444; www.travignerestaurant.com

Almost like dining at an Italian vineyard, this wine country restaurant has a rustic setting with views of the fields beyond and a neoclassical Italian menu. Fresh pastas are made with local ingredients (try the rigatoni alla carbonara). Entrées like wood oven roasted whole fish with arugla and shaved artichoke salad are simple enough to let the freshness of the food shine through.

Italian. Lunch, dinner. Reservations recommended. Outdoor seating. Bar. $36-85

★★★WINE SPECTATOR GREYSTONE
2555 Main St., St. Helena, 707-967-1010, 800-333-9242; www.ciachef.edu

Regulars come to this former old stone winery, which is part of the Culinary Institute of America's western campus, for the ambiance, wine country cuisine and all-California wine list. The restaurant has a high-beamed ceiling and massive fireplace. The menu changes daily, and guests can watch the professional culinary staff (assisted by students from institute) craft their plate-bound delicacies in the open kitchen.

YOSEMITE VALLEY

To best view Yosemite Valley's grand peaks, try this picturesque route. From Fresno, follow Highway 41 north toward the park. Take Highway 49 northwest to the gold rush town of Mariposa (Spanish for "butterfly"), where Highway 140 heads north and then east toward Yosemite. On the way into the park, you'll pass along a stretch of the Merced River, popular with rafters in summer. From the park's western entrance, follow the signs leading to the valley.

The best times to visit are fall and spring. Expect heavy traffic over holidays or on weekends in the height of summer (cars are occasionally banned from the valley). Beware of slick roads in winter, where four-wheel drive or tire chains are sometimes required and some high-elevation roads typically close.

South side and north side drives make a loop around the valley, passing spectacular waterfalls (best in spring) and imposing granite monoliths such as Half Dome (4,737 feet) and El Capitan (3,000 feet). There are plenty of pullouts for snapshots or short hikes. Make -reservations if you plan to stay overnight in the valley.

On the way out, take Highway 41 south. If the access road to Glacier Point is open (it closes in winter) and you have an extra hour or two drive. Follow the signs to panoramic views of the valley, Yosemite Falls and half dome. Continue south on Highway 41 through the park's Wawona section, where the Mariposa Grove of big trees awaits; a short hike leads to several ancient giant sequoias. Return to Highway 41 south to head back to Fresno. Approximately 200 miles.

International. Lunch, dinner. Reservations recommended. Outdoor seating. Children's menu. Bar. $36-85

SPAS

★★★★THE SPA AT MEADOWOOD

900 Meadowood Lane, St. Helena, 800-458-8080; www.meadowood.com

Massages delivered fireside, a rejuvenating facial with organic ingredients, a relaxing yoga class. These are just some of the incredibly indulgent services available at this wine country spa, located at Meadowood resort. Signature treatments include the Meadowood Harvest Wrap, which begins with a tea tree exfoliant and ends with your body swaddled in warm towels and blankets while you soak in the benefits of a hydrating body masque. Those short on time can opt for the 30-minute foot relief, which includes just enough pressure-point relieving massage to invigorate you for another day of wine tasting.

YOSEMITE NATIONAL PARK

See also Fresno, Lake Tahoe Area, Mammoth Lakes

Yosemite is one of the most popular and best-known national parks in the world. John Muir, the naturalist instrumental in the founding of this national park, wrote that here are "the most songful streams in the world, the noblest forests, the loftiest granite domes, the deepest ice sculptured canyons." Within 1,169 square miles, there are sheer cliffs, high-wilderness country, alpine meadows, lakes, snowfields, trails, streams and river beaches. Waterfalls are particularly magnificent during spring and early summer. More than three million people visit each year, but the views tend to distract from the crowds. The entrance fee (good for seven days) is $20 per vehicle. Routes to Yosemite National Park involve some travel over steep grades, which may extend driving times. The portion of Tioga Road (Highway 120) that travels over Tioga Pass to Lee Vining/Highway 395 is closed in winter. Highway 120 is open year-round to Crane Flat, where the Big Oak Flat Road continues into Yosemite Valley.

WHAT TO SEE
ANSEL ADAMS GALLERY
9031 Village Drive, Yosemite National Park, 209-372-4413; www.anseladams.com
Within Yosemite Village, you'll find the Ansel Adams Gallery, formerly known as Best's Studio, featuring the photography that made the park's landmarks recognizable to people across the country. Prints of Adams' work are available here along with contemporary photography and other fine art, handicrafts, books and souvenirs.
Daily 10 a.m.-5 p.m.

BADGER PASS SKI AREA
Glacier Point Road, Yosemite National Park, 559-253-5635; www.badgerpass.com
If you visit the park in winter, you'll have the opportunity to cross-country ski, ice skate in Yosemite Valley and snowshoe in the Badger Pass area. Badger Pass makes a good family ski destination with 85 percent of the mountain devoted to beginner and intermediate trails. The area is equipped with one triple, three double and one cable tow lift, ski patrol, and rentals. There is an ice skating rink, ski tours, snow tubing and snowshoeing among other activities. Mid-December-late March,
Daily 9 a.m.-4 p.m.; depending on conditions.

CAMPING
www.nps.gov/yose
According to his good friend Teddy Roosevelt, John Muir said that camping is "the only way in which to see at their best the majesty and charm of the Sierras," and if you're down with dirt, we second that. Yosemite has 13 campgrounds, including accommodations for traditional tent camping, RVs and canvas tents, and of course, an extensive backcountry for the more adventurous. Camping is limited to 30 days in a calendar year; May to mid-September, camping is limited to seven days in Yosemite Valley, in the rest of the park to 14 days. Campsites in the valley campgrounds, Hodgdon Meadow, Crane Flat, Wawona and half of Tuolumne Meadows campgrounds may be reserved in advance (877-444-6777; www.recreation.gov). Reservations are highly recommended, as these sites are routinely booked solid in the summer. Other park campgrounds are on a first-come, first serve basis and typically fill very early in the day. Winter camping is permitted in the Valley, Hodgdon Meadow and Wawona only.

GLACIER POINT
The exquisite panorama at Glacier Point from the rim 3,214 feet above Yosemite Valley captures views of the high Sierra and the valley below and faces Half Dome head-on in all its glory. Across the valley from here are Yosemite Falls, the Royal Arches, North Dome, Basket Dome, Mount Watkins and Washington Column. Up the Merced Canyon are Vernal and Nevada

falls. Grizzly Peak, Liberty Cap, and the towering peaks along the Sierras' crest and the Clark Range mark the skyline. The road is closed to vehicles in winter but open to skiers and snowshoers.

MARIPOSA GROVE

This is the largest and most visited of Yosemite's three groves of giant sequoia trees. The two-mile road to the grove is closed to cars from November to April, depending on conditions, but can be walked, skied, or snowshoed anytime. Merced and Tuolumne groves are near Crane Flat, northwest of Yosemite Valley. The Grizzly Giant in Mariposa Grove, 209 feet high and 34.7 feet in diameter at its base, is estimated to be 2,700 years old.

MONO LAKE

Highway 395 and Third Street, Lee Vining, 760-647-6595; www.monolake.org
One of North America's oldest lakes, located in the Mono Basin National Forest Scenic Area, Mono contains 250 percent more salt than the Pacific Ocean, and millions of migratory waterfowl feed here on brine shrimp and alkali flies. But, there are no fish. There are interpretive educational programs offered here from seminars to walks. Come to explore and bird-watch, bike and picnic at the Mono Lake Country Park (only 5 miles north of Lee Vining). Mark Twain wrote about the lake and its islands, volcanoes and gulls in *Roughing It*.
Daily.

YOSEMITE MUSEUM

209-372-0200; www.nps.gov/yose
Next to the visitor center, this museum has displays that explore the cultural history of the indigenous Miwok and Paiute peoples and an art gallery. Just behind the museum is the Indian Village of Ahwahnee, a reconstructed Miwok-Paiute village with a self-guided trail, which is always open.
Daily 9 a.m.-4:30 p.m.

YOSEMITE MOUNTAIN SUGAR PINE RAILROAD

Fish Camp, 56001 Highway 41, Yosemite National Park, 559-683-7273;
www.ymsprr.com
Take a four-mile historic narrow-gauge steam train excursion through scenic Sierra National Forest, which is south of Yosemite. These locomotives were used to haul log trains through the mountains. Take either the Logger steam train, Jenny Railcars which is narrated, or the moonlight special which includes a barbecue and live entertainment. See Web site for schedule and pricing.

YOSEMITE VALLEY

209-372-0200; www.nps.gov/yose
A must-see, and the main reason most people come to this park, the valley lies at the foot of such wonders as the 5,000-foot Half Dome, the 3,000-foot sheer granite wall of El Capitan and roaring Yosemite and Bridalveil Falls. One of the most famous views the Tunnel View, in which you gaze up at Cloud's Rest, with El Capitan on the left and Bridal Veil Falls on the right.

Follow signs for Yosemite Village to reach the Yosemite Valley Visitor Center (www.yosemite.org), the largest information station in the park, where you'll find details on all there is to see and do during your stay.

WHERE TO STAY
★★★THE AHWAHNEE HOTEL
Yosemite Valley, Yosemite National Park, 801-559-4884; www.yosemitepark.com
Opened in 1927, this storied hotel, located within Yosemite National Park, is a celebration of Native American and colonial American designs. Its wooded, natural setting is perfectly complemented by the Native American décor, including artifacts and artwork created by the Yosemite Miwok. The rooms and suites may appear rustic, but the public spaces are glorious, with impressive stained-glass windows, intricate stonework and mosaics in the lobby, as well as a lounge, solarium and dining room.
123 rooms. Restaurant, bar. $351 and up

★★★TENAYA LODGE AT YOSEMITE
1122 Highway 41, Fish Camp, 559-683-6555, 888-514-2167; www.tenayalodge.com
Situated on 35 acres adjacent to the Sierra National Forest and just two miles from Yosemite, this elegant mountain retreat is just the place to see the sights without forsaking the comforts of home. The newly renovated guest rooms and suites share an upscale yet rustic appeal. Guests are supplied with all-natural, eco-friendly bath amenities. Activities are plentiful, both on the property and off, including a terrific children's program. Enjoy fine dining at Sierra, while Jackalopes Bar & Grill is ideal for the entire family.
244 rooms. Restaurant, bar. Fitness center. Pool. Spa. $151-250

★★WAWONA HOTEL
Yosemite National Park, Wawona, 801-559-4884; www.yosemitepark.com
104 rooms. Restaurant, bar. Pool. $61-150

★★YOSEMITE LODGE AT THE FALLS
Highway 41/140, Yosemite National Park, 559-252-4848; www.yosemitepark.com
249 rooms. Restaurant, bar. Pool. $151-250

WHERE TO EAT
★★THE VICTORIAN ROOM
The Groveland Hotel, 18767 Main St., Groveland, 209-962-4000, 800-273-3314; www.groveland.com
American. Dinner. Closed Monday. Reservations recommended. Outdoor seating. Children's menu. Bar. $16-35

THE AHWAHNEE DINING ROOM
The Ahwahnee Hotel, Yosemite National Park, Yosemite Valley, 209-372-1489, 801-559-4884; www.yosemitepark.com
The architecture is enough to make a meal here worthwhile, with a grand 34-foot-high beamed ceiling and floor-to-ceiling windows exposing the beauty beyond the glass. But the gourmet California cuisine, including organic, sustainable and locally grown ingredients, could easily stand alone.

Try a specialty such as the roast prime rib of California grassfed beef au jus or the spinach and chickpea crêpes.

American. Breakfast, lunch, dinner, Sunday brunch. Reservations recommended. Bar. $16-35

YOUNTVILLE

See also Napa, St. Helena

This Napa Valley town Yountville has become a major tourist destination without sacrificing its turn-of-the-20th-century charm. The quiet farming community dates to 1831, when George Yount, a North Carolina trapper, settled in the area. Surrounded by world-famous wineries, there is no better place for true gourmet sustenance than Yountville—at least in wine country. In fact, it's often referred to as the "culinary capital of the Napa Valley" and with good reason. There is a slew of fine restaurants here to keep your wine-tasting well balanced. When you're not feasting, take a stroll down Washington Street (the main strip), where you'll find inviting inns and quaint boutique shops.

WHAT TO SEE

CLIFF LEDE VINEYARDS

1473 Yountville Cross Road, Yountville, 707-944-8642, 800-428-2259; www.cliffledevineyards.com

Claiming 60 acres of Napa Valley's Stags Leap District, the Cliff Lede Vineyards utilize state-of-the-art techniques, including gravity-flow and berry-by-berry sorting systems to produce some of the best cabernet sauvignon in the region, along with sauvignon blanc and claret varietals. Tours of the vineyard, which commence in the restored craftsman-style tasting room, are small and informative, but the real treat is relaxing on one of the cozy porch swings, which offers views of the Lede vineyards and beyond. Another great post-tasting option is to stroll through the property's art gallery.

Daily 10 a.m.-5 p.m.; private tours by appointment.

DOMAINE CHANDON

1 California Drive, Yountville, 707-944-2280, 800-736-2892; www.chandon.com

Founded in 1973 by the French Champagne maker Moet & Chandon, Domaine Chandon is one of the leading sparking wine producers in the United States. You'll feel the true romance of the place when you tour the winery and the beautifully landscaped premises. On the terrace adjacent to the Tasting Salon, you can sip some bubbly and enjoy lunch outdoors, a fitting conclusion to a jaunt into wine country. Tours and times may vary so check the Web site for more information.

DOWNTOWN YOUNTVILLE

Beard Plaza, Yountville, 707-944-0850; www.yountville.com

If you want to bring home more than wine from your visit to the Napa Valley area, spend an afternoon wandering among the boutiques, art galleries and antique shops in downtown Yountville. Begin on Washington Street and stop at Beard Plaza, a showcase for high-end shops, including Vintage 1870, a converted 130-year-old winery that now houses 36 specialty shops and galleries, and a host of home accessories and design stores.

NAPA VALLEY MUSEUM

55 Presidents Circle, Yountville, 707-944-0500; www.napavalleymuseum.org

This small museum's permanent exhibits tell stories of the land and people of Napa Valley, as well as the art and science of California wines. A permanent exhibit, The Land and People of the Napa Valley, contains history of the Wappo Native Americans, pioneers and settlers, viticulture and more. Admission: adults $4.50, students and seniors $3.50, children 7-17 $2.50, children under 7 free. Wednesday-Monday 10 a.m.-5 p.m.

VINTAGE 1870

6525 Washington St., Yountville, 707-944-2451; www.vintage1870.com

This restored brick winery complex now houses four restaurants, a bakery, art galleries and more than 40 specialty shops. V Wine Cellar offers wine tasting and sells a range of different wines and cigars. A hot air balloon company is also located here, in case you want to take flight above Napa Valley. Daily 10 a.m.-5:30 p.m.

SPECIAL EVENTS
NAPA VALLEY MUSTARD FESTIVAL

Various venues, Yountville, 707-944-1133; www.mustardfestival.org

This celebration was first conceived to enliven the valley during the typically slow winter months. But there's nothing particularly wintry about the area in January, February and March—much of the valley is covered in brilliant yellow wild mustard flowers. The now popular celebration includes grand dinners, jazz concerts, art exhibitions, a mustard recipe competition, rare wine auctions, a photography contest and wine tasting. January-March.

WHERE TO STAY
★★NAPA VALLEY LODGE

2230 Madison St., Yountville, 707-944-2468, 888-455-3545; www.napavalleylodge.com

55 rooms. Complimentary breakfast. Fitness center. Pool. $251-350

★★★VILLAGIO INN & SPA

6481 Washington St., Yountville, 707-944-8877, 800-351-1133; www.villagio.com

An Italian-style retreat, this inn has rooms with fireplaces, sunken bathtubs, private patios or balconies and beds topped with luxury bedding. Amenities including a swimming pool and tea, coffee and cookies served every afternoon. The onsite spa has an expansive menu, from massages to wraps. 112 rooms. Restaurant, bar Complimentary breakfast. Pool. Spa. $251-350

★★★VINTAGE INN

6541 Washington St., Yountville, 707-944-1112, 800-351-1133; www.vintageinn.com

Inspired by the country inns of France, this inn sits on three-and-a-half acres in the heart of wine country. After a day of vineyard hopping, relax in bright, spacious rooms with private patios or balconies, wood-beamed ceilings, sunken whirlpool bathtubs and large fireplaces. The daily champagne breakfast buffet is a local favorite and if you're still hungry, there's afternoon tea or coffee and cookies. 80 rooms. Restaurant, bar. Complimentary breakfast. $251-350

★★★YOUNTVILLE INN

6462 Washington St., Yountville, 707-944-5600, 888-366-8166; www.yountvilleinn.com

The high-ceilinged, wood-beamed rooms at this inn, which feature fireplaces and views of the surrounding gardens, are perfect to retreat to after a day of touring local wineries. Some rooms have French doors that open to private patios. Guests receive a pass that delivers special offers at local wineries. 51 rooms. Complimentary breakfast. $251-350

WHERE TO EAT

★★★AD HOC

6476 Washington St., Yountville, 707- 944-2487; www.adhocrestaurant.com

An experiment gone right, Ad Hoc originated as a temporary venture by the legendary chef Thomas Keller and his crew. Planning to serve a four-course family style meal five days a week for a temporary time, the place became so popular that they just couldn't close. The set menus might start with assorted charcuterie, followed by a Colorado rack of lamb with frisée and currants, and an almond and broccolini cous cous. The menus change depending on what's in season, but the fried chicken makes a regular appearance, and is a local favorite.

Contemporary American. Dinner, Sunday brunch. Closed Tuesday-Wednesday. Reservations recommended. Bar. $36-85

★★BISTRO JEANTY

6510 Washington St., Yountville, 707-944-0103; www.bistrojeanty.com

French. Lunch, dinner, late-night. Reservations recommended. Outdoor seating. Bar. $36-85

★★★BOUCHON

6534 Washington St., Yountville, 707-944-8037; www.bouchonbistro.com

If you can't get into The French Laundry, try Thomas Keller's more casual French bistro. Like most Napa Valley restaurants, the fare is seasonal, but Bouchon maintains a decidedly bistro flavor, right down to the pommes frites, chalkboard specials and newspaper rack by the nickel bar. You can't go wrong with any of the fresh seafood, and the comfort dishes like slow-braised pork short ribs and croque madame are especially enjoyable. Desserts include pot de crème and profiteroles. Be sure to stop by the next-door Bouchon Bakery. The éclairs and macarons are spectacular.

French. Lunch, dinner, late-night. Reservations recommended. Outdoor seating. Bar. $36-85

★★★BRIX

7377 St. Helena Highway, Yountville, 707-944-2749; www.brix.com

Healthful and flavorful cuisine is served against a backdrop of vineyards, landscaping and the Mayacamas Mountains, captured by a wall of windows and glass doors in the stylish, contemporary dining room. There is also a long bar and an extensive L-shaped exhibition kitchen with a wood-burning oven. A wine and gift shop lies just past the entrance.

French, Italian. Lunch, dinner, brunch. Reservations recommended. Outdoor seating. Bar. $36-85

★★★ÉTOILE

1 California Drive, Yountville, 707-944-8844; 800-736-2892; www.chandon.com

An acclaimed restaurant inside the Domaine Chandon winery, Étoile serves California cuisine with a French influence in a sophisticated, candlelit setting. Choose from the prix fixe menu or from the a la carte menu. Dishes include duck breast with green lentils and baby turnips or fava bean ravioli with black summer truffle. All dishes can be paired with wines from the Domaine Chandon vineyards.

American, French. Lunch, dinner. Closed Tuesday-Wednesday; January. Reservations recommended. Outdoor seating. Bar. $36-85

★★★★★THE FRENCH LAUNDRY

6640 Washington St., Yountville, 707-944-2380; www.frenchlaundry.com

At this former French steam laundry, chef Thomas Keller has raised the standard for fine dining in America. While the country locale—a circa-1900 rock and timber cottage—makes diners feel at home, tables topped with limoges china, crystal stemware and floor-length linens, set the tone for the nine-course French or vegetarian tasting menus that change daily but always rely on seasonal produce and organic meats. Dishes are small and prompt contemplation on the perfect marriage of fresh, pristine ingredients on each plate. The affable staff keeps the experience casual and comfortable, yet refined and memorable. Reservations are taken two months in advance, so be prepared if you're hoping to snag a table at this perennially outstanding American classic.

French. Lunch (Friday-Sunday), dinner. Closed two weeks in January and one week in late July-early August. Reservations required. $86 and up

★★★REDD

6480 Washington St., Yountville, 707-944-2222; www.reddnapavalley.com

Locals love to love Redd, Napa's newest epicurean destination. This chic restaurant represents chef/owner Richard Reddington's view of wine country cuisine with influences from all over the map. The unadorned white-walled interior and wood doorframe speak to the simplicity of Reddington's cooking. You'll be won over by such dishes as Alaskan halibut with chickpea purée, sweet peppers, prosciutto and salt cod beignets, and organic chicken with faro, bacon and asparagus saltimbocca.

Contemporary American. Lunch, dinner, Sunday brunch. Reservations recommended. Outdoor seating. Bar. $36-85

INDEX

Y

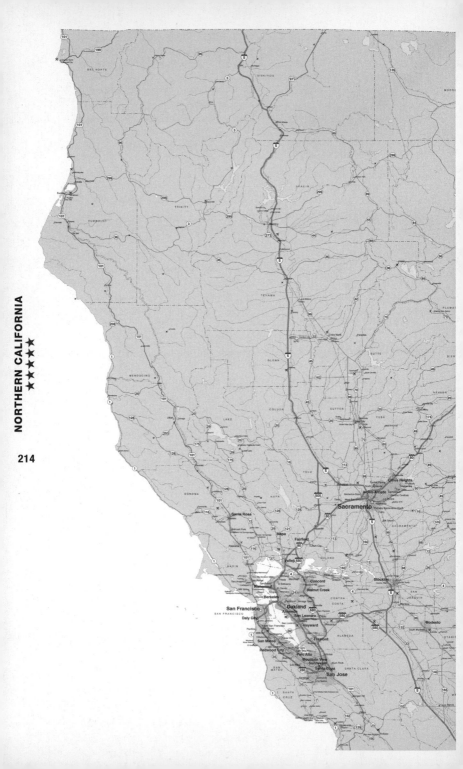

NORTHERN CALIFORNIA

SACRAMENTO

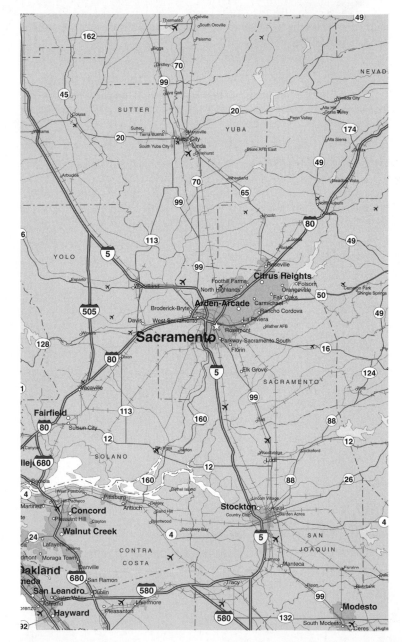

SAN FRANCISCO

NOTES

NOTES

NOTES

NOTES

NOTES

NOTES

NOTES